RELATIONS OF MUSLIMS AND NON-MUSLIMS

RELATIONS OF MUSLIMS AND NON-MUSLIMS

SHAYKH-UL-ISLAM
Dr MUHAMMAD TAHIR-UL-QADRI

Preface by
Dr Kemal Argon

Author: Dr Muhammad Tahir-ul-Qadri

Published by
Minhaj-ul-Quran Publications
292–296 Romford Road
Forest Gate
London, E7 9HD
United Kingdom

All proceeds from the books, literature and audio-visual media (all multimedia) delivered by Dr Muhammad Tahir-ul-Qadri are entirely donated to Minhaj-ul-Quran International (MQI).

Research Assistants
Abdul Aziz Suraqah, Shaykh Abdul Aziz Dabbagh, Muhammad Hanif

A catalogue record for this book is available from the British Library.

ISBN–13: 978–1–908229–32–8 (pbk)

www.minhaj.org | www.minhajuk.org
www.minhajpublications.com

First published June 2015

Printed by TJ International, Cornwall, UK

بِسۡمِ ٱللَّهِ ٱلرَّحۡمَٰنِ ٱلرَّحِيمِ

In the name of God, Most Compassionate, Ever-Merciful

Saying of God ﷻ

﴿مَن قَتَلَ نَفۡسَۢا بِغَيۡرِ نَفۡسٍ أَوۡ فَسَادٖ فِي ٱلۡأَرۡضِ فَكَأَنَّمَا قَتَلَ ٱلنَّاسَ جَمِيعٗا﴾

﴿Whoever kills a person [unjustly], except as a punishment for murder or [as a prescribed punishment for spreading] disorder in the land, it is as if he killed all of humanity.﴾

[Qur'ān 5:32]

Saying of the Prophet ﷺ

عَنْ أَبِي بَكْرَةَ رضي الله عنه عَنِ النَّبِيِّ ﷺ أَنَّهُ قَالَ: «إِنَّ دِمَاءَكُمْ وَأَمْوَالَكُمْ وَأَعْرَاضَكُمْ عَلَيْكُمْ حَرَامٌ، كَحُرْمَةِ يَوْمِكُمْ هَذَا، فِي شَهْرِكُمْ هَذَا، فِي بَلَدِكُمْ هَذَا، إِلَى يَوْمِ تَلْقَوْنَ رَبَّكُمْ»

Abū Bakra رضي الله عنه reported that the Prophet ﷺ said, "Indeed, your blood and your property and your honour are inviolable, like the inviolability of this day of yours and this month of yours and this land of yours until the day you meet your Lord".

[al-Bukhārī and Muslim]

Shaykh-ul-Islam Dr Muhammad Tahir-ul-Qadri

Shaykh-ul-Islam Dr Muhammad Tahir-ul-Qadri was born in 1951 in the city of Jhang, Pakistan, hailing from a family of Islamic saints, scholars and teachers. His formal religious education was initiated in Medina at the age of 12 in Madrasa al-ʿUlūm al-Sharʿiyya, a traditional school situated in the blessed house of the Companion of the Prophet Muhammad ﷺ, Abū Ayyūb al-Anṣārī ؓ. He completed the traditional studies of classical and Arabic sciences under the tutelage of his father and other eminent scholars of the time. He continued to travel around the Islamic world in the pursuit of sacred knowledge, and studied under many famous scholars of Mecca, Medina, Syria, Baghdad, Lebanon, the Maghreb, India and Pakistan, and received around five hundred authorities and chains of transmission from them in hadith and classical Islamic and spiritual sciences. Amongst them is an unprecedented, unique and highly honoured chain of authority which connects him, through four teachers, to al-Shaykh ʿAbd al-Razzāq, the son of al-Shaykh ʿAbd al-Qādir al-Jīlānī al-Ḥasanī al-Ḥusaynī (of Baghdad), al-Shaykh al-Akbar Muḥyī al-Dīn b. ʿArabī [(the author of *al-Futūḥāt al-Makkiyya*) (Damascus)] and Imam Ibn Ḥajar al-ʿAsqalānī, the great hadith authority of Egypt. Through another chain he is linked to Imam Yūsuf b. Ismāʿīl al-Nabhānī directly via only one teacher. His chains of transmission are published in two of his *thabts* (detailed lists): *al-Jawāhir al-Bāhira fī al-Asānīd al-Ṭāhira* and *al-Subul al-Wahabiyya fī al-Asānīd al-Dhahabiyya*.

In the academic sphere, Dr Qadri received a First Class Honours Degree from the University of the Punjab in 1970. After earning his MA in Islamic studies with University Gold Medal in 1972 and achieving his LLB in 1974, Dr Qadri began to practise law in the district courts of Jhang. He moved to Lahore in 1978 and joined the University of the Punjab as a lecturer in law and completed his doctorate in Islamic Law. He was later appointed as a professor of Islamic Law and was head of the department of Islamic legislation for LLM.

Dr Qadri was also a jurist advisor to the Federal Shariat Court and Appellate Shariah Bench of the Supreme Court of Pakistan and advisor on the development of Islamic Curricula to the Federal Ministry of Education. Within a short span of time, Dr Qadri emerged as one of the Pakistan's leading Islamic jurists and scholars and one of the world's most renowned and leading authorities on Islam. A prolific author, researcher and orator, Dr Qadri has written around one thousand books, of which more than four hundred and fifty have been published, and has delivered over six thousand lectures (in Urdu, English and Arabic) on a wide range of subjects.

In 2010, Shaykh-ul-Islam Dr Muhammad Tahir-ul-Qadri issued his historic and world-renowned fatwa on the critical matter of suicide bombings and terrorism carried out in the name of Islam. It has been regarded as a significant and historic step, the first time that such an explicit and unequivocal decree against the perpetrators of terror has been broadcast so widely. The original fatwa was written in Urdu, and amounts to 600 pages of research and references from the Qur'ān, hadith, the opinions of the Companions ﷺ, and the widely accepted classical texts of Islamic scholarship. This historic work has been published in English, Indonesian and Hindi, while translation into Arabic, Norwegian, Danish, Spanish, French and other major languages is also in process. The Islamic Research Academy of Jamia al-Azhar Egypt wrote a detailed description of the fatwa and verified its contents. It gained worldwide media attention and acclaim as an indispensable tool in the intellectual and ideological struggle against violent extremism.

Also Dr Qadri is the founder and head of Minhaj-ul-Quran International (MQI), an organisation with branches and centres in more than ninety countries around the globe; he is the chairman of the Board of Governors of Minhaj University Lahore, which is chartered by the Government of Pakistan; he is the founder of Minhaj Education Society, which has established more than 600 schools and colleges in Pakistan; and he is the chairman of Minhaj Welfare Foundation, an organization involved in humanitarian and social welfare activities globally.

Dr Qadri has spent his life, and especially the last decade, in an indefatigable effort to counter religious extremism and promote peace and harmony between communities. His painstaking research into the Qurʾān, hadith and classical Islamic authorities has resulted in landmark works, some published, and others soon to be published, demonstrating Islam as a religion that not only safeguards human rights, but promotes peace, tolerance and socioeconomic progress. He has travelled extensively to lecture at the invitation of government and non-government agencies, and has organised and took part in international conferences in order to promote peace. He has arrayed spiritual and educational training programmes across the Western world with a focus on addressing the roots of religious extremism. He is recognised for his commitment to interfaith dialogue, with over 12,000 people attending his Peace for Humanity Conference in 2011, probably the largest interfaith gathering ever held in the UK, and which announced the London Declaration, a charter for world peace, signed online by a quarter of a million people. He has been politically active in his native Pakistan, organising massive pro-democracy and anti-corruption demonstrations. When not travelling, he is based in Canada, busy in his research activities and producing vital works of Islamic scholarship relevant to Muslims in this day and age.

Transliteration Key

ا/آ/ى	ā	ظ	ẓ
ب	b	ع	ʿ
ت	t	غ	gh
ث	th	ف	f
ج	j	ق	q
ح	ḥ	ك	k
خ	kh	ل	l
د	d	م	m
ذ	dh	ن	n
ر	r	ه	h
ز	z	و	w/ū
س	s	ي	y/ī
ش	sh	ة	a
ص	ṣ	ء	ʾ
ض	ḍ	أ	a
ط	ṭ	إ	i

Formulaic Arabic Expressions

(*Subḥānahū wa taʿālā*) an invocation to describe the Glory of Almighty Allah: 'the Exalted and Sublime'

(*Ṣalla-llāhu ʿalayhi wa ālihī wa sallam*) an invocation of God's blessings and peace upon the Prophet Muhammad and his family: 'God's blessings and peace be upon him and his family'

(*ʿAlayhis-salām*) an invocation of God's blessings and peace upon a Prophet or an angel: 'May peace be upon him'

(*ʿAlayhas-salām*) an invocation of God's blessings and peace upon a Prophet's mother, wife, daughter and other pious woman: 'May peace be upon her'

(*ʿAlayhimas-salām*) an invocation of God's blessings and peace upon two Prophets or two angels: 'May peace be upon both of them'

(*ʿAlayhimus-salām*) an invocation of God's blessings and peace upon three or more Prophets: 'May peace be upon them'

(*Raḍiya-llāhu ʿanhu*) an invocation of God's pleasure with a male Companion of the Prophet: 'May God be pleased with him'

(*Raḍiya-llāhu ʿanhā*) an invocation of God's pleasure with a female Companion of the Prophet: 'May God be pleased with her'

(*Raḍiya-llāhu ʿanhumā*) an invocation of God's pleasure with two Companions of the Prophet: 'May God be pleased with both of them'

(*Raḍiya-llāhu ʿanhum*) an invocation of God's pleasure with more than two Companions of the Prophet: 'May God be pleased with them'

Contents

Preface

This new work by Dr Muhammad Tahir-ul-Qadri comes at a very important time in relations between Muslims and non-Muslims and is an important text for many different concerns and interests, Muslim and non-Muslim. Muslim and non-Muslim scholars, leaders and activists will find within its contents strong arguments and ample original sources and citations, that promote bridge-building, peace and harmony between communities. These sources and citations can be useful in formal education about Islam as well as in less formal discourses about Muslims' relations with non-Muslims.

This book comes in the wake of Dr Qadri's earlier critical fatwa of 2010, the "Fatwa Against Terrorism and Suicide Bombings." Whereas the fatwa from 2010 was an important and convincing work of Islamic scholarship, that was extensively researched and evidenced, this later book stands as an important sequel to the earlier work, providing a different focus with additional and complementary information not found in the 2010 text's contents.

The 2010 fatwa was and is strategically very important on a number of points. The fatwa provides a scholarly standard for Muslims and non-Muslims wondering what is representative of a balanced and moderate Muslim perspective for comparison. The 2010 fatwa was also highly relevant for guiding a younger generation of Muslims away from extreme and unbalanced perspectives and ideologies. While both of Dr Qadri's works are important, this later text has another focus, dealing with questions and concerns about long-term and sustained good and peaceful relations between Muslims and non-Muslims. These long-term and sustained good peaceful relations could be between Muslims and non-Muslim minorities either in Muslim majority countries or between minority Muslims and others in non-Muslim societies. While both works are relevant to both these above situations, the latter work provides content with a focus shifted to a concern for sustained, long-term good relations.

Dr Qadri's later work redirects our attention to a humanitarian interpretation of the religion that guides to bridge-building and good, peaceful relations between Muslims and non-Muslims. This is done in two parts, the first part being about more individual relations and community relations and the second part being about "categories of abodes."

The first part provides ample evidences for very important aspects of individual and community relations. Non-Muslims in their treatment by Muslims, as a rule, are to be secure in their lives and in their belongings. Evidences are presented showing that women, children, elderly and priests are also protected as are diplomats, farmers, traders and non-combatants. Non-Muslims have freedom of faith and beliefs and the Muslims have been ordered to protect the places of worship belonging to the non-Muslims, despite religious differences. In addition, there is to be justice in all judgments and rulings for non-Muslims. Muslims are to treat non-Muslims with piety and excellent social morality. Muslims are to be non-revengeful, forbearing and tolerant towards non-Muslims. They are to keep and fulfill their agreements and covenants with non-Muslims. Dr Qadri provides evidences that there should be support for elderly, infirm, and feeble non-Muslims. Ample evidences are provided for good treatment of non-Muslims by Muslims.

The second part of the book, on categories of abodes, makes this work one of geopolitical relevance. Dr Qadri provides evidences and nuanced interpretations of the concepts, the "Abode of Islam, the Abode of Reconciliation, the Abode of Treaty, the Abode of Peace, and the Abode of War." Clear definitions of these categories are offered, along with how different countries can and cannot be classified in each of these categories.

This section raises many interesting points, relevant to long-term sustained good relations. Amongst these many points, we can take as an example the assertion that many non-Muslim states are in the Abode of Treaty because of membership in the United Nations. (see pages 161–162). In addition, on page 162 Dr Qadri states,

> "We miserably lack Islamic knowledge...the great jurists do not feel any hesitation in calling a non-Muslim state an Abode of Islam on very insignificant conditions...on the contrary, a small number of terrorists, owing to the dearth of wisdom, intellect and insight into the Islamic law issue verdicts of bloodshed and terrorism in the same countries."

This statement encapsulates the wisdom, which this whole work points in the direction of, away from wayward drift, extremism and unbalance back to knowledge and benevolent relations.

In contrast to the arguments made by Dr Qadri, one may note that a clearer focus of arguments and their evidences on the humanitarian core of Islam is too often obscured by attention being focused on extreme and unbalanced interpretation and opinions, Muslim and non-Muslim. Clearly education and a pertinent discourse about Islam is necessary. Muslim and non-Muslim critics of the Muslim community and of certain Islamic scholarship might continue to point to extant examples of Islamic scholarship and activism that are extreme and non-representative of the greater historical tradition. In addition, individual Muslims looking for guidance may be confused by Islamic activism which has drifted away to some extent from the mainstream tradition, offering perspectives which may be mildly inaccurate or even reactionary and unbalanced. In regard to any pertinent discourse about these concerns, and to aid in individuals' quest for answers in this regard, Dr Muhammad Tahir ul-Qadri's new book presents a high standard of Islamic scholarship for different audiences, Muslim and non-Muslim. Members of these different communities may benefit by comparing their own viewpoints, perspectives, understandings, and opinions with this one important example of a high scholarly standard.

Dr Kemal Argon
Assistant Professor of World Religions, Faculty of Divinity,
Necmettin Erbakan University, Konya, Turkey

Part I

اَلْبَابُ الْأَوَّلُ

قَتْلُ نَفْسِ الْإِنْسَانِ مِنْ أَعْظَمِ الْكَبَائِرِ

Chapter One

To Murder a Human Being is to Commit One of the Worst of the Major Sins

Qur'ān

﴿مَن قَتَلَ نَفْسًا بِغَيْرِ نَفْسٍ أَوْ فَسَادٍ فِي ٱلْأَرْضِ فَكَأَنَّمَا قَتَلَ ٱلنَّاسَ جَمِيعًا وَمَنْ أَحْيَاهَا فَكَأَنَّمَآ أَحْيَا ٱلنَّاسَ جَمِيعًا﴾

﴾Whoever killed a person (unjustly), except as a punishment for murder or for (spreading) disorder in the land, it would be as if he killed all the people (of society); and whoever (saved him from unjust murder and) made him survive, it would be as if he saved the lives of all the people (of society, i.e., he rescued the collective system of human life).﴿[1]

Hadith

١/١. عَنْ أَبِي بَكْرَةَ رضي الله عنه قَالَ: خَطَبَنَا النَّبِيُّ ﷺ يَوْمَ النَّحْرِ. قَالَ: إِنَّ دِمَاءَكُمْ وَأَمْوَالَكُمْ وَأَعْرَاضَكُمْ عَلَيْكُمْ حَرَامٌ، كَحُرْمَةِ يَوْمِكُمْ هَذَا، فِي شَهْرِكُمْ هَذَا، فِي بَلَدِكُمْ هَذَا، إِلَى يَوْمِ تَلْقَوْنَ رَبَّكُمْ.

مُتَّفَقٌ عَلَيْهِ.

1/1. Abū Bakra ﷺ related that the Prophet ﷺ addressed them on the Day of Sacrifice and said:

"Indeed, your blood, your property and your honour are inviolable, like the inviolability of this day of yours and this month of yours, (as fixed) in this land of yours, until the day you meet your Lord."[2]

---

1 Qur'ān 5:32.

2 Set forth by •al-Bukhārī in *al-Ṣaḥīḥ*: *Kitāb al-Ḥajj* [The Book of Pilgrimage], chapter: "The sermon during the days of Mina," 2:620 §1654. •Muslim in *al-*

Agreed upon by al-Bukhārī and Muslim.

٢/ ٢. عَنْ عَبْدِ اللهِ بْنِ عُمَرَ ﷺ: إِنَّ مِنْ وَرَطَاتِ الْأُمُوْرِ الَّتِي لَا مَخْرَجَ لِمَنْ أَوْقَعَ نَفْسَهُ فِيْهَا، سَفْكَ الدَّمِ الْحَرَامِ بِغَيْرِ حِلِّهِ.

رَوَاهُ الْبُخَارِيُّ وَالْبَيْهَقِيُّ.

2/2. ʿAbd Allāh b. ʿUmar ﷺ said:

"Of the fatal matters—those in which one's (lower) self is entangled and finds no slit from which to escape—is the act of shedding inviolable blood."[1]

Reported by al-Bukhārī and al-Bayhaqī.

٣/ ٣. عَنْ عَبْدِ اللهِ قَالَ: قَالَ رَسُوْلُ اللهِ ﷺ: أَوَّلُ مَا يُقْضَى بَيْنَ النَّاسِ يَوْمَ الْقِيَامَةِ فِي الدِّمَاءِ.

مُتَّفَقٌ عَلَيْهِ.

3/3. ʿAbd Allāh b. Masʿūd ﷺ related that Allah's Messenger ﷺ said:

"The first issue that will be judged between people on the Day of Resurrection is that of blood [i.e., murder]."[2]

Ṣaḥīḥ: *Kitāb al-qasāma wa al-muḥāribīn wa al-qiṣāṣ wa al-diyāt* [The Book of Apportioning Wealth, Warmongers, Legal Retribution and Bloodwit], chapter: "The inviolability of a believer's blood, honour and property," 3:1305–1306 §1679.

[1] Set forth by •al-Bukhārī in *al-Ṣaḥīḥ: Kitāb al-diyāt* [The Book of Blood Money], chapter: "Whoever Kills a Believer Intentionally, His Recompense is Hell," 6:2517 §6470. •al-Bayhaqī in *al-Sunan al-kubrā*, 8:21 §15637.

[2] Set forth by •al-Bukhārī in *al-Ṣaḥīḥ*: *Kitāb al-diyāt* [The Book of Blood Money], chapter: "Whoever Kills a Believer intentionally," 6:2517 §6471. •Muslim in *al-Ṣaḥīḥ*: *Kitāb al-qasāma wa al-muḥāribīn wa al-qiṣāṣ wa al-diyāt* [The Book of Taking an Oath, Warmongers, Legal Retribution and Bloodwit], chapter: "The (cases of) Bloodshed would be Decided first of all on the Day of Resurrection," 3:1304 §1678. •Aḥmad b. Ḥanbal in *al-Musnad*, 1:442 §4213. •al-Tirmidhī in *al-Sunan: Kitāb al-diyāt* [The Book of Blood Money], chapter: "The Legal Ruling Concerning Blood," 4:17 §1397. •al-

Agreed upon by al-Bukhārī and Muslim.

٤/ ٤. عَنِ الْبَرَاءِ بْنِ عَازِبٍ ﷺ قَالَ: قَالَ رَسُوْلُ اللهِ ﷺ: لَزَوَالُ الدُّنْيَا جَمِيْعًا أَهْوَنُ عِنْدَ اللهِ مِنْ سَفْكِ دَمٍ بِغَيْرِ حَقٍّ.

رَوَاهُ ابْنُ أَبِي الدُّنْيَا وَابْنُ أَبِي عَاصِمٍ وَالْبَيْهَقِيُّ.

4/4. Al-Barā' b. ʿĀzib ﷺ reported that Allah's Messenger ﷺ said:

"Certainly, in the estimation of Allah, the obliteration of the whole world is lesser than unjustly shedding the blood of a human being."[1]

Reported by Ibn Abī Dunya, Ibn Abī ʿĀṣim and al-Bayhaqī.

Saying of Imam Abū Manṣūr al-Māturīdī

قَالَ الْإِمَامُ أَبُوْ مَنْصُورٍ الْـمَاتُرِيْدِيُّ فِي تَفْسِيْرِ هَذِهِ الْآيَةِ ﴿مَن قَتَلَ نَفْسًۢا بِغَيْرِ نَفْسٍ أَوْ فَسَادٍ فِي ٱلْأَرْضِ فَكَأَنَّمَا قَتَلَ ٱلنَّاسَ جَمِيعًا﴾.

مَنِ اسْتَحَلَّ قَتْلَ نَفْسٍ حَرَّمَ اللهُ قَتْلَهَا بِغَيْرِ حَقٍّ، فَكَأَنَّمَا اسْتَحَلَّ قَتْلَ النَّاسِ جَمِيْعًا، لِأَنَّهُ يَكْفُرُ بِاسْتِحْلَالِهِ قَتْلَ نَفْسٍ مُحَرَّمٍ قَتْلُهَا، فَكَانَ كَاسْتِحْلَالِ قَتْلِ النَّاسِ جَمِيْعًا، لِأَنَّ مَنْ كَفَرَ بِآيَةٍ مِّنْ كِتَابِ اللهِ يَصِيْرُ كَافِرًا بِالْكُلِّ. ...

وَتَحْتَمِلُ الْآيَةُ وَجْهًا آخَرَ، وَهُوَ مَا قِيْلَ: إِنَّهُ يَجِبُ عَلَيْهِ مِنَ الْقَتْلِ مِثْلُ

Nasā'ī in *al-Sunan: Kitāb taḥrīm al-dam* [The Book on the Prohibition of Bloodshed], chapter: "The Sanctity of Blood," 7:83 §3994. •Ibn Mājah in *al-Sunan: Kitāb al-Diyāt* [The Book of Blood Money], chapter: "The Gravity of unjustly Killing a Muslim," 2:873 §2615. •Ibn Ḥibbān in *al-Ṣaḥīḥ*, 16:339 §7344. •Abū Yaʿlā in *al-Musnad*, 9:35 §5099. •Ibn al-Mubārak in *al-Musnad*, 1:59 §97.

[1] Set forth by •Ibn Abī al-Dunyā in *al-Ahwāl*, p. 190 §183. •Ibn Abī ʿĀṣim in *al-Diyāt*, p. 2 §2. •al-Bayhaqī in *Shuʿab al-īmān*, 4:345 §5344.

مَا أَنَّهُ لَوْ قَتَلَ النَّاسَ جَمِيْعًا.

وَوَجْهٌ آخَرُ: أَنَّهُ يَلْزَمُ النَّاسَ جَمِيْعًا دَفْعُ ذَلِكَ عَنْ نَفْسِهِ وَمَعُوْنَتُهُ لَهُ، فَإِذَا قَتَلَهَا أَوْ سَعَى عَلَيْهَا بِالْفَسَادِ، فَكَأَنَّمَا سَعَى بِذَلِكَ عَلَى النَّاسِ كَافَّةً. ... وَهَذَا يَدُلُّ أَنَّ الْآيَةَ نَزَلَتْ بِالْحُكْمِ فِي أَهْلِ الْكُفْرِ وَأَهْلِ الْإِسْلَامِ جَمِيْعًا، إِذَا سَعَوْا فِي الْأَرْضِ بِالْفَسَادِ.

Imam Abū Manṣūr al-Māturīdī (one of the Imams of *Ahl al-Sunna* in theology) has interpreted the verse: ﴿*Whoever killed a person (unjustly), except as a punishment for murder or for (spreading) disorder in the land, it would be as if he killed all the people (of society).*﴾.[1]

Declaring that murder can be an act of disbelief, he wrote:

Whoever declares lawful the killing of a person whose killing has been forbidden by Allah (except when there is a valid reason), it is as if he considers it lawful to kill all of humanity. This is because he disbelieves by his declaring lawful the killing of one whose killing is unlawful, which is akin to declaring lawful the killing of entire humanity because the one who disbelieves in one verse from God's Book disbelieves in the whole of it.

This verse contains another possible angle of interpretation, and it is as has been said: His murder of one person entails the same burden [in the Hereafter] as if he killed the entire humanity. Another possible angle of interpretation is that it is necessary for everyone to make a collective effort to help and save the peaceful person from murder. Therefore, when the murderer kills that harmless soul or attempts to harm it, it is as if he is attempting to do that to everyone... This indicates that the verse has been revealed as a ruling both for the people of disbelief and the people of Islam together, if they sow corruption in the earth.[2]

---

[1] Qur'ān 5:32.

[2] •Abū Manṣūr al-Māturīdī, *Ta'wīlāt Ahl al-Sunna,* 3:501.

The Exegetes' Views on the Gravity of Killing a Human Being

قَالَ الْعَلاَّمَةُ أَبُو حَفْصٍ الْـحَنْبَلِيُّ فِي تَفْسِيْرِهِ «اللُّبَابِ فِي عُلُوْمِ الْكِتَابِ» فِي تَفْسِيْرِ الآيَةِ ﴿فَكَأَنَّمَا قَتَلَ ٱلنَّاسَ جَمِيعًا﴾ بِأَنَّ قَتْلَ إِنْسَانٍ وَاحِدٍ قَتْلُ جَمِيْعِ النَّاسِ:

١. قَالَ مُجَاهِدٌ: مَنْ قَتَلَ نَفْساً مُحَرَّمَةً يَصْلَى النَّارَ بِقَتْلِهَا، كَمَا يَصْلاَهَا لَوْ قَتَلَ النَّاسَ جَمِيْعًا.

٢. وَقَالَ قَتَادَةُ: أَعْظَمَ اللهُ أَجْرَهَا وَعَظَّمَ وِزْرَهَا، مَعْنَاهُ: مَنِ اسْتَحَلَّ قَتْلَ مُسْلِمٍ بِغَيْرِ حَقِّهِ، فَكَأَنَّمَا قَتَلَ النَّاسَ جَمِيْعاً.

٣. وَقَالَ الْـحَسَنُ: ﴿فَكَأَنَّمَا قَتَلَ ٱلنَّاسَ جَمِيعًا﴾، يَعْنِي: أَنَّهُ يَجِبُ عَلَيْهِ مِنَ الْقِصَاصِ بِقَتْلِهَا، مِثْلُ الَّذِي يَجِبُ عَلَيْهِ لَوْ قَتَلَ النَّاسَ جَمِيْعًا.

In his exegesis *al-Lubāb fī ʿulūm al-Kitāb,* Abū Ḥafṣ al-Ḥanbalī interpreted the Qurʾānic verse ﴾*as if he killed all the people (of society)*﴿[1] and declared that the murder of one individual is comparable to the killing of all of humanity. He quoted the sayings of different Imams in support of this position.

1. Mujāhid said: "If someone kills a soul unjustly, he will go to Hell due to that murder, just as he would have gone to Hell if he had killed the whole of humanity."
2. Qatāda said: "Allah has made the reward for saving it [a life] tremendous and made the chastisement of sin [for taking a life unjustly] tremendous, too. This means that whoever declares it lawful for himself to kill a Muslim, it is as if he killed all humanity."
3. Interpreting the same verse, al-Ḥasan al-Baṣrī said: "This

[1] Qurʾān 5:32.

means that he is liable to legal retribution [*qiṣāṣ*] for killing it [the harmless soul] as would be the person who killed all of humanity."[1]

قَالَ ابْنُ كَثِيرٍ فِي تَفْسِيرِ هَذِهِ الآيَةِ: ﴿وَمَن يَقْتُلْ مُؤْمِنًا مُّتَعَمِّدًا فَجَزَآؤُهُۥ جَهَنَّمُ خَٰلِدًا فِيهَا وَغَضِبَ ٱللَّهُ عَلَيْهِ وَلَعَنَهُۥ وَأَعَدَّ لَهُۥ عَذَابًا عَظِيمًا ﴿٩٣﴾﴾:

هَذَا تَهْدِيْدٌ شَدِيْدٌ وَوَعِيْدٌ أَكِيْدٌ لِـمَنْ تَعَاطَى هَذَا الذَّنْبَ الْعَظِيْمَ، الَّذِي هُوَ مَقْرُوْنٌ بِالشِّرْكِ بِالله فِي غَيْرِ مَا آيَةٌ فِي كِتَابِ الله، حَيْثُ يَقُوْلُ سُبْحَانَهُ فِي سُوْرَةِ الْفُرْقَانِ: ﴿وَٱلَّذِينَ لَا يَدْعُونَ مَعَ ٱللَّهِ إِلَٰهًا ءَاخَرَ وَلَا يَقْتُلُونَ ٱلنَّفْسَ ٱلَّتِي حَرَّمَ ٱللَّهُ إِلَّا بِٱلْحَقِّ وَلَا يَزْنُونَ﴾. وَقَالَ تَعَالَى: ﴿قُلْ تَعَالَوْا۟ أَتْلُ مَا حَرَّمَ رَبُّكُمْ عَلَيْكُمْ ۖ أَلَّا تُشْرِكُوا۟ بِهِۦ شَيْـًٔا﴾ إِلَى أَنْ قَالَ: ﴿وَلَا تَقْتُلُوا۟ ٱلنَّفْسَ ٱلَّتِي حَرَّمَ ٱللَّهُ إِلَّا بِٱلْحَقِّ ۚ ذَٰلِكُمْ وَصَّىٰكُم بِهِۦ لَعَلَّكُمْ تَعْقِلُونَ﴾.

Ibn Kathīr wrote in the details of this verse: ﴾*But he who kills a Muslim deliberately, his sentence will be Hell wherein will he abide for ages. Allah will afflict him with His wrath and will cast His curse on him. And He has prepared for him a dreadful torment.*﴿.[2]

This is a stern warning and emphatic Divine threat to those who perpetrate this grievous sin that is connected—in more than one verse in Allah's Book—with the taking of partners in worship along with Allah. Allah has revealed in *sūra al-Furqān*: ﴾*And these are the people who do not worship any other god apart from Allah, nor do they kill the soul whose killing without any lawful cause Allah has forbidden, nor do they commit adultery*﴿.[3] And Allah has also revealed:

---

1 •Abū Ḥafṣ al-Ḥanbalī, *al-Lubāb fī ʿulūm al-Kitāb*, 7:301.

2 Qurʾān 4:93.

3 Ibid., 25:68.

﴾*Say: 'Come, I will recite to you those things which your Lord has forbidden to you: Do not set up anything as a partner with Him; be morally excellent with parents; and do not kill your children owing to poverty. We alone give you sustenance and (will provide for) them as well. And do not draw near to shameful deeds (whether) open or hidden. And do not kill the soul whose (killing) Allah has forbidden, except when it is rightfully due (according to law in self-defence against disruption and whilst combating terrorism). It is these (injunctions) He has enjoined upon you so that you may apply reason.*[1] ﴿.[2]

[1] Ibid., 6:151.

[2] •Ibn Kathīr, *Tafsīr al-Qur'ān al-'Aẓīm*, 1:535.

اَلْبَابُ الثَّانِي

حِفْظُ نُفُوْسِ غَيْرِ الْمُسْلِمِيْنَ وَأَعْرَاضِهِمْ وَأَمْوَالِهِمْ مِنْ أَعْظَمِ الْفَرَائِضِ

CHAPTER TWO

THE PROTECTION OF LIFE, PROPERTY AND HONOUR OF NON-MUSLIMS IS AMONGST THE SUPREME DUTIES OF ISLAM

Qur'ān

١. ﴿يَـٰٓأَيُّهَا ٱلَّذِينَ ءَامَنُوا۟ كُتِبَ عَلَيْكُمُ ٱلْقِصَاصُ فِى ٱلْقَتْلَى﴾

1. ﴾*O believers! Retribution (the law of equality in punishment) is prescribed for you in the case of those who are unjustly slain.*﴿[1]

٢. ﴿وَلَكُمْ فِى ٱلْقِصَاصِ حَيَوٰةٌ يَـٰٓأُو۟لِى ٱلْأَلْبَـٰبِ لَعَلَّكُمْ تَتَّقُونَ﴾

2. ﴾*And there is a (guarantee of) life for you in retribution (i.e., vengeance of murder), O wise people, so that you may guard (against bloodshed and destruction).*﴿[2]

٣. ﴿وَلَا تَأْكُلُوٓا۟ أَمْوَٰلَكُم بَيْنَكُم بِٱلْبَـٰطِلِ وَتُدْلُوا۟ بِهَآ إِلَى ٱلْحُكَّامِ لِتَأْكُلُوا۟ فَرِيقًا مِّنْ أَمْوَٰلِ ٱلنَّاسِ بِٱلْإِثْمِ وَأَنتُمْ تَعْلَمُونَ﴾

3. ﴾*And do not eat up one another's wealth amongst yourselves through injustice, nor take wealth to the authorities (as a bribe) so that, this way, you may (also) swallow a portion of others' wealth unfairly, whilst you are aware (that this is a sin).*﴿[3]

٤. ﴿وَكَتَبْنَا عَلَيْهِمْ فِيهَآ أَنَّ ٱلنَّفْسَ بِٱلنَّفْسِ وَٱلْعَيْنَ بِٱلْعَيْنِ وَٱلْأَنفَ بِٱلْأَنفِ وَٱلْأُذُنَ بِٱلْأُذُنِ وَٱلسِّنَّ بِٱلسِّنِّ وَٱلْجُرُوحَ قِصَاصٌ﴾

4. ﴾*In that (the Torah) We had prescribed for them: a life for a life, an eye for an eye, a nose for a nose, an ear for an*

[1] Qur'ān 2:178.

[2] Ibid., 2:179.

[3] Ibid., 2:188.

ear, and a tooth for a tooth, and in the case of injuries (too) there is a requital.﴾[1]

٥. ﴿فَلَمَّا نَسُواْ مَا ذُكِّرُواْ بِهِۦٓ أَنجَيۡنَا ٱلَّذِينَ يَنۡهَوۡنَ عَنِ ٱلسُّوٓءِ وَأَخَذۡنَا ٱلَّذِينَ ظَلَمُواْ بِعَذَابِۭ بَـِٔيسِۭ بِمَا كَانُواْ يَفۡسُقُونَ﴾

5. ﴾*Then, when they forgot (all) they had been advised, We delivered those who were engaged in forbidding evil (i.e., performing the duty of preaching don'ts), and seized (the rest of) the people who committed injustice (actively or passively) with a very harsh punishment because they were disobeying.*﴿[2]

٦. ﴿وَلَا تَقۡتُلُواْ ٱلنَّفۡسَ ٱلَّتِي حَرَّمَ ٱللَّهُ إِلَّا بِٱلۡحَقِّۗ وَمَن قُتِلَ مَظۡلُومٗا فَقَدۡ جَعَلۡنَا لِوَلِيِّهِۦ سُلۡطَٰنٗا فَلَا يُسۡرِف فِّي ٱلۡقَتۡلِۖ إِنَّهُۥ كَانَ مَنصُورٗا﴾

6. ﴾*And do not kill any soul whose (killing) Allah has declared unlawful unless (killing him) is just (according to the law and decree of the court). But whoever is killed unjustly, We have indeed given his heir the right (of retribution according to the legal procedure), but he too must not exceed the limits in (retributive) killing. He is indeed helped (by Allah. The responsibility of his legal help and support will be on the government.)*﴿[3]

HADITH

٥/١. عَنْ عَبْدِ اللهِ بْنِ عَمْرٍو رضي الله عنهما عَنِ النَّبِيِّ ﷺ قَالَ: مَنْ قَتَلَ مُعَاهَدًا لَمْ يَرِحْ رَائِحَةَ الْجَنَّةِ، وَإِنَّ رِيْحَهَا تُوْجَدُ مِنْ مَسِيْرَةِ أَرْبَعِيْنَ عَامًا.

رَوَاهُ الْبُخَارِيُّ وَابْنُ مَاجَه وَالْبَزَّارُ.

[1] Ibid., 5:45.

[2] Ibid., 7:165.

[3] Ibid., 17:33.

5/1. ʿAbd Allāh b. ʿAmr ﷺ related that the Prophet ﷺ said:
"Anyone who kills a non-Muslim under treaty [*muʿāhad*] will not smell the fragrance of Paradise, even though its fragrance can be smelt at a distance of forty years."[1]

Reported by al-Bukhārī, Ibn Mājah and al-Bazzār.

٦/ ٢. وَفِي رِوَايَةٍ عَنْهُ، قَالَ: قَالَ رَسُوْلُ اللهِ ﷺ: مَنْ قَتَلَ قَتِيْلًا مِنْ أَهْلِ الذِّمَّةِ لَمْ يَجِدْ رِيْحَ الْجَنَّةِ، وَإِنَّ رِيْحَهَا لَيُوْجَدُ مِنْ مَسِيْرَةِ أَرْبَعِيْنَ عَامًا.

رَوَاهُ أَحْمَدُ وَالنَّسَائِيُّ وَاللَّفْظُ لَهُ، وَالْبَزَّارُ وَابْنُ الْجَارُوْدِ وَالْحَاكِمُ وَالْبَيْهَقِيُّ وَذَكَرَهُ الْمُنْذِرِيُّ فِي التَّرْغِيْبِ وَالتَّرْهِيْبِ. وَقَالَ الْحَاكِمُ: هَذَا حَدِيْثٌ صَحِيْحٌ.

6/2. ʿAbd Allāh b. ʿAmr ﷺ related that Allah's Messenger ﷺ said:
"Anyone who kills a non-Muslim citizen will not smell the fragrance of Paradise, while its fragrance can be smelt at a distance of forty years."[2]

Reported by Aḥmad, al-Nasāʾī (the wording is his), al-Bazzār, Ibn al-Jārūd, al-Ḥākim, al-Bayhaqī and cited by al-Mundhirī in *al-Targhīb wa al-tarhīb*. According to al-Ḥākim: "This is an authentic tradition."

---

[1] Set forth by •al-Bukhārī in *al-Ṣaḥīḥ*: *Kitāb al-jizya* [The Book of Annual Security Tax for Non-Muslims Living in an Islamic State], chapter: "The Sin of Someone Who Kills a Non-Muslim Citizen without his having Committed a Crime," 3:1155 §2995; and in *Kitāb al-Diyāt* [The Book of Blood Money], chapter: "The Sin Of Someone Who Kills a Soul Without His Having Committed A Crime," 6:2533 §6516. •Ibn Mājah in *al-Sunan*: *Kitāb al-diyāt* [The Book of Blood Money], chapter:"Someone Who Kills a Non-Muslim Citizen," 2:896 §2686. •al-Bazzār in *al-Musnad*, 6:368 §2383.

[2] Set forth by •al-Nasāʾī in *al-Sunan*: *Kitāb al-qasāma* [The Book of Taking an Oath], chapter: "The Gravity of Killing a Non-Muslim Citizen," 8:25 §4750; and in *al-Sunan al-Kubrā*, 4:221 §6952. •Aḥmad b. Ḥanbal in *al-Musnad*, 2:186§6745. •al-Bazzār in *al-Musnad*, 6:361 §3273. •al-Ḥākim in *al-Mustadrak*, 2:137 §2580. •Ibn al-Jārūd in *al-Muntaqā*, 1:212 §834. •al-Bayhaqī in *al-Sunan al-kubrā*, 8:133 §16260.

٧ / ٣. وَفِي رِوَايَةِ أَبِي هُرَيْرَةَ ﴿ عَنِ النَّبِيِّ ﴾ قَالَ: أَلَا مَنْ قَتَلَ نَفْسًا مُعَاهِدًا لَهُ ذِمَّةُ
اللهِ وَذِمَّةُ رَسُولِهِ، فَقَدْ أَخْفَرَ بِذِمَّةِ اللهِ، فَـلَا يُرَحْ رَائِحَةَ الْـجَنَّةِ، وَإِنَّ رِيْحَهَا لَيُوْجَدُ مِنْ
مَسِيْرَةِ سَبْعِيْنَ خَرِيْفًا.

رَوَاهُ التِّرْمِذِيُّ وَابْنُ مَاجَه وَأَبُوْ يَعْلَى وَالْـحَاكِمُ وَالْبَيْهَقِيُّ. وَقَالَ
التِّرْمِذِيُّ: حَدِيْثُ أَبِي هُرَيْرَةَ ﴿ حَدِيْثٌ حَسَنٌ صَحِيْحٌ.

7/3. Abū Hurayra ﷺ related that the Prophet ﷺ said:

"Listen! Anyone who kills a non-Muslim citizen who is under the protection of Allah and His Messenger violates the protection of Allah; he will not smell the fragrance of Paradise, while its fragrance reaches out as far as a distance of seventy years."[1]

Reported by al-Tirmidhī, Ibn Mājah, Abū Yaʿlā, al-Ḥākim and al-Bayhaqī. According to al-Tirmidhī: "The tradition reported by Abū Hurayra ﷺ is an authentic tradition."

٨ / ٤. وَفِي رِوَايَةِ الْقَاسِمِ بْنِ مُخَيْمِرَةَ عَنْ رَجُلٍ مِنْ أَصْحَابِ النَّبِيِّ ﴿ أَنَّ رَسُوْلَ اللهِ
﴾ قَالَ: مَنْ قَتَلَ رَجُـلًا مِنْ أَهْلِ الذِّمَّةِ لَـمْ يَجِدْ رِيْحَ الْـجَنَّةِ وَإِنَّ رِيْحَهَا لَيُوْجَدُ مِنْ
مَسِيْرَةِ سَبْعِيْنَ عَامًا.

رَوَاهُ أَحْمَدُ وَالنَّسَائِيُّ وَاللَّفْظُ لَهُ.

8/4. Qāsim b. Mukhaymira reported that he heard from a noble Companion of the Messenger of Allah ﷺ, who said:

"Anyone who kills a non-Muslim citizen under protection will not smell the fragrance of Paradise, even though its fragrance can be

---

[1] Set forth by •al-Tirmidhī in al-Sunan: Kitāb al-diyāt [The Book of Blood Money], chapter: "What has Come to us Concerning Someone Who Kills a Non-Muslim Citizen," 4:20 §1403. •Ibn Mājah in al-Sunan: Kitāb al-diyāt [The Book of Blood Money], chapter: "Someone Who Kills a Non-Muslim Citizen," 2:896 §2687. •Abū Yaʿlā in al-Musnad, 11:335 §6452. •al-Ḥākim in al-Mustadrak, 2:138 §2581. •al-Bayhaqī in al-Sunan al-kubrā, 9:205 §18511.

smelt at a distance of seventy years."[1]

Reported by Aḥmad and al-Nasāʾī and the wording is his.

٩ / ٥. وَفِي رِوَايَةِ أَبِي بَكْرَةَ، قَالَ: قَالَ النَّبِيُّ ﷺ مَنْ قَتَلَ نَفْسًا مُعَاهَدَةً بِغَيْرِ حِلِّهَا فَحَرَامٌ عَلَيْهِ الْـجَنَّةُ أَنْ يَّشُمَّ رِيْحَهَا وَإِنَّ رِيْحَهَا لَيُوْجَدُ مِنْ مَسِيْرَةِ مِئَةِ عَامٍ.

رَوَاهُ النَّسَائِيُّ وعَبْدُ الرَّزَّاقِ وَابْنُ حِبَّانَ وَالْبَزَّارُ وَالطَّبَرَانِيُّ.

9/5. Abū Bakra ﷻ related that the Prophet ﷺ said:

"Anyone who unjustly kills a non-Muslim under treaty [muʿāhad] will be forbidden to smell the fragrance of Paradise, even though its fragrance can be smelt at a distance of a hundred years."[2]

Reported by al-Nasāʾī, ʿAbd al-Razzāq, Ibn Ḥibbān, al-Bazzār and al-Ṭabarānī.

١٠ / ٦. وَفِي رِوَايَةٍ عَنْهُ أَنَّ رَسُوْلَ اللهِ ﷺ قَالَ: مَنْ قَتَلَ نَفْسًا مُعَاهَدَةً بِغَيْرِ حَقِّهَا لَـمْ يَجِدْ رَائِحَةَ الْـجَنَّةِ وَإِنَّ رَائِحَتَهَا تُوْجَدُ مِنْ مَسِيْرَةِ خَمْسِمِائَةِ عَامٍ.

رَوَاهُ الْـحَاكِمُ وَقَالَ: هَذَا حَدِيْثٌ صَحِيْحٌ عَلَى شَرْطِ مُسْلِمٍ.

10/6. Abū Bakra ﷻ also related that Allah's Messenger ﷺ said:

"Anyone who unjustly kills a non-Muslim under treaty will not approach the fragrance of Paradise, even though its fragrance can be smelt at a distance of five hundred years."[3]

---

[1] Set forth by •Aḥmad b. Ḥanbal in al-Musnad, 4:237, 5:369 §§18097, 23177. •al-Nasāʾī in al-Sunan: Kitāb al-qasāma [The Book of Taking an Oath], chapter: "The Enormity of Murdering a Non-Muslim Citizen," 8:25 §4749; and in al-Sunan al-kubrā, 4:221 §6951. Cited by •al-Mundhirī in al-Targhīb wa al-Tarhīb, 3:204 §3695.

[2] Set forth by •al-Nasāʾī in al-Sunan: Kitāb al-qasāma [The Book of Taking an Oath], chapter: "The Enormity of Murdering a Non-Muslim Citizen," 8:25 §4748; and in al-Sunan al-kubrā, 4:221 §6950. •ʿAbd al-Razzāq in al-Muṣannaf, 10:102 §18521. •Ibn Ḥibbān in al-Ṣaḥīḥ, 16:391 §8382. •al-Bazzār in al-Musnad, 9:138 §3696. •al-Ṭabarānī in al-Muʿjam al-awsaṭ, 1:207 §663.

[3] Set forth by •al-Ḥākim in al-Mustadrak ʿalā al-Ṣaḥīḥayn, 1:105 §133.

Reported by al-Ḥakim. According to al-Ḥākim: "This is an authentic tradition in conformity with the stipulation of Muslim."

١١/٧. وَفِي رِوَايَةٍ عَنْهُ قَالَ: سَمِعْتُ رَسُوْلَ اللهِ ﷺ يَقُوْلُ: مَنْ قَتَلَ نَفْسًا مُعَاهَدَةً بِغَيْرِ حَقِّهَا حَرَّمَ اللهُ عَلَيْهِ الْجَنَّةَ أَنْ يَشُمَّ رِيحَهَا وَرِيحُهَا يُوْجَدُ مِنْ مَسِيْرَةِ خَمْسِمِائَةِ عَامٍ.

رَوَاهُ الْحَاكِمُ وَابْنُ أَبِي شَيْبَةَ.

11/7. Abū Bakra ؓ also related that he heard Allah's Messenger ﷺ say:

"Allah has forbidden the fragrance of Paradise to him who unjustly kills a non-Muslim, even though its fragrance will be available at a distance of five hundred years."[1]

Reported by al-Ḥākim and Ibn Abī Shayba.

١٢/٨. عَنْ أَبِي بَكْرَةَ ؓ قَالَ: قَالَ رَسُوْلُ اللهِ ﷺ: مَنْ قَتَلَ مُعَاهِدًا فِي غَيْرِ كُنْهِهِ حَرَّمَ اللهُ عَلَيْهِ الْجَنَّةَ.

رَوَاهُ أَحْمَدُ وَأَبُوْ دَاوُدَ وَالنَّسَائِيُّ وَالدَّارِمِيُّ وَالْبَزَّارُ وَابْنُ أَبِي شَيْبَةَ، وَالْحَاكِمُ. وَقَالَ الْحَاكِمُ: هَذَا حَدِيثٌ صَحِيْحُ الْإِسْنَادِ.

12/8. Abū Bakra ؓ also related that Allah's Messenger ﷺ said:

"Any Muslim who unjustly kills a non-Muslim with whom there is a peace treaty [*muʿāhad*], Allah will make Paradise forbidden for him."[2]

---

[1] Set forth by •al-Ḥākim in *al-Mustadrak ʿalā al-Ṣaḥīḥayn*, 1:105 §134. •Ibn Abī Shayba in *al-Muṣannaf*, 5:457 §27944.

[2] Set forth by •Aḥmad b. Ḥanbal in *al-Musnad*, 5:36–38 §§20393, 20419. •Abū Dāwūd in *al-Sunan*: *Kitāb al-jihād* [The Book of Struggle], chapter: "Fulfilling the Contract of a Non-Muslim Citizen and the Sanctity of His Contract," 3:83 §2760. •al-Nasāʾī in *al-Sunan*: *Kitāb al-qasāma* [The Book

Reported by Aḥmad, Abū Dāwūd, al-Nasāʾī, al-Dārimī, al-Bazzār, Ibn Abī Shayba and al-Ḥākim. Al-Ḥākim said: "This tradition has an authentic chain of transmission."

١٣/ ٩. وَفِي رِوَايَةٍ عَنْهُ قَالَ: قَالَ رَسُوْلُ اللهِ ﷺ: مَنْ قَتَلَ نَفْساً مُعَاهَدَةً بِغَيْرِ حِلِّهَا (وَفِي رِوَايَةٍ بِغَيْرِ حَقِّهَا) حَرَّمَ اللهُ عَلَيْهِ الْـجَنَّةَ أَنْ يَجِدَ رِيْحَهَا.

رَوَاهُ أَحْمَدُ وَالْـحَاكِمُ.

13/9. Abū Bakra ﵁ also related that Allah's Messenger ﷺ said: "Any Muslim who unlawfully kills a non-Muslim (in one tradition, "unjustly" is reported), Allah has forbidden even the fragrance of Paradise to him."[1]

Reported by Aḥmad and al-Hakim.

قَالَ الْكَاشْمِيْرِيُّ فِي شَرْحِ هَذَا الْـحَدِيْثِ:

قَوْلُهُ ﷺ: "مَنْ قَتَل مُعَاهَدًا لَـمْ يَرِحْ رَائِحَةَ الْـجَنَّةِ" وَمُخُّ الْـحَدِيْثِ: إِنَّكَ أَيُّهَا الْـمُخَاطَبُ، قَدْ عَلِمْتَ مَا فِي ْ قَتْلِ الْـمُسْلِمِ مِنَ الْإِثْمِ، فَإِنَّ شَنَاعَتَهُ بَلَغَتْ مَبْلَغَ الْكُفْرِ، حَيْثُ أَوْجَبَ التَّخْلِيْدَ. أَمَّا قَتْلُ مُعَاهَدٍ، فَأَيْضًا لَيْسَ بِهَيِّنٍ، فَإِنَّ قَاتِلَهُ أَيْضًا لَا يَجِدُ رَائِحَةَ الْـجَنَّةِ.

Commenting on this hadith—*anyone who kills a non-Muslim citizen will not smell the fragrance of Paradise*—Anwar Shāh Kāshmīrī writes in his book *Fayḍ al-Bārī*:

---

of Taking an Oath], chapter: "The Gravity of Killing a Non-Muslim Citizens," 8:24 §4747; and in *al-Sunan al-kubrā*, 4:221, §6949. •al-Dārimī in *al-Sunan*, 2:308 §2504. •al-Bazzār in *al-Musnad*, 9:129 §3679. •Ibn Abī Shayba in *al-Muṣannaf*, 5:457 §27946. •al-Ḥākim in *al-Mustadrak*, 2:154 §2631. •al-Ṭabarānī in *al-Muʿjam al-awsaṭ*, 8:76 §8011. •Ibn al-Jārūd in *al-Muntaqā*, 1:213 §835. •al-Ṭayālisī in *al-Musnad*, 1:118 §879. •al-Bayhaqī in *al-Sunan al-kubrā*, 9:231 §18629.

[1] Set forth by •Aḥmad b. Ḥanbal in *al-Musnad*, 5:36 §20399. •al-Ḥākim in *al-Mustadrak ʿalā al-Ṣaḥīḥayn*, 1:105 §135.

(As for) his (ﷺ) statement, "Anyone who kills a non-Muslim under treaty [*muʿāhad*] will not smell the fragrance of Paradise, even though its fragrance can be smelt at a distance of forty years," its essence, dear brother, can be expressed like this: You know the gravity of the sin of killing a Muslim—its odiousness has reached the point of disbelief—and it necessitates that [the killer abides in Hell] forever. As for killing a non-Muslim citizen [*muʿāhad*], it is similarly no small matter, for the one who does it will not smell the fragrance of Paradise.[1]

١٤/ ١٠. عَنْ خَالِدِ بْنِ الْوَلِيدِ ﵁، قَالَ: غَزَوْنَا مَعَ رَسُولِ اللهِ ﷺ غَزْوَةَ خَيْبَرَ، فَأَسْرَعَ النَّاسُ فِي حَظَائِرِ يَهُودَ، فَأَمَرَنِي أَنْ أُنَادِيَ: الصَّلَاةُ. ... ثُمَّ قَالَ: أَيُّهَا النَّاسُ، إِنَّكُمْ قَدْ أَسْرَعْتُمْ فِي حَظَائِرِ يَهُودَ. أَلَا! لَا تَحِلُّ أَمْوَالُ الْـمُعَاهَدِينَ إِلَّا بِحَقِّهَا.

رَوَاهُ أَحْمَدُ وَأَبُوْ دَاوُدَ وَالشَّيْبَانِيُّ وَابْنُ زَنْجَوَيْهِ.

14/10. Khālid b. al-Walīd ﵁ said:

"We fought in the Battle of Khaybar [showing great *esprit de corps* owing to being] in the companionship of Allah's Messenger ﷺ and [as victory loomed] some people hastened to enter the compounds of the Jews. The Prophet ﷺ then ordered me to deliver the call to prayer ... then he said, 'O people! You have hastened to enter the compounds of the Jews, but beware; the property of the non-Muslim citizens is not lawful to you except that which is due.'"[2]

Reported by Aḥmad, Abū Dāwūd, al-Shaybānī and Ibn Zanjawayh.

١٥/ ١١. وَفِي رِوَايَةٍ عَنْهُ، عَنِ النَّبِيِّ ﷺ: أَلَا! وَإِنِّيْ أُحَرِّمُ عَلَيْكُمْ أَمْوَالَ الْـمُعَاهِدِيْنَ

[1] •Anwar Shāh Kāshmīrī, *Fayḍ al-Bārī ʿalā Ṣaḥīḥ al-Bukhārī*, 4:288.

[2] Set forth by •Aḥmad b. Ḥanbal in *al-Musnad*, 4:89 §16862. •Abū Dāwūd in *al-Sunan*: *Kitāb al-aṭʿima* [The Book of Foodstuffs], chapter: "The Unlawfulness of Eating Beasts of Prey," 3:356 §3806. •al-Shaybānī in *al-Āḥād wa al-mathānī*, 2:29 §703. •Ibn Zanjawayh in *Kitāb al-amwāl,* p. 379 §618.

بِغَيْرِ حَقِّهَا.

رَوَاهُ الطَّبَرَانِيُّ وَابْنُ زَنْجَوَيْهِ.

15/11. Khālid b. al-Walīd ﷺ also reported that the Prophet ﷺ said:

"Beware! I forbid you to take the wealth of the non-Muslim citizens unjustly."[1]

Reported by al-Ṭabarānī and Ibn Zanjawayh.

١٦/ ١٢. وَفِي رِوَايَةٍ عَنْهُ: حَرَّمَ رَسُوْلُ اللهِ ﷺ يَوْمَ خَيْبَرَ أَمْوَالَ الْـمُعَاهَدِينَ.

رَوَاهُ الدَّارَقُطْنِيُّ.

16/12. Khālid b. al-Walīd ﷺ also said:

"On the day of Khaybar, Allah's Messenger ﷺ forbade seizing the wealth of the non-Muslim citizens."[2]

Reported by al-Dāraquṭnī.

١٧/ ١٣. عَنْ عَاصِمٍ يَعْنِي ابْنَ كُلَيْبٍ عَنْ أَبِيهِ عَنْ رَجُلٍ مِنَ الْأَنْصَارِ قَالَ: خَرَجْنَا مَعَ رَسُولِ اللهِ ﷺ فِي سَفَرٍ، فَأَصَابَ النَّاسَ حَاجَةٌ شَدِيدَةٌ وَجَهْدٌ، وَأَصَابُوا غَنَمًا، فَانْتَهَبُوهَا. فَإِنَّ قُدُورَنَا لَتَغْلِي إِذْ جَاءَ رَسُولُ اللهِ ﷺ يَمْشِي عَلَى قَوْسِهِ، فَأَكْفَأَ قُدُورَنَا بِقَوْسِهِ، ثُمَّ جَعَلَ يُرَمِّلُ اللَّحْمَ بِالتُّرَابِ. ثُمَّ قَالَ: إِنَّ النُّهْبَةَ لَيْسَتْ بِأَحَلَّ مِنَ الْـمَيْتَةِ أَوْ إِنَّ الْـمَيْتَةَ لَيْسَتْ بِأَحَلَّ مِنَ النُّهْبَةِ.

رَوَاهُ أَبُوْ دَاوُدَ وَالْبَيْهَقِيُّ.

17/13. ʿĀṣim b. Kulayb narrated on the authority of his father that one of the *Anṣār* related:

"We set out on a journey with Allah's Messenger ﷺ. The people

---

[1] Set forth by •al-Ṭabarānī in *al-Muʿjam al-kabīr*, 4:111 §3828. •Ibn Zanjawayh in *Kitāb al-amwāl*, p. 380 §619.

[2] Set forth by •al-Dāraquṭnī in *al-Sunan*, 4:287 §63.

were suffering hunger and were in need, so they forcibly took some goats and slaughtered them. The pots were boiling when the Prophet ﷺ came over, holding his bow, and he started turning our pans upside down with the bow and mixing the meat with the soil. Then he said, 'Eating stolen food is not less unlawful than eating carrion,' or he said: 'Carrion is not more unlawful than plunder!'"[1]

Reported by Abū Dāwūd and al-Bayhaqī.

١٨/ ١٤. وَفِي رِوَايَةِ الْعِرْبَاضِ بْنِ سَارِيَةَ السُّلَمِيِّ قَالَ: نَزَلْنَا مَعَ النَّبِيِّ ﷺ خَيْبَرَ وَمَعَهُ مَنْ مَعَهُ مِنْ أَصْحَابِهِ. وَكَانَ صَاحِبُ خَيْبَرَ رَجُلًا مَارِدًا مُنْكَرًا فَأَقْبَلَ إِلَى النَّبِيِّ ﷺ فَقَالَ: يَا مُحَمَّدُ، أَلَكُمْ أَنْ تَذْبَحُوا حُمُرَنَا وَتَأْكُلُوا ثَمَرَنَا وَتَضْرِبُوا نِسَاءَنَا؟ فَغَضِبَ يَعْنِي النَّبِيَّ ﷺ وَقَالَ: يَا ابْنَ عَوْفٍ، ارْكَبْ فَرَسَكَ ثُمَّ نَادِ: أَلَا إِنَّ الْجَنَّةَ لَا تَحِلُّ إِلَّا لِمُؤْمِنٍ وَأَنْ اجْتَمِعُوا لِلصَّلَاةِ قَالَ: فَاجْتَمَعُوا ثُمَّ صَلَّى بِهِمُ النَّبِيُّ ﷺ ثُمَّ قَامَ فَقَالَ: أَيَحْسَبُ أَحَدُكُمْ مُتَّكِئًا عَلَى أَرِيكَتِهِ قَدْ يَظُنُّ أَنَّ اللهَ لَمْ يُحَرِّمْ شَيْئًا إِلَّا مَا فِي هَذَا الْقُرْآنِ؟ أَلَا وَإِنِّي وَاللهِ قَدْ وَعَظْتُ وَأَمَرْتُ وَنَهَيْتُ عَنْ أَشْيَاءَ إِنَّهَا لَمِثْلُ الْقُرْآنِ أَوْ أَكْثَرُ. وَإِنَّ اللهَ ﷻ لَمْ يُحِلَّ لَكُمْ أَنْ تَدْخُلُوا بُيُوتَ أَهْلِ الْكِتَابِ إِلَّا بِإِذْنٍ، وَلَا ضَرْبَ نِسَائِهِمْ، وَلَا أَكْلَ ثِمَارِهِمْ.

رَوَاهُ أَبُو دَاوُدَ وَالْبَيْهَقِيُّ.

18/14. ʿIrbāḍ b. Sāriya al-Sulamī ؓ said:

"We disembarked at Khaybar with the Prophet ﷺ and many of his Companions were with him. One of the chiefs of Khaybar who was arrogant and contentious came to the Prophet ﷺ and asked: 'Is it fair that you slaughter our donkeys, eat our fruits, and beat our women?' The Prophet ﷺ became annoyed and said: 'O Ibn ʿAwf! Ride your steed and declare that Paradise is only for the believers, and that they should gather for prayer.' They all gathered, and the Prophet ﷺ

[1] Set forth by •Abū Dāwūd in *al-Sunan*: *Kitāb al-jihād* [The Book of Jihad], 3:66 §2705. •al-Bayhaqī in *al-Sunan al-kubrā*, 9:61 §17789.

led them in prayer, stood up, and said: 'Does any of you recline on his couch and imagine that Allah has not forbidden anything save that which has been mentioned in the Qur'ān? Beware, by Allah, I have exhorted, issued commands and forbade various matters. They are as numerous as what is found in the Qur'ān, or more. Allah has not permitted you to enter the houses of the People of the Book without permission, or to beat their women, or to eat their fruit.'"[1]

Reported by Abū Dāwūd and al-Bayhaqī.

١٥ / ١٩. عَنْ يَحْيَى بْنِ سَعِيدٍ، قَالَ: حُدِّثْتُ، أَنَّ أَبَا بَكْرٍ بَعَثَ جُيُوْشًا إِلَى الشَّامِ فَخَرَجَ يَتْبَعُ يَزِيدَ بْنَ أَبِي سُفْيَانَ، فَقَالَ: إِنِّي أُوْصِيكَ بِعَشْرٍ: لَا تَقْتُلَنَّ صَبِيًّا، وَلَا امْرَأَةً، وَلَا كَبِيْرًا هَرِمًّا، وَلَا تَقْطَعَنَّ شَجَرًا مُثْمِرًا، وَلَا تُخَرِّبَنَّ عَامِرًا، لَا تَعْقِرَنَّ شَاةً وَلَا بَعِيْرًا إِلَّا لِمَأْكَلَةٍ، وَلَا تُغْرِقَنَّ نَخْلاً، وَلَاَ تُحَرِّقَنَّهُ، وَلَا تَغْلُلْ، وَلَا تَجْبُنْ.

رَوَاهُ مَالِكٌ وَابْنُ أَبِي شَيْبَةَ وَاللَّفْظُ لَهُ.

19/15. Yaḥyā b. Saʿīd states that he was told that while seeing off the Muslim forces for Syria, Abū Bakr al-Ṣiddīq ؓ came to Yazīd b. Abī Sufyān and told him:

"I command you to observe ten things: Do not kill a young child, a woman or an elderly infirm man. Do not cut down fruit-bearing trees or demolish buildings. Do not slaughter a sheep or a camel except for food. Do not drown or burn date-palm trees. And do not steal from the war booty or show cowardice."[2]

Reported by Mālik and Ibn Abī Shayba (the wording is his).

٢٠ / ١٦. وَفِي رِوَايَةِ سَعِيدِ بْنِ الْـمُسَيِّبِ أَنَّ أَبَا بَكْرٍ ؓ لَـمَّا بَعَثَ الْـجُنُوْدَ نَحْوَ

---

[1] Set forth by •Abū Dāwūd in al-Sunan: Kitāb al-kharāj wa al-imāra wa al-fayʾ [The Book of Land Tax, Leadership and the Spoils Acquired without Fighting], 3:170 §3050. •al-Bayhaqī in al-Sunan al-kubrā, 9:204 §18508. •Ibn ʿAbd al-Barr in al-Tamhīd, 1:149.

[2] Set forth by •Mālik in al-Muwaṭṭā, 2:447 §965. •Ibn Abī Shayba in al-Muṣannaf, 6:483 §33121.

الشَّامِ يَزِيْدَ بْنَ أَبِي سُفْيَانَ وَعَمْرَو بْنَ الْعَاصِ وَشُرَحْبِيْلَ بْنَ حَسَنَةَ قَالَ ... ثُمَّ جَعَلَ يُوْصِيْهِمْ فَقَالَ ... وَلَا تُفْسِدُوْا فِي الْأَرْضِ وَلَا تَعْصَوْا مَا تُؤْمَرُوْنَ ... وَلَا تُغْرِقُنَّ نَخْلًا وَلَا تُحْرِقُنَّهَا، وَلَا تَعْقِرُوْا بَهِيْمَةً وَلَا شَجَرَةً تُثْمِرُ، وَلَا تَهْدِمُوْا بِيْعَةً، وَلَا تَقْتُلُوا الْوِلْدَانَ وَلَا الشُّيُوْخَ وَلَا النِّسَاءَ. وَسَتَجِدُوْنَ أَقْوَامًا حَبَسُوْا أَنْفُسَهُمْ فِي الصَّوَامِعِ، فَدَعُوْهُمْ، وَمَا حَبَسُوْا أَنْفُسَهُمْ لَهُ.

رَوَاهُ مَالِكٌ وَعَبْدُ الرَّزَّاقِ وَالْبَيْهَقِيُّ وَاللَّفْظُ لَهُ.

20/16. According to Saʿīd b. al-Musayyib ﷺ, Abū Bakr al-Ṣiddīq ﷺ said while sending the troops to Syria under the leadership of Yazīd b. Abī Sufyān, ʿAmr b. al-ʿĀṣ and Shuraḥbīl b. Ḥasana:

"Neither sow corruption in the land nor defy what you are commanded to do. Do not drown or burn date-palm trees. Do not kill any animal. Do not cut down a fruit-bearing tree. Do not demolish a church. And do not kill any children or old people or women. Soon you shall come upon people who have secluded themselves in cloisters; you must leave them to engage in that for which they have secluded themselves."[1]

Reported by Mālik, ʿAbd al-Razzāq and al-Bayhaqī (the wording is his).

وَفِي رِوَايَةٍ زَادَ الْـهِنْدِيُّ: وَلَا مَرِيْضًا وَلَا رَاهِبًا.

ذَكَرَهُ الْـهِنْدِيُّ.

And in one version, al-Hindī added the following words:
"Do not kill a sick person or a priest."[2]

---

[1] Set forth by •Mālik in *al-Muwaṭṭā*, 2:448 §966. •ʿAbd al-Razzāq in *al-Muṣannaf*, 5:199. •al-Bayhaqī in *al-Sunan al-kubrā*, 9:85. Cited by •al-Hindī in *Kanz al-ʿummāl*, 1:296. •Ibn Qudāma in *al-Mughnī*, 8:451–452, 477 §17904.

[2] Cited by •al-Hindī in *Kanz al-ʿummāl*, 4:474 §11409.

Reported by al-Hindī.

٢١/١٧. وَفِي رِوَايَةِ ابْنِ عُمَرَ ﵄ قَالَ أَبُوبَكْرٍ الصَّدِّيقُ لِيَزِيدَ بْنِ أَبِي سُفْيَانَ: وَلَا تَهْدِمُوا بِيعَةً ... وَلَا تَقْتُلُوا شَيْخًا كَبِيرًا، وَلَا صَبِيًّا وَلَا صَغِيرًا وَلَا امْرَأَةً.

ذَكَرَهُ الْـهِنْدِيُّ.

21/17. According to ʿAbd Allāh b. ʿUmar ﵄, Abū Bakr al-Ṣiddīq ﵁ said to Yazīd b. Abī Sufyān:

"Do not demolish the cloisters, do not kill any old man or infant or a young child or woman."[1]

Reported by al-Hindī.

٢٢/١٨. قَالَ الْأَوْزَاعِيُّ: وَنَهَى أَبُو بَكْرٍ الصَّدِّيقُ أَنْ يَقْطَعَ شَجَرًا مُثْمِرًا أَوْ يُخَرَّبَ عَامِرًا، وَعَمِلَ بِذَلِكَ الْـمُسْلِمُونَ بَعْدَهُ.

رَوَاهُ التِّرْمِذِيُّ.

22/18. Al-Awzāʿī said:

"Abū Bakr al-Ṣiddīq ﵁ forbade people from cutting down fruit-bearing trees or destroying buildings [during war]—and the Muslims abided by his instructions after that."[2]

Reported by al-Tirmidhī.

٢٣/١٩. وَفِي رِوَايَةٍ: كَتَبَ عُمَرُ بْنُ الْـخَطَّابِ ﵁ إِلَى أَبِي عُبَيْدَةَ ابْنِ الْـجَرَّاحِ، وَقَالَ: وَامْنَعِ الْـمُسْلِمِينَ مِنْ ظُلْمِهِمْ وَالْإِضْرَارِ بِهِمْ وَأَكْلِ أَمْوَالِـهِمْ إِلَّا بِحِلِّهَا.

ذَكَرَهُ أَبُو يُوسُفَ.

23/19. In another narration: The letter ʿUmar b. al-Khaṭṭāb ﵁ wrote

---

[1] Ibid., 4:475 §11411.

[2] Set forth by •al-Tirmidhī in *al-Sunan: Kitāb al-siyar* [The Book of Military Expeditions], 4:122 §1552.

to Abū ʿUbayda b. al-Jarrāḥ 🕮, the Governor of Syria, contained:

"[In your capacity as Governor] see to it that you prohibit the Muslims [under your command] from oppressing them [the non-Muslim citizens], harming them or illegally eating up their wealth, except what is lawful."[1]

Narrated by Abū Yūsuf.

٢٤ / ٢٠. وَفِي رِوَايَةٍ، قَالَ عَلِيٌّ 🕮: إِنَّمَا بَذَلُوا الْـجِزْيَةَ لِتَكُونَ دِمَاؤُهُمْ كَدِمَائِنَا وَأَمْوَالُـهُمْ كَأَمْوَالِنَا.

ذَكَرَهُ النَّوَوِيُّ.

24/20. In one tradition, ʿAlī b. Abī Ṭālib 🕮 said:

"The non-Muslim citizens pay the security tax so that their blood and property should be as inviolable as ours."[2]

Narrated by al-Nawawī.

TRADITIONS OF PIOUS SCHOLARS OF EARLY TIMES

• قَالَ الإِمَامُ النَّوَوِيُّ الشَّافِعِيُّ فِي شَرْحِهِ: فَإِنَّ مَالَ الذِّمِّيِّ وَالْـمُعَاهَدِ وَالْـمُرْتَدِّ فِي هَذَا كَمَالِ الْـمُسْلِمِ.

Imam Yaḥyā b. Sharaf al-Nawawī writes: "In this context, the wealth of the non-Muslim citizen, the non-Muslim under agreement of protection and even the apostate is certainly like that of a Muslim."[3]

• قَالَ الإِمَامُ ابْنُ قُدَامَةَ الْـحَنْبَلِيُّ: فَإِنَّ الْـمُسْلِمَ يُقْطَعُ بِسَرِقَةِ مَالِهِ.

Imam Ibn Qudāma al-Ḥanbalī said: "Indeed, the prescribed punishment shall be enforced if a Muslim happens

---

[1] Cited by •Abū Yūsuf in al-Kharāj, p. 141.

[2] Cited by •Ibn Qudāma in al-Mughnī, 9:181. •al-Zaylaʿī in Naṣb al-rāya, 3:381.

[3] •Al-Nawawī, Sharḥ Ṣaḥīḥ Muslim, 12:7.

to steal the possessions of a non-Muslim."[1]

- قَالَ الْإِمَامُ أَبُوْ مُحَمَّدٍ ابْنُ حَزْمٍ الظَّاهِرِيُّ: لَا خِلَافَ فِي أَنَّ الْـمُسْلِمَ يُقْطَعُ إِنْ سَرَقَ مِنْ مَالِ الذِّمِّيِّ وَالْـمُسْتَأْمِنِ.

Imam Abū Muhammad Ibn Ḥazm al-Ẓāhirī holds: "There is no disagreement on subjecting a Muslim to the prescribed punishment if he steals the possessions of a non-Muslim citizen."[2]

- قَالَ الْإِمَامُ ابْنُ رُشْدٍ الْـمَالِكِيُّ: وَأَمَّا مِنْ طَرِيْقِ الْقِيَاسِ فَإِنَّهُمُ اعْتَمَدُوْا عَلَى إِجْمَاعِ الْـمُسْلِمِيْنَ أَنَّ يَدَ الْـمُسْلِمِ تُقْطَعُ إِذَا سَرَقَ مِنْ مَالِ الذِّمِّيِّ.

Imam Ibn Rushd al-Mālikī said: "There is a consensus on the prescribed punishment that it shall be awarded to the Muslim who steals the possessions of a non-Muslim citizen."[3]

- وَقَالَ الْإِمَامُ الْـحَصْكَفِيُّ الْـحَنَفِيُّ: وَيَضْمَنُ الْـمُسْلِمُ قِيْمَةَ خَمْرِهِ وَخِنْزِيْرِهِ إِذَا أَتْلَفَهُ.

Imam al-Ḥaṣkafī al-Ḥanafī has observed: "The Muslim who destroys his [the Christian's] wine and pork is legally responsible to pay for it."[4]

- وَذَكَرَ الْقُرَافِيُّ الْـمَالِكِيُّ: وَكَذَلِكَ حَكَى ابْنُ حَزْمٍ فِي «مَرَاتِبِ الْإِجْمَاعِ» لَهُ: أَنَّ مَنْ كَانَ فِي الذِّمَّةِ وَجَاءَ أَهْلُ الْحَرْبِ إِلَى بِلَادِنَا يَقْصِدُوْنَهُ، وَجَبَ عَلَيْنَا أَنْ نَخْرُجَ لِقِتَالِـهِمْ بِالْكُرَاعِ وَالسِّلَاحِ، وَنَمُوْتُ دُوْنَ ذَلِكَ.

Imam al-Qurāfī al-Mālikī writes that Ibn Ḥazm has

1 •Ibn Qudāma, *al-Mughnī*, 9:112.

2 •Ibn Ḥazm, *al-Muḥallā*, 10:351.

3 •Ibn Rushd al-Mālikī, *Bidāyat al-mujtahid*, 2:299.

4 •Al-Ḥaṣkafī, *al-Durr al-mukhtār*, 2:223. •Ibn ʿĀbidīn al-Shāmī, *Radd al-muḥtār*, 3:273.

described in his book *Marātib al-ijmāʿ*:

"Indeed for the *dhimmīs* (non-Muslim citizens), it is binding on our Islamic state that, for the protection of non-Muslim citizens, we wage war with military might against those combatants who aggress against them, even though our troops may die (in fighting against the aggressors)".[1]

وَذَكَرَ الْقُرَافِيُّ الْمَالِكِيُّ أَيْضًا: إِنَّ عَقْدَ الذِّمَّةِ لَمَّا كَانَ عَقْدًا عَظِيْمًا، فَيُوْجِبُ عَلَيْنَا حُقُوْقًا لَهُمْ مِنْهَا مَا حَكَى ابْنُ حَزْمٍ فِي «مَرَاتِبِ الْإِجْمَاعِ». وَنَجْعَلُهُمْ فِي جِوَارِنَا وَفِي حَقِّ رَبِّنَا وَفِي ذِمَّةِ اللهِ تَعَالَى وَذِمَّةِ رَسُوْلِ اللهِ ﷺ وَذِمَّةِ دِيْنِ الْإِسْلَامِ.

وَالَّذِيْ إِجْمَاعُ الأُمَّةِ عَلَيْهِ أَنَّ مَنْ كَانَ فِي الذِّمَّةِ وَجَاءَ أَهْلُ الْحَرْبِ إِلَى بِلَادِنَا يَقْصِدُوْنَهُ، وَجَبَ عَلَيْنَا أَنْ نَّخْرُجَ لِقِتَالِهِمْ بِالْكُرَاعِ وَالسِّلَاحِ، وَنَمُوْتُ دُوْنَ ذَلِكَ صَوْنًا لِمَنْ هُوَ فِي ذِمَّةِ اللهِ تَعَالَى وَذِمَّةِ رَسُوْلِهِ ﷺ. فَإِنَّ تَسْلِيْمَهُ دُوْنَ ذَلِكَ إِهْمَالٌ لِعَقْدِ الذِّمَّةِ.

وَمِنْهَا أَنَّ مَنِ اعْتَدَى عَلَيْهِمْ وَلَو بِكَلِمَةِ سُوْءٍ أَوْ غِيْبَةٍ فِي عِرْضِ أَحَدِهِمْ أَوْ نَوْعٍ مِنْ أَنْوَاعِ الْأَذِيَّةِ أَوْ أَعَانَ عَلَى ذَلِكَ، فَقَدْ ضَيَّعَ ذِمَّةَ اللهِ تَعَالَى وَذِمَّةَ رَسُوْلِهِ.

Imam al-Qurāfī al-Mālikī has also demonstrated:

The *dhimma* contract concluded with the non-Muslims is a great treaty that establishes certain rights they have upon us. Some of these rights are those which Ibn Ḥazm has described in his book *Marātib al-ijmāʿ*. Hence, we keep the non-Muslim citizens protected in our proximity under the bountiful obligation of their rights prescribed by our Lord,

[1] •al-Qurāfī, *al-Furūq*, 3:29.

> Almighty Allah, the Messenger of God ﷺ and the religion of Islam.
>
> There exists among *Umma* a consensus on it. Indeed, when the *dhimmīs* (non-Muslim citizens) are there and the aggressing combatants intrude into the boundaries of our state with the intention to commit aggression against them, it is incumbent upon the Islamic state to fight (against the aggressors) with troops and military arsenal, even if (while fighting, the soldiers) lay down their lives. (The state is) to protect the Non-Muslim citizens, for they are under the bountiful obligation of Allah and His Messenger. Handing them over to the aggressing combatants without fighting a defensive war will be in sheer negligence of and indifference to the *dhimma* contract.
>
> One of the rights of the Non-Muslim citizens is also that if an individual aggresses against the Non-Muslim citizens—even if defaming someone by an evil word, through backbiting, afflicting with torture or supporting someone against them—he will render the bountiful obligation of Allah and His Messenger ﷺ null and void.[1]

The aforementioned sayings of the jurists prove that it is obligatory for all Muslims to protect the honour and wealth of non-Muslim citizens.

---

[1] •al-Qurāfī, *al-Furūq*, 3:29.

اَلْبَابُ الثَّالِثُ

مَنْعُ قَتْلِ النِّسَاءِ وَالْوِلْدَانِ وَالشُّيُوْخِ وَالرُّهْبَانِ

CHAPTER THREE

THE PROHIBITION OF KILLING WOMEN, CHILDREN, THE ELDERLY AND PRIESTS

٢٥ / ١. عَنِ ابْنِ عُمَرَ ﷺ قَالَ: وُجِدَتِ امْرَأَةٌ مَقْتُوْلَةً فِي بَعْضِ مَغَازِي رَسُوْلِ اللهِ ﷺ فَنَهَى رَسُوْلُ اللهِ ﷺ عَنْ قَتْلِ النِّسَاءِ وَالصِّبْيَانِ.

مُتَّفَقٌ عَلَيْهِ.

25/1. ᶜAbd Allāh b. ᶜUmar ﷺ said:

"A woman was found slain in one of the expeditions. Upon this Allah's Messenger ﷺ forbade the killing of women and children."[1]

Agreed upon by al-Bukhārī and Muslim.

٢٦ / ٢. وَفِي رِوَايَةٍ طَوِيْلَةٍ عَنْ يَزِيدَ بْنِ هُرْمُزَ فَمِنْهَا، فَكَتَبَ إِلَيْهِ (أَيْ النَّجْدَةَ) ابْنُ عَبَّاسٍ فَقَالَ: وَإِنَّ رَسُولَ اللهِ ﷺ لَـمْ يَكُنْ يَقْتُلُ الصِّبْيَانَ فَلَا تَقْتُلِ الصِّبْيَانَ.

رَوَاهُ مُسْلِمٌ.

26/2. Yazīd b. Hurmuz narrated in a detailed report:

"ᶜAbd Allah b. ᶜAbbās wrote in reply to a letter from Najda: 'Indeed, the Messenger of Allah ﷺ did not kill children; so you must not kill them either.'"[2]

---

[1] Set forth by •al-Bukhārī in *al-Ṣaḥīḥ*: *Kitāb al-jihād wa al-siyar* [The Book of Jihad and Battles], chapter: "Killing Women in War," 3:1098 §2852. •Muslim in *al-Saḥīḥ: Kitāb al-jihād wa al-siyar* [The Book of Jihad and Battles], chapter: "The Unlawfulness of Killing Women and Children during War," 3:1364 §1744. •Aḥmad b. Ḥanbal in *al-Musnad*, 2:22 §4739. •al-Tirmidhī in *al-Sunan*: *Kitāb al-siyar* [The Book of Military Expeditions], chapter: "What Has Come to Us about the Killing of Women and Children," 4:136 §1569. •Ibn Mājah in *al-Sunan*: *Kitāb al-jihād* [The Book of Jihad], chapter, "Indiscriminate night attacks and killing women and children," 2:947 §2841. •al-Nasā'ī in *al-Sunan al-kubrā*, 5:185 §8618. •al-Dārimī in *al-Sunan*, 2:293 §2462. •Ibn Ḥibbān in al-Ṣaḥīḥ, 1:344 §135.

[2] Set forth by •Muslim in *al-Ṣaḥīḥ: Kitāb al-jihād wa al-siyar* [The Book of

Reported by Muslim.

٢٧/ ٣. وَفِي رِوَايَةِ رَبَاحِ بْنِ رَبِيْعٍ ﵁ قَالَ: كُنَّا مَعَ رَسُوْلِ اللهِ ﷺ فِي غَزْوَةٍ، فَرَأَى النَّاسَ مُجْتَمِعِيْنَ عَلَى شَيءٍ، فَبَعَثَ رَجُلًا فَقَالَ: انْظُرْ عَلَامَ اجْتَمَعَ هَؤُلَاءِ؟ فَجَاءَ فَقَالَ: عَلَى امْرَأَةٍ قَتِيْلٍ، فَقَالَ: مَا كَانَتْ هَذِهِ لِتُقَاتِلَ. قَالَ: وَعَلَى الْمُقَدِّمَةِ خَالِدُ بْنُ الْوَلِيْدِ، فَبَعَثَ رَجُلًا فَقَالَ: قُلْ لِخَالِدٍ: لَا يَقْتُلَنَّ امْرَأَةً وَلَا عَسِيْفًا.

وفي رواية: لَا تَقْتُلَنَّ ذُرِّيَّةً وَلَا عَسِيْفًا.

رَوَاهُ أَحْمَدُ وأَبُوْ دَاوُدَ وَاللَّفْظُ لَهُ وَابْنُ مَاجَه وَالنَّسَائِيُّ وَابْنُ حِبَّانَ وَابْنُ أَبِي شَيْبَةَ وَأَبُوْ يَعْلَى وَالْحَاكِمُ.

27/3. According to Rabāḥ b. Rabīʿ ﵁:

"We were with Allah's Messenger ﷺ in one of the battle expeditions, and he saw some people gathered around something. He sent a man out, saying: 'Go and see what they are gathering around.' The man returned and informed him, saying: 'They are gathering around a slain woman.' The Prophet ﷺ said: 'She was not amongst those who fight!' The head of the group was Khālid b. al-Walīd, so the Prophet sent a man to go and inform him: 'Neither an [idolatrous] woman nor a hired servant should be killed.'"[1]

In another report, it is stated: "neither [idolatrous]

Jihad and Battles], chapter: "Women participants in jihid to be given a prize but not a regular share in the booty, and prohibition to kill children of the enemy," 3:1444 §1812.

[1] Set forth by •Aḥmad b. Ḥanbal in *al-Musnad*, 3:488 §16035. •Abū Dāwūd in *al-Sunan*: *Kitāb al-jihād* [The Book of Jihad], chapter: "The Killing of Women," 3:53 §2669. •Ibn Mājah in *al-Sunan*: *Kitāb al-jihād* [The Book of Jihad], chapter: "Making a sudden raid at night and the killing women and children," 2:948 §2842. •al-Nasāʾī in *al-Sunan al-kubrā*, 5:186–187 §§8625, 8627. •Ibn Ḥibbān in *al-Ṣaḥīḥ*, 11:110 §4789. •Ibn Abī Shayba in *al-Muṣannaf*, 6:482 §33117. •Abū Yaʿlā in *al-Musnad*, 3:115–116 §1546. •al-Ḥākim in *al-Mustadrak*, 2:133 §2565. •al-Ṭabarānī in *al-Muʿjam al-kabīr*, 4:10 §3489. •al-Bayhaqī in *al-Sunan al-kubrā*, 9:82 §17883.

children nor a hired servant should be killed."

Reported by Aḥmad, Abū Dāwūd (the wording is his), Ibn Mājah, al-Nasā'ī, Ibn Ḥibbān, Ibn Abī Shayba, Abū Ya'lā and al-Ḥākim.

٢٨/ ٤. عَنْ أَنَسٍ ﷺ، كَانَ رَسُولُ اللهِ ﷺ إِذَا غَزَا قَوْمًا لَمْ يُغِرْ حَتَّى يُصْبِحَ.

رَوَاهُ الْبُخَارِيُّ وَأَحْمَدُ وَابْنُ حِبَّانَ وَأَبُو يَعْلَى.

28/4. According to Anas b. Mālik ﷺ:

"Allah's Messenger ﷺ would not attack any nation until daybreak."[1]

Reported by al-Bukhārī, Aḥmad, Ibn Ḥibbān and Abū Ya'lā.

٢٩/ ٥. وَفِي رِوَايَةٍ عَنْهُ: أَنَّ النَّبِيَّ ﷺ خَرَجَ إِلَى خَيْبَرَ فَجَاءَهَا لَيْلًا. وَكَانَ إِذَا جَاءَ قَوْمًا بِلَيْلٍ لَا يُغِيْرُ عَلَيْهِمْ حَتَّى يُصْبِحَ.

رَوَاهُ الْبُخَارِيُّ وَالتِّرْمِذِيُّ وَالنَّسَائِيُّ وَابْنُ حِبَّانَ.

29/5. Anas b. Mālik ﷺ also said:

"The Prophet ﷺ set out towards Khaybar. He arrived there at night. When he came to a people [a force] at night, he would not attack them until daybreak."[2]

Reported by al-Bukhārī, al-Tirmidhī, al-Nasā'ī and Ibn Ḥibbān.

---

[1] Set forth by •al-Bukhārī in *al-Ṣaḥīḥ*: *Kitāb al-jihād wa al-siyar* [The Book of Struggle and Military Expeditions], chapter: "The Prophet's summons to Islam and Prophethood," 3:1077 §2784. •Aḥmad b. Ḥanbal in *al-Musnad*, 3:159 §12639. •Abū Ya'lā in *al-Musnad*, 6:431 §3804. •Ibn Ḥibbān in *al-Ṣaḥīḥ*, 11:49 §4745.

[2] Set forth by •al-Bukhārī in *al-Ṣaḥīḥ*: *Kitāb al-jihād wa al-siyar* [The Book of Struggle and Military Expeditions], chapter: "The Prophet ﷺ calling people to Islam and Prophethood," 3:1077 §2785. •al-Tirmidhī in *al-Sunan*: *Kitāb al-siyar* [The Military Expeditions], chapter: "Waging night offences and indiscriminate nocturnal attacks," p. 335," 4:121 §1550. •al-Nasā'ī in *al-Sunan al-kubrā*, 5:178 §8598. •Ibn Ḥibbān in *al-Ṣaḥīḥ*, 11:51 §4746.

٣٠/ ٦. عَنِ الأَسْوَدِ بْنِ سَرِيْعٍ ﷺ قَالَ: كُنَّا فِي غَزَاةٍ فَأَصَبْنَا ظَفَرًا وَقَتَلْنَا مِنَ الْـمُشْرِكِيْنَ حَتَّى بَلَغَ بِهِمُ الْقَتْلُ إِلَى أَنْ قَتَلُوْا الذُّرِّيَّةَ فَبَلَغَ ذَلِكَ النَّبِيَّ ﷺ فَقَالَ: مَا بَالُ أَقْوَامٍ بَلَغَ بِهِمُ الْقَتْلُ إِلَى أَنْ قَتَلُوْا الذُّرِّيَّةَ؟ أَ لَا، لَا تَقْتُلُنَّ ذُرِّيَّةً! أَ لَا، لَا تَقْتُلُنَّ ذُرِّيَّةً! قِيْلَ: لِـمَ، يَا رَسُوْلَ اللهِ، أَلَيْسَ هُمْ أَوْلَادَ الْـمُشْرِكِيْنَ؟ قَالَ: أَوَ لَيْسَ خِيَارُكُمْ أَوْلَادَ الْـمُشْرِكِيْنَ؟

وفِي رِوايةٍ زاد: فَقَالَ رَجُلٌ: يَا رَسُوْلَ اللهِ، إِنَّمَا هُمْ أَبْنَاءُ الْـمُشْرِكِيْنَ. فَقَالَ: خِيَارُكُمْ أَبْنَاءُ الْـمُشْرِكِيْنَ. أَ لَا، لَا تُقْتَلُ الذُّرِّيَّةُ! كُلُّ نَسَمَةٍ تُوْلَدُ عَلَى الْفِطْرَةِ، حَتَّى يُعْرِبَ عَنْهَا لِسَانُهَا، فَأَبَوَاهَا يُهَوِّدَانِهَا وَيُنَصِّرَانِهَا.

رَوَاهُ أَحْمَدُ وَالنَّسَائِيُّ وَالدَّارِمِيُّ وَابْنُ أَبِي شَيْبَةَ. وَقَالَ الْـحَاكِمُ: هَذَا حَدِيْثٌ صَحِيْحٌ عَلَى شَرْطِ الشَّيْخَيْنِ، وَقَالَ الْهَيْثَمِيُّ: رَوَاهُ أَحْمَدُ بِأَسَانِيْدَ وَبَعْضُ أَسَانِيْدِ أَحْمَدَ رِجَالُهُ رِجَالُ الصَّحِيْحِ.

30/6. Al-Aswad b. Sarīʿ ﷺ narrated:

"We were once in a battle and gained the upper hand and killed many of the pagans, including some children. The news reached the Prophet ﷺ and he said, 'What is wrong with some people that they went so far as to kill children? Beware! Do not kill children at all! Beware! Do not kill children at all!" Someone asked: 'Why, O Messenger of Allah? Are they not the children of the pagans?' He replied: 'Are the best amongst you not from the children of pagans?'"[1]

---

[1] Set forth by •Aḥmad b. Ḥanbal in *al-Musnad*, 3:435 §15626-15627 and in 4:24 §16342. •al-Nasāʾī in *al-Sunan al-kubrā*: *Kitāb al-siyar* [The Book of Military Expeditions], chapter: "The Prohibition of Killing the Children of the Pagans," 5:184 §8616. •al-Dārimī in *al-Sunan*, 2:294 §2463. •Ibn Abī Shayba in *al-Muṣannaf*, 6:484 §33131. •Ibn Ḥibbān in *al-Ṣaḥīḥ*, 1:341 §132. •al-Ḥākim in *al-Mustadrak*, 2:133–134 §2566–2567. •al-Ṭabarānī in *al-Muʿjam al-kabīr*, 1:284 §829. •al-Shaybānī in *al-Āḥād wa al-Mathānī*, 2:375 §1160. •Abū Nuʿaym in *Ḥilya al-Awliyāʾ*, 8:263. •al-Bayhaqī in *al-Sunan al-kubrā*, 9:77 §17868. Cited by •al-Haythamī in *Majmaʿ al-zawāʾid*, 5:316.

In another narration it reads: "A man said: 'O Messenger of Allah! They are only the children of the pagans!' He ﷺ replied: 'The best of you are the children of pagans. Beware! Children must not be killed. Every soul is born upon the primordial nature (*fiṭra*), until his language manifests it and his parents make him a Jew or a Christian.'"

Reported by Aḥmad, al-Nasā'ī, al-Dārimī and Ibn Abī Shayba. Al-Ḥākim said: "This is an authentic tradition in conformity with the stipulation of al-Bukhārī and Muslim." According to al-Haythamī: "Aḥmad narrated it from several chains and the sources of some chains are authentic."

٣١/ ٧. وَفِي رِوَايَةٍ عَنْهُ: فَقَالَ أَلَا أَنَّ خِيَارَكُمْ أَبْنَاءُ الْـمُشْرِكِيْنَ ثُمَّ قَالَ: أَلا لَاتَقْتُلُوْا ذُرِّيَّةً أَلَا لَا تَقْتُلُوا ذُرِّيَّةً.

رَوَاهُ أَحْمَدُ وَالْبَيْهَقِيُّ.

31/7. Al-Aswad b. Sarīʿ has also reported that Allah's Messenger ﷺ said:

"Beware! The best among you were the sons of pagans. Beware! Do not kill children at all! Beware! Do not kill children at all!"[1]

Reported by Aḥmad and al-Bayhaqī.

٣٢/ ٨. عَنِ ابْنِ عَبَّاسٍ قَالَ: كَانَ رَسُولُ اللهِ ﷺ إِذَا بَعَثَ جُيُوشَهُ قَالَ: اخْرُجُوْا بِسْمِ اللهِ. تُقَاتِلُوْنَ فِي سَبِيْلِ اللهِ مَنْ كَفَرَ بِاللهِ. لَا تَغْدِرُوا، وَلَا تَغُلُّوْا، وَلَا تُمَثِّلُوْا، وَلَا تَقْتُلُوا الْوِلْدَانَ، وَلَا أَصْحَابَ الصَّوَامِعِ.

رَوَاهُ أَحْمَدُ وَابْنُ أَبِي شَيْبَةَ وأَبُوْ يَعْلَى.

32/8. Ibn ʿAbbās ؓ reported:

---

[1] Set forth by •Aḥmad b. Ḥanbal in *al-Musnad*, 3:435 §15626–15627. •al-Bayhaqī in *al-Sunan al-kubrā*, 9:77 §17868.

"While dispatching the troops, the Messenger of Allah ﷺ used to give the instructions: 'Depart in the name of Allah. You are going to fight with infidels in the way of Allah; do not break a promise or a treaty; do not steal from the spoils of war; do not mutilate the bodies; and do not slay children and monks.'"[1]

Reported by Aḥmad, Ibn Abī Shayba and Abū Yaʿlā.

٣٣/ ٩. وَفِي رِوَايَةٍ عَنْهُ قَالَ: إِنَّ النَّبِيَّ ﷺ كَانَ إِذَا بَعَثَ جُيُوْشَهُ قَالَ: لَا تَقْتُلُوا أَصْحَابَ الصَّوَامِعِ.

رَوَاهُ ابْنُ أَبِي شَيْبَةَ وَالطَّحَاوِيُّ وَالدَّيْلَمِيُّ.

33/9. Ibn ʿAbbās ﵄ has reported:

"The Prophet ﷺ would enjoin as he dispatched an army: 'Do not kill those (priests) who tend to monasteries.'"[2]

Reported by Ibn Abī Shayba, al-Ṭaḥāwī and al-Daylamī.

٣٤/ ١٠. وَفِي رِوَايَةٍ عَنْ عَلِيِّ بْنِ أَبِي طَالِبٍ ﵁ قَالَ: كَانَ نَبِيُّ اللهِ ﷺ إِذَا بَعَثَ جَيْشًا مِّنَ الْـمُسْلِمِيْنَ إِلَى الْـمُشْرِكِيْنَ قَالَ: انْطَلِقُوْا بِاسْمِ اللهِ فَذَكَرَ الْـحَدِيْثَ وَفِيْهِ وَلَا تَقْتُلُوا وَلِيدًا طِفْـلًا، وَلَا امْرَأَةً، وَلَا شَيْخًا كَبِيْرًا، وَلَا تَغُوْرُنَّ عَيْنًا، وَلَا تَعْقِرُنَّ شَجَرَةً إِلَّا شَجَرًا يَمْنَعُكُمْ قِتَالاً أَوْ يَحْجُزُ بَيْنَكُمْ وَبَيْنَ الْـمُشْرِكِيْنَ، وَلَا تُمَثِّلُوْا بِآدَمِيٍّ وَلَا بَهِيْمَةٍ، وَلَا تَغْدِرُوْا وَلَا تَغُلُّوْا.

رَوَاهُ الْبَيْهَقِيُّ وَذَكَرَهُ الْـهِنْدِيُّ.

34/10. ʿAlī b. Abī Ṭālib ﵁ said that when the Prophet ﷺ dispatched

[1] Set forth by •Aḥmad b. Ḥanbal in *al-Musnad*, 1:300 §2728. •Ibn Abī Shayba in *al-Muṣannaf*, 6:484 §33132. •Abū Yaʿlā in *al-Musnad*, 4:422 §2549. Cited by •Ibn Rushd in *Bidāya al-mujtahid*, 1:281.

[2] Set forth by •Ibn Abī Shayba in *al-Mussannaf*, 6:484 §33132. •Abū Yaʿlā in *al-Musnad*, 5:59 §2650. •al-Ṭaḥāwī in *Sharḥ maʿānī al-āthār*, 3:225. •al-Daylamī in *Musnad al-firdaws*, 5:45 §7410.

the Muslim army towards the pagans, he would advise them to proceed in the name of Allah and then enjoin:

"Do not kill a young boy, a woman or an old man. Do not cause fountains to dry up and do not destroy any trees, except those that cause hindrance during war. Mutilate neither a human nor an animal, and do not break a promise or breach a trust."[1]

Reported by al-Bayhaqī and cited by al-Hindī.

٣٥ / ١١. عَنْ أَنَسِ بْنِ مَالِكٍ أَنَّ رَسُوْلَ الله ﷺ قَالَ: وَلَا تَقْتُلُوا شَيْخًا فَانِيًا وَلَا طِفْلاً وَلَا صَغِيرًا وَلَا امْرَأَةً.

رَوَاهُ أَبُوْ دَاوُدَ وَابْنُ أَبِي شَيْبَةَ وَالْبَيْهَقِيُّ.

35/11. Anas b. Mālik ☝ related that Allah's Messenger ﷺ said:

"Do not kill any infirm old man, or any infant or young child or woman."[2]

Reported by Abū Dāwūd, Ibn Abī Shayba and al-Bayhaqī.

٣٦ / ١٢. وَفِي رِوَايَةِ رَاشِدِ بْنِ سَعْدٍ قَالَ: نَهَى رَسُوْلُ الله ﷺ عَنْ قَتْلِ النِّسَاءِ وَالذُّرِّيَّةِ وَالشَّيْخِ الْكَبِيرِ الَّذِي لَا حِرَاكَ بِهِ.

رَوَاهُ ابْنُ أَبِي شَيْبَةَ.

36/12. Rāshid b. Saʿd narrated:

"The Messenger of Allah ﷺ forbade the killing of women, children and the debilitated and infirm old man."[3]

Reported by Ibn Abī Shayba.

---

[1] Set forth by •al-Bayhaqī in al-Sunan al-kubrā, 9:90 §17934. Cited by •al-Hindī in Kanz al-ʿummāl, 4:205 §11425.

[2] Set forth by •Abū Dāwūd in al-Sunan: Kitāb al-jihād [The Book of Jihad], 3:37 §2614. •Ibn Abī Shayba in al-Muṣannaf, 6:483 §33118. •al-Bayhaqī in al-Sunan al-kubrā, 9:90 §17932.

[3] Set forth by •Ibn Abī Shayba in al-Muṣannaf, 6:483 §33135.

٣٧/ ١٣. وَفِي رِوَايَةِ ابْنِ كَعْبِ بْنِ مَالِكٍ ﵁ أَنَّ النَّبِيَّ ﷺ حِينَ بَعَثَ إِلَى ابْنِ أَبِي حَقِيقٍ، نَهَى حِينَئِذٍ عَنْ قَتْلِ النِّسَاءِ وَالصِّبْيَانِ.

رَوَاهُ عَبْدُ الرَّزَّاقِ وَالشَّافِعِيُّ وَالطَّحَاوِيُّ وَالْبَيْهَقِيُّ.

37/13. Ibn Ka'b b. Mālik 🙵 narrated:

"When the Prophet 🙙 dispatched an army to Ibn Abī Ḥaqīq, he forbade the killing of women and children."[1]

Reported by 'Abd al-Razzāq, al-Shāfi'ī, al-Ṭaḥāwī and al-Bayhaqī.

٣٨/ ١٤. وَفِي رِوَايَةِ عَطِيَّةَ الْقُرَظِيِّ قَالَ: كُنْتُ فِيمَنْ حَكَمَ فِيهِمْ سَعْدُ بْنُ مُعَاذٍ، فَشَكُّوا فِيَّ: أَمِنَ الذُّرِّيَّةِ أَنَا أَمْ مِنَ الْـمُقَاتِلَةِ؟ فَنَظَرُوا إِلَى عَانَتِي فَلَمْ يَجِدُوهَا نَبَتَتْ، فَأُلْقِيتُ فِي الذُّرِّيَّةِ، وَلَـمْ أُقْتَلْ.

رَوَاهُ ابْنُ حِبَّانَ وَعَبْدُ الرَّزَّاقِ وَالطَّبَرَانِيُّ وَالْبَيْهَقِيُّ.

38/14. According to 'Aṭiya al-Quraẓī 🙵:

"I was amongst those judged by Sa'd b. Mu'ādh [when he was given the authority to decide the fate of the plotters of Banū Qurayẓa], but they were in doubt about me—was I to be counted amongst the children or amongst those who engaged in hostilities?—so, to find the answer, they examined my pubic regions and saw that I had yet to grow pubic hair [and thus was underage], so they grouped me with the children and I was spared."[2]

---

[1] Set forth by •'Abd al-Razzāq in *al-Muṣannaf*, 5:202 §9385. •al-Shāfi'ī in *al-Musnad*, p. 238. •al-Ṭaḥāwī in *Sharḥ ma'ānī al-āthār*, 3:221. •al-Bayhaqī in *al-Sunan al-kubrā*, 9:77 §17865.

[2] Set forth by •Ibn Ḥibbān in *al-Ṣaḥīḥ*: *Kitāb al-siyar* [The Book of Military Expeditions], chapter: "An assertive act of resistance against the head of the state and the method of jihad," 11:109 §4788. •'Abd al-Razzāq in *al-Muṣannaf*, 10:179 §18742. •al-Ṭabarānī in *al-Mu'jam al-kabīr*, 17:164 §434. •al-Bayhaqī in *al-Sunan al-kubrā*, 6:166 §11098.

Reported by Ibn Ḥibbān, ʿAbd al-Razzāq, al-Ṭabarānī and al-Bayhaqī.

٣٩/ ١٥. وَفِي رِوَايَةٍ عَنْ أَبِي ثَعْلَبَةَ الْـخُشَنِيِّ قَالَ: نَهَى رَسُوْلُ اللهِ ﷺ عَنْ قَتْلِ النِّسَاءِ وَالْوِلْدَانِ.

رَوَاهُ الطَّبَرَانِيُّ.

39/15. Abū Thaʿlaba al-Khushanī reported:

"The Messenger of Allah ﷺ prohibited the killing of women and children."[1]

Reported by al-Ṭabarānī.

- قَالَ الْإِمَامُ السَّرْخَسِيُّ فِي كِتَابِهِ الْـمَشْهُوْرِ «الْـمَبْسُوْطِ»: قَالَ ﷺ: وَلَا تَقْتُلُوْا وَلِيدًا وَالْوَلِيْدُ الْـمَوْلُوْدُ فِي اللُّغَةِ وَكُلُّ آدَمِيٍّ مَوْلُوْدٌ، وَلَكِنَّ هَذَا اللَّفْظُ إِنَّمَا يُسْتَعْمَلُ فِي الصِّغَارِ عَادَةً. فَفِيْهِ دَلِيْلٌ عَلَى أَنَّهُ لَا يَحِلُّ قَتْلُ الصِّغَارِ مِنْهُمْ، إِذَا كَانُوْا لَا يُقَاتِلُوْنَ. وَقَدْ جَاءَ فِي الْـحَدِيْثِ أَنَّ النَّبِيَّ ﷺ نَهَى عَنْ قَتْلِ النِّسَآءِ وَالْوِلْدَانِ. وَقَالَ: اقْتُلُوْا شُيُوْخَ الْـمُشْرِكِيْنَ، وَاسْتَحْيُوْا شُرُوْخَهُمْ. وَالْـمُرَادُ بِالشُّيُوخِ الْبَالِغُوْنَ وَبِالشُّرُوْخِ، اَلْأَتْبَاعُ مِنَ الصِّغَارِ وَالنِّسَآءِ، وَالْاِسْتِحْيَاءُ الْاِسْتِرْقَاقُ. قَالَ اللهُ: ﴿وَيَسْتَحْيُونَ نِسَآءَهُمْ﴾. وَفِي وَصِيَّةِ أَبِي بَكْرٍ ﷺ لِيَزِيْدَ بْنِ أَبِي سُفْيَانَ: لَا تَقْتُلْ شَيْخًا ضَرِعًا وَلَا صَبِيًّا ضَعِيْفًا، يَعْنِي شَيْخًا فَانِيًا وَصَغِيْرًا لَا يُقَاتِلُ.

Regarding the prohibition of killing non-Muslim women, children and elderly folk during war, the eminent Ḥanafī jurist Imam al-Sarakhsī wrote in his magnum opus, *al-Mabsūṭ*:

---

[1] Set forth by •al-Ṭabarānī in *al-Muʿjam al-awsaṭ*, 7:113 §7011.

The Prophet ﷺ said: "Do not kill children [*walīd*]." In the [Arabic] language, the word *walīd* means the one who is born [*mawlūd*]; and every human being [*ādamī*] is born. However, customarily this word is only used for young children. Therefore, it proves that it is impermissible to kill the young children amongst them [the non-Muslims], as long as they are not fighting. It is mentioned in a hadith that the Prophet ﷺ forbade the killing of women and children, and said: "Kill the [warring] elders of the pagans [during war] and keep alive their subordinates." The "elders" refer to the adults amongst them, and the "subordinates" signify their followers amongst the young and the womenfolk. To "keep alive" here means to take them as captives. Allah says, ﴾*And they kept their women alive*﴿.[1] And it is mentioned in Abū Bakr's ؓ dictated commands to Yazīd b. Abī Sufyān: "Kill neither a feeble old man nor a fragile young child"—in other words, an elderly man and a young child do not fight.[2]

---

[1] Qur'ān 40:25.

[2] •Al-Sarakhsī, *al-Mabsūṭ*, 10:5–6.

اَلْبَابُ الرَّابِعُ

مَنْعُ قَتْلِ السُّفَرَاءِ وَالزُّرَّاعِ وَالتُّجَّارِ وَغَيْرِ الْمُتَحَارِبِيْنَ

CHAPTER FOUR

THE UNLAWFULNESS OF KILLING DIPLOMATS, FARMERS, TRADERS AND NON-COMBATANTS

١/٤٠. عَنْ أَبِي هُرَيْرَةَ ﷺ قَالَ: قَالَ رَسُوْلُ اللهِ ﷺ (فِي يَوْمِ فَتْحِ مَكَّةَ): مَنْ دَخَلَ دَارَ أَبِي سُفْيَانَ فَهُوَ آمِنٌ، وَمَنْ أَلْقَى السِّلَاحَ فَهُوَ آمِنٌ، وَمَنْ أَغْلَقَ بَابَهُ فَهُوَ آمِنٌ.

رَوَاهُ مُسْلِمٌ وَأَبُوْ دَاوُدَ وَالْبَزَّارُ.

40/1. Abū Hurayra ﷺ related that Allah's Messenger ﷺ said (on conquering Mecca):

"Whoever enters Abū Sufyān's house is safe, and whoever lays down his weapon is safe, and whoever shuts his door is safe."[1]

Reported by Muslim, Abū Dāwūd and al-Bazzār.

٢/٤١. عَنْ نَعِيْمِ بْنِ مَسْعُوْدٍ الْأَشْجَعِيِّ قَالَ: سَمِعْتُ رَسُوْلَ اللهِ ﷺ يَقُوْلُ حِيْنَ قَرَأَ كِتَابَ مُسَيْلَمَةَ الْكَذَّابِ، قَالَ لِلرَّسُوْلَيْنِ: فَمَا تَقُوْلَانِ أَنْتُمَا؟ قَالَا: نَقُوْلُ كَمَا قَالَ. فَقَالَ رَسُوْلُ اللهِ ﷺ: وَاللهِ، لَوْ لَا أَنَّ الرُّسُلَ لَا تُقْتَلُ لَضَرَبْتُ أَعْنَاقَكُمَا.

رَوَاهُ أَحْمَدُ وَأَبُوْ دَاوُدَ وَالْحَاكِمُ. وَقَالَ الْحَاكِمُ: هَذَا حَدِيْثٌ صَحِيْحٌ عَلَى شَرْطِ مُسْلِمٍ.

41/2. Naʿīm b. Masʿūd al-Ashjaʿī related:

"I heard Allah's Messenger ﷺ saying to the two envoys after he had read the letter from Musaylama the Liar: 'What do both of you

---

[1] Set forth by •Muslim in *al-Ṣaḥīḥ: Kitāb al-jihād wa al-siyar* [The Book of Jihad and Military Expeditions], Chapter:"The Conquest of Mecca," 3:1407 §1780. •Abū Dāwūd in *al-Sunan*: *Kitāb al-kharāj wa al-imāra wa al-fay'* [The Book of Land Tax, Leadership and the Spoils Acquired without Fighting], chapter: "What has been Narrated about Mecca," 3:162 §3021. •al-Bazzār in *al-Musnad*, 4:122 §1292. •al-Dāraquṭnī in *al-Sunan*, 3:60 §233. •Abū ʿAwāna in *al-Musnad*, 4:290 §6780. •Ibn Rahawayh in *al-Musnad*, 1:300 §278.

say (believe)?' They said: 'We say (believe) what he does.' He said: 'By Allah! Were it not for the fact that envoys are not to be killed, I would have struck your necks!'"[1]

Reported by Aḥmad, Abū Dāwūd and al-Ḥākim. Al-Ḥākim said: "This is an authentic tradition in conformity with the stipulation of Muslim."

٤٢/ ٣. وَفِي رِوَايَةٍ عَبْدِ اللهِ ﷺ، فَقَالَ لَـهُمَـا رَسُوْلُ اللهِ ﷺ: أَتَشْهَدَانِ أَنِّي رَسُوْلُ اللهِ؟ قَالَا: نَشْهَدُ أَنَّ مُسَيْلِمَةَ رَسُولُ اللهِ. فَقَالَ: لَوْ كُنْتُ قَاتِلًا رَسُولًا لَضَرَبْتُ أَعْنَاقَكُمَـا.

قَالَ: فَجَرَتْ سُنَّةٌ أَنْ لَّا يُقْتَلُ الرَّسُوْلُ.

رَوَاهُ أَحْمَدُ وَالدَّارِمِيُّ وَأَبُوْ يَعْلَى.

42/3. ʿAbd Allāh (b. Masʿūd) ﷺ related:

"Allah's Messenger ﷺ asked both envoys [ʿAbd Allāh b. Nuwāḥa and Ibn Athāl] about Musaylama the Liar: 'Do you bear witness that I am Allah's Messenger?' They said: 'We bear witness that Musaylama is the Messenger of Allah!' The Messenger ﷺ of Allah said: 'Were I to execute envoys, I would have executed you!'"

The transmitter said: "From that day forward, the rule was that no envoy was to be killed."[2]

Reported by Aḥmad, al-Dārimī and Abū Yaʿlā.

٤٣/ ٤. وَفِي رِوَايَةٍ عَنْهُ قَالَ: فَقَالَ النَّبِيُّ ﷺ: آمَنْتُ بِاللهِ وَرُسُلِهِ. لَوْ كُنْتُ قَاتِلاً رَسُوْلًا لَقَتَلْتُكُمَـا. قَالَ عَبْدُ اللهِ: قَالَ: فَمَضَتِ السُّنَّةُ أَنَّ الرُّسُلَ لَا تُقْتَلُ.

---

[1] Set forth by •Aḥmad b. Ḥanbal in *al-Musnad*, 3:487 §16032. •Abū Dāwūd in *al-Sunan*, chapter: "On Envoys," 3:83 §2761. •al-Ḥākim in *al-Mustadrak ʿalā al-Ṣaḥīḥayn*, 2:155 §2632 and 3:54 §4377.

[2] Set forth by •Aḥmad b. Ḥanbal in *al-Musnad*, 1:390 §3708 and 1:404 §3837. •al-Nasāʾī in *al-Sunan al-kubrā*, 5:205 §8675. •al-Dārimī in *al-Sunan*, 2:307 §2503. •Abū Yaʿlā in *al-Musnad*, 9:31 §5097.

رَوَاهُ أَحْمَدُ وَالطَّيَالِسِيُّ وَذَكَرَهُ ابْنُ الْقَيِّمِ.

43/4. ʿAbd Allāh b. Masʿūd ﷺ related:

"The Prophet ﷺ said: 'I believe in Allah ﷻ and His Messengers. Had it been permissible for me to slay envoys, I would have executed both of you [the two envoys of Musaylama the Liar (due to the denigration they had perpetrated)].'"[1] According to ʿAbd Allāh b. Masʿūd, from that day forward, the rule was that no envoy was to be killed.

Reported by Aḥmad and al-Ṭayālisī, and cited by Ibn al-Qayyim.

٤٤/ ٥. عَنْ جَابِرِ بْنِ عَبْدِ اللهِ ﷺ، قَالَ: كَانُوْا لَا يَقْتُلُوْنَ تُجَّارَ الْـمُشْرِكِيْنَ.

رَوَاهُ ابْنُ أَبِي شَيْبَةَ وَالْبَيْهَقِيُّ.

44/5. Jābir b. ʿAbd Allāh ﷺ said:

"They [the Muslim soldiers] did not kill the merchants amongst the pagans."[2]

Reported by Ibn Abī Shayba and al-Bayhaqī.

٤٥/ ٦. عَنْ زَيْدِ بْنِ وَهْبٍ قَالَ: أَتَانَا كِتَابُ عُمَرَ: لَا تَغُلُّوْا وَلَا تَغْدِرُوْا، وَلَا تَقْتُلُوْا وَلِيْدًا، وَاتَّقُوا اللهَ فِي الْفَلَّاحِيْنَ.

رَوَاهُ ابْنُ أَبِي شَيْبَةَ وَابْنُ آدَمَ الْقُرَشِيُّ.

45/6. Zayd b. Wahb related that ʿUmar ﷺ sent them [the Muslim forces] a letter in which he said:

"Do not take anything without right when distributing the spoils

[1] Set forth by •Aḥmad in *al-Musnad*, 1:396 §3761. •al-Ṭayālisī in *al-Musnad*, 1:34 §251. Cited by •Ibn al-Qayyim in *Zād al-maʿād*, 3:611.

[2] Set forth by •Ibn Abī Shayba in *al-Muṣannaf*, 6:484 §33129. •al-Bayhaqī in *al-Sunan al-kubrā*, 9:91 §17939. Cited by •Ibn Ādam al-Qurashī in *Kitāb al-Kharāj*, 1:52 §133.

of war, and do not commit any treachery or kill children. And fear Allah regarding farmers."[1]

Reported by Ibn Abī Shayba and Ibn Ādam al-Qurashī.

٤٦ / ٧. وَفِي رِوَايَةٍ عَنْهُ، أَنَّهُ قَالَ: اتَّقُوا اللهَ فِي الْفَلَّاحِينَ، فَـلَا تَقْتُلُوهُمْ إِلَّا أَنْ يَنْصِبُوا لَكُمُ الْـحَرْبَ.

رَوَاهُ الْبَيْهَقِيُّ.

46/7. In one report from Zayd b. Wahb, ʿUmar ⬧ said:

"Fear Allah regarding the farmers and do not kill them unless they wage war against you."[2]

Reported by al-Bayhaqī.

٤٧ / ٨. عَنِ ابْنِ عَبَّاسٍ ⬧، أَنَّ النَّبِيَّ ﷺ كَانَ إِذَا بَعَثَ جُيُوشَهُ قَالَ: لَا تَقْتُلُوا أَصْحَابَ الصَّوَامِعِ.

رَوَاهُ ابْنُ أَبِي شَيْبَةَ وَأَبُو يَعْلَى وَالطَّحَاوِيُّ وَالدَّيْلَمِيُّ.

47/8. (ʿAbd Allāh) b. ʿAbbās ⬧ related:

"When the Prophet ﷺ sent his troops, he would enjoin: 'Do not kill those (priests) who tend to the monasteries.'"[3]

Reported by Ibn Abī Shayba, Abū Yaʿlā, al-Ṭaḥāwī, and al-Daylamī.

٤٨ / ٩. وَفِي رِوَايَةِ ثَابِتِ بْنِ الْـحَجَّاجِ الْكِلَابِيِّ قَالَ: قَامَ أَبُو بَكْرٍ فِي النَّاسِ، فَحَمِدَ اللهَ وَأَثْنَى عَلَيْهِ، ثُمَّ قَالَ: أَ لَا! لَا يُقْتَلُ الرَّاهِبُ فِي الصَّوْمَعَةِ.

---

[1] Set forth by •Ibn Abī Shayba in *al-Muṣannaf*, 6:483 §33120. Cited by •Ibn Ādam al-Qurashī in *Kitāb al-Kharāj*, 1:52 §132.

[2] Set forth by •al-Bayhaqī in *al-Sunan al-kubrā*, 9:91 §17938.

[3] Set forth by •Ibn Abī Shayba in *al-Muṣannaf*, 6:484 §33132. •Abū Yaʿlā in *al-Musnad*, 5:59 §2650. •al-Ṭaḥāwī in *Sharḥ maʿānī al-āthār*, 3:225. •al-Daylamī in *Musnad al-firdaws*, 5:45 §7410.

رَوَاهُ ابْنُ أَبِي شَيْبَةَ.

48/9. According to Thābit b. al-Ḥajjāj al-Kilābī, Abū Bakr ﷺ stood up among the people, praised and glorified Allah and said (to people):

"Beware! No [non-combatant] priest tending to his monastery should be killed."[1]

Reported by Ibn Abī Shayba.

٤٩/ ١٠. وَفِي رِوَايَةِ سَعِيدِ بْنِ الْمُسَيِّبِ أَنَّ أَبَا بَكْرٍ ﷺ لَمَّا بَعَثَ الْجُنُوْدَ نَحْوَ الشَّامِ قَالَ: لَمَّا رَكِبُوْا، مَشَى أَبُوْ بَكْرٍ مَعَ أُمَرَاءِ جُنُوْدِهِ يُوَدِّعُهُمْ حَتَّى بَلَغَ ثَنِيَّةَ الْوَدَاعِ، فَقَالُوْا: يَا خَلِيْفَةَ رَسُوْلِ اللهِ، أَتَمْشِي وَنَحْنُ رُكْبَانٌ؟ فَقَالَ: إِنِّي أَحْتَسِبُ خُطَايَ هَذِهِ فِي سَبِيْلِ اللهِ ثُمَّ جَعَلَ يُوْصِيْهِمْ. فَقَالَ: أُوْصِيكُمْ بِتَقْوَى اللهِ. اغْزُوْا فِي سَبِيْلِ اللهِ فَقَاتِلُوا مَنْ كَفَرَ بِاللهِ فَإِنَّ اللهَ نَاصِرُ دِيْنِهِ، وَلَا تَقْتُلُوْا الْوِلْدَانِ وَلَا الشُّيُوْخَ وَلَا النِّسَاءَ وَسَتَجِدُوْنَ أَقْوَامًا حَبَسُوا أَنْفُسَهُمْ فِي الصَّوَامِعِ فَدَعُوْهُمْ وَمَا حَبَسُوْا أَنْفُسَهُمْ لَهُ.

رَوَاهُ الْبَيْهَقِيُّ وَالطَّحَاوِيُّ وَابْنُ عَسَاكِرَ وَذَكَرَهُ الْهِنْدِيُّ.

49/10. Saʿīd b. al-Musayyib related:

"When Abū Bakr al-Ṣiddīq ﷺ dispatched an army towards Syria, he came walking with the commanders of the army until he reached the mountains to bid them farewell. At that time, the commander said: 'O successor of Allah's Messenger! (Is it not against reverence for us that) you walk while we are riding?' He said: 'I count these steps of mine in the way of Allah.' Then he instructed the army: 'I enjoin you to fear Allah (in every matter), fight (against the oppressors) for the cause of Allah and strive face-to-face with the disbelievers. Indeed, Allah helps His *Dīn* [religion]. Do not kill any children or elderly people or women. You shall come upon a people who have secluded themselves in cloisters; you must leave them to engage in that for whose sake they

---

[1] Set forth by •Ibn Abī Shayba in *al-Muṣannaf*, 6:483 §33127.

have secluded themselves.'"[1]

Reported by al-Bayhaqī, al-Ṭaḥāwī, and Ibn ʿAsākir, and cited by al-Hindī.

٥٠ / ١١. وَفِي رِوَايَةِ صَالِحِ بْنِ كَيْسَانَ قَالَ: لَـمَّا بَعَثَ أَبُوْ بَكْرٍ ﵁ يَزِيدَ بْنَ أَبِي سُفْيَانَ إِلَى الشَّامِ فَقَالَ (لَهُ): وَلاَ تَقْتُلُوا كَبِيرًا هَرِمًا وَلاَ امْرَأَةً وَلاَ وَلِيدًا وَلاَ تُخَرِّبُوا عُمْرَانًا وَلاَ تَقْطَعُوا شَجَرَةً إِلاَّ لِنَفْعٍ وَلاَ تَعْقِرَنَّ بَهِيمَةً إِلاَّ لِنَفْعٍ وَلاَ تُحْرِقَنَّ نَخْلاً وَلاَ تُغْرِقَنَّهُ وَلاَ تَغْدِرْ وَلاَ تُمَثِّلْ وَلاَ تَجْبُنْ وَلاَ تَغْلُلْ.

رَوَاهُ الْبَيْهَقِيُّ.

50/11. According to Ṣāliḥ b. Kaysān, when Abū Bakr al-Ṣiddīq ﵁ dispatched Yazīd b. Abī Sufyān (and the Muslim troops to Syria), he addressed them:

"Do not kill an old, feeble man or a woman or a child. Do not damage any populated area. Do not cut down trees needlessly. Do not kill animals unless it is for a benefit [to feed others]. Do not burn down date-palm trees or destroy them. Do not commit any treachery. Do not mutilate (anyone). Do not behave cowardly. And do not take anything without right when distributing the spoils of war."[2]

Reported by al-Bayhaqī.

٥١ / ١٢. وَفِي رِوَايَةٍ: قَالَ عَلِيُّ ابْنُ أَبِي طَالِبٍ ﵁: لَا يُذَفَّفُ عَلَى جَرِيْحٍ، وَلَا يُقْتَلُ أَسِيرٌ، وَلَا يُتْبَعُ مُدْبِرٌ.

رَوَاهُ عَبْدُ الرَّزَّاقِ.

51/12. ʿAlī b. Abī Ṭālib ﵁ said:

---

[1] Set forth by •al-Bayhaqī in *al-Sunan al-kubrā*, 9:85 §17904. •al-Ṭaḥāwī in *Sharḥ Mushkil al-āthār*, 3:144. •Ibn ʿAsākir in *Tārīkh Madīna Dimashq*, 2:75. Cited by •al-Hindī in *Kanz al-ʿummāl*, 4:203 §11408.

[2] Set forth by •al-Bayhaqī in *al-Sunan al-kubrā*, 9:90 §17929.

"The injured person or prisoner should not be killed, nor should be chased those who flee."[1]

Reported by ʿAbd al-Razzāq.

٥٢/١٣. وَفِي رِوَايَةٍ عَنْ جُوَيْبِرٍ قَالَ: أَخْبَرَتْنِي امْرَأَةٌ مِنْ بَنِي أَسَدٍ قَالَتْ: سَمِعْتُ عَمَّارًا بَعْدَ مَا فَرَغَ عَلِيٌّ مِنْ أَصْحَابِ الْجَمَلِ يُنَادِي: لَا تَقْتُلُوْا مُقْبِلًا، وَلَا مُدْبِرًا، وَلَا تُذَفِّفُوْا عَلَى جَرِيْحٍ، وَلَا تَدْخُلُوْا دَارًا. مَنْ أَلْقَى السِّلَاحَ فَهُوَ آمِنٌ، وَمَنْ أَغْلَقَ بَابَهُ فَهُوَ آمِنٌ.

رَوَاهُ عَبْدُ الرَّزَّاقِ.

52/13. Juwaybir related that a woman from the tribe of Banū Asad told him that she heard ʿAmmār ﷺ declare after ʿAlī ﷺ had finished the Battle of the Camel:

"Do not kill anyone coming up or going back; do not kill an injured person; and do not enter the house of someone who has laid down his arms, for he is considered safe. Similarly, the one who shuts his door is considered safe."[2]

Reported by ʿAbd al-Razzāq.

• قَالَ الْإِمَامُ الْأَوْزَاعِيُّ: لَا يُقْتَلُ الْحُرَّاثُ إِذَا عُلِمَ أَنَّهُ لَيْسَ مِنَ الْمُقَاتِلَةِ.

Imam al-Awzāʿī said: "Farmers are not to be killed [during war] if it is known that they are not from the combatants."[3]

• قَالَ الْإِمَامُ ابْنُ الْقُدَّامَةِ الْمَقْدِسِيُّ: فَأَمَّا الْفَلَّاحُ الَّذِي لَا يُقَاتِلُ فَيَنْبَغِي أَلَّا يُقْتَلَ، لِمَا رُوِيَ عَنْ عُمَرَ بْنِ الْخَطَّابِ ﷺ أَنَّهُ قَالَ: اتَّقُوْا اللهَ فِي

[1] Set forth by •ʿAbd al-Razzāq in *al-Muṣannaf*, 10:123 §18590.

[2] Set forth by •ʿAbd al-Razzāq in *al-Muṣannaf*, 10:124 §18591.

[3] Cited by •Ibn al-Qayyim in *Aḥkām ahl al-dhimma*, 1:165.

الْفَلَّاحِيْنَ، الَّذِيْنَ لَا يَنْصِبُوْنَ لَكُمْ فِي الْـحَرْبِ.

Ibn Qudāma al-Maqdisī said: "As for the farmer who is a non-combatant, he should not be killed, because it was narrated from ʿUmar b. al-Khaṭṭāb ﷺ that he said: 'Fear Allah regarding the farmers who do not wage war against you.'"[1]

• قَالَ الْعَلَّامَةُ ابْنُ الْقَيِّمِ: فَإِنَّ أَصْحَابَ النَّبِيِّ ﷺ لَـمْ يَقْتُلُوْهُمْ حِيْنَ فَتَحُوْا الْبِلَادَ، وَلِأَنَّهُمْ لَا يُقَاتِلُوْنَ، فَأَشْبَهُوْا الشُّيُوْخَ وَالرُّهْبَانَ.

Ibn al-Qayyim said: "Indeed, when the Companions of the Prophet ﷺ conquered the various lands, they did not kill them [farmers and merchants] because the latter did not fight [against them], and so in that sense they [the civilians] resembled the elderly and the religious leaders."[2]

• وَقَالَ الْعَلَّامَةُ ابْنُ الْقَيِّمِ: وَإِنَّ الْعَبْدَ مَحْقُوْنُ الدَّمِ فَأَشْبَهَ النِّسَاءَ وَالصِّبْيَانَ.

Ibn al-Qayyim also said: "Like the women and children, the servants who work at home are also safe from bloodshed."[3]

---

1 •Ibn Qudāma al-Maqdisī, *al-Mughnī*, 9:251.

2 •Ibn al-Qayyim, *Aḥkām ahl al-dhimma*, 1:165.

3 Ibid., 1:172.

اَلْبَابُ الخَامِسُ

حُرِّيَّةُ مَذْهَبِهِمْ وَعَقَائِدِهِمْ

CHAPTER FIVE

FREEDOM OF FAITH AND BELIEFS FOR NON-MUSLIMS

QUR'ĀN

١. ﴿لَآ إِكۡرَاهَ فِي ٱلدِّينِۖ قَد تَّبَيَّنَ ٱلرُّشۡدُ مِنَ ٱلۡغَيِّ﴾

1. ﴿*There is no compulsion in* Dīn *(Religion). Surely, the guidance has been evidently distinguished from error.*﴾[1]

٢. ﴿وَلَا تَسُبُّواْ ٱلَّذِينَ يَدۡعُونَ مِن دُونِ ٱللَّهِ فَيَسُبُّواْ ٱللَّهَ عَدۡوَۢا بِغَيۡرِ عِلۡمٍ﴾

2. ﴿*And, (O Muslims,) do not abuse these (false gods) that these (polytheists) worship besides Allah, lest these people should (also, in retaliation,) revile against Allah's Glory wrongfully due to ignorance.*﴾[2]

٣. ﴿قُلۡ يَٰٓأَهۡلَ ٱلۡكِتَٰبِ تَعَالَوۡاْ إِلَىٰ كَلِمَةٖ سَوَآءِۭ بَيۡنَنَا وَبَيۡنَكُمۡ أَلَّا نَعۡبُدَ إِلَّا ٱللَّهَ وَلَا نُشۡرِكَ بِهِۦ شَيۡـٔٗا وَلَا يَتَّخِذَ بَعۡضُنَا بَعۡضًا أَرۡبَابٗا مِّن دُونِ ٱللَّهِۚ فَإِن تَوَلَّوۡاْ فَقُولُواْ ٱشۡهَدُواْ بِأَنَّا مُسۡلِمُونَ﴾

3. ﴿*Say: "O People of the Book, come to that matter which is common between us and you (namely that): we shall worship none other than Allah, and we shall not associate any partner with Him. Nor shall any of us take one another as Lords apart from Allah." Then if they turn away, say: "Bear witness that we are but Allah's obedient servants (Muslims)."*﴾[3]

---

1 Qur'ān 2:256.

2 Ibid., 6:108.

3 Ibid., 3:64.

٤. ﴿وَلَا تَكۡسِبُ كُلُّ نَفۡسٍ إِلَّا عَلَيۡهَاۚ وَلَا تَزِرُ وَازِرَةٞ وِزۡرَ أُخۡرَىٰ﴾

4. ﴾*And whatever (sin) each soul earns, (its evil outcome) falls back upon it. And no bearer of burden will bear another's burden.*﴿[1]

٥. ﴿وَلَوۡ شَآءَ رَبُّكَ لَأٓمَنَ مَن فِي ٱلۡأَرۡضِ كُلُّهُمۡ جَمِيعًاۚ أَفَأَنتَ تُكۡرِهُ
ٱلنَّاسَ حَتَّىٰ يَكُونُواْ مُؤۡمِنِينَ﴾

5. ﴾*And had Allah so willed, certainly all inhabitants on the earth would have believed. (When your Lord has not made them believe by force,) will you coerce the people until they become believers?*﴿[2]

٦. ﴿وَقُلِ ٱلۡحَقُّ مِن رَّبِّكُمۡۖ فَمَن شَآءَ فَلۡيُؤۡمِن وَمَن شَآءَ فَلۡيَكۡفُرۡۚ إِنَّآ
أَعۡتَدۡنَا لِلظَّٰلِمِينَ نَارًا﴾

6. ﴾*And say: "(This) truth is from your Lord. So whoever desires may believe and whoever desires may deny." Indeed, We have prepared for the wrongdoers the Fire (of Hell).*﴿[3]

٧. ﴿وَلَوۡلَا دَفۡعُ ٱللَّهِ ٱلنَّاسَ بَعۡضَهُم بِبَعۡضٖ لَّهُدِّمَتۡ صَوَٰمِعُ وَبِيَعٞ
وَصَلَوَٰتٞ وَمَسَٰجِدُ يُذۡكَرُ فِيهَا ٱسۡمُ ٱللَّهِ كَثِيرٗا﴾

7. ﴾*And had Allah not been repelling one class of human society by the other (through progressive struggle and persistent toil), the cloisters, synagogues, churches and mosques (i.e., religious centres and places of worship of all religions) would have been ruined where Allah's Name is*

---

[1] Ibid., 6:164.

[2] Ibid., 10:99.

[3] Ibid., 18:29.

abundantly commemorated.﴾[1]

٨. ﴿فَذَكِّرْ إِنَّمَآ أَنتَ مُذَكِّرٌ ۝٢١ لَّسْتَ عَلَيْهِم بِمُصَيْطِرٍ﴾

8. ﴾*So, continuously admonish them, for you are but an admonisher. You are not imposed upon them (as) an oppressor and persecutor.*﴿[2]

٩. ﴿لَكُمْ دِينُكُمْ وَلِيَ دِينِ﴾

9. ﴾*(So) you have your* dīn *(religion), and I have my Dīn (Religion).*﴿[3]

Hadith

١/٥٣. عَنْ عِدَّةٍ (وعند البيهقي: عَنْ ثَلَاثِيْنَ) مِنْ أَبْنَاءِ أَصْحَابِ رَسُوْلِ اللهِ ﷺ، عَنْ آبَائِهِمْ دِنْيَةً، عَنْ رَسُوْلِ اللهِ ﷺ قَالَ: أَلَا مَنْ ظَلَمَ مُعَاهِدًا، أَوِ انْتَقَصَهُ، أَوْ كَلَّفَهُ فَوْقَ طَاقَتِهِ، أَوْ أَخَذَ مِنْهُ شَيْئًا بِغَيْرِ طِيْبِ نَفْسٍ فَأَنَا حَجِيْجُهُ يَوْمَ الْقِيَامَةِ.

رَوَاهُ أَبُوْ دَاوُدَ وَالْبَيْهَقِيُّ وَذَكَرَهُ الْمُنْذِرِيُّ وَالْعَجْلُوْنِيُّ وَقَالَ الْعَجْلُوْنِيُّ: إِسْنَادُهُ حَسَنٌ.

53/1. It is related by a number of the Companions' sons (about thirty of their sons, as reported by al-Bayhaqī), on the authority of their nearest relatives, that Allah's Messenger ﷺ said:

"Beware! Whoever wrongs a non-Muslim citizen, or diminishes any of his (religious, social, economic, political and cultural) rights, or loads him with more (work) than he can bear, or takes anything from him without his consent, I shall plead on his [the latter's] behalf on the Day of Resurrection."[4]

---

[1] Ibid., 22:40.

[2] Ibid., 88:21–22.

[3] Ibid., 109:6.

[4] Set forth by •Abū Dāwūd in *al-Sunan*: *Kitāb al-kharāj wa al-imāra wa al-*

Reported by Abū Dāwūd and Bayhaqī and cited by al-Mundhirī and al-ʿAjlūnī. According to al-ʿAjlūnī: "It has a fine chain of transmission."

٢/٥٤. عَنِ ابْنِ إِسْحَاقَ قَالَ: وَفَدَ عَلَى رَسُوْلِ اللهِ وَفْدُ نَصَارَى نَجْرَانَ بِالْمَدِيْنَةِ حَدَّثَنِي مُحَمَّدُ بْنُ جَعْفَرِ بْنِ النَّدَى بْنِ النَّدَى قَالَ: لَمَّا قَدِمَ وَفْدُ نَجْرَانَ عَلَى رَسُوْلِ اللهِ دَخَلُوا عَلَيْهِ مَسْجِدَهُ بَعْدَ الْعَصْرِ، فَحَانَتْ صَلَاتُهُمْ، فَقَامُوْا يُصَلُّوْنَ فِي مَسْجِدِهِ، فَأَرَادَ النَّاسُ مَنْعَهُمْ، فَقَالَ رَسُوْلُ اللهِ: دَعُوْهُمْ فَاسْتَقْبَلُوا الْمَشْرِقَ فَصَلَّوْا صَلَاتَهُمْ.

رَوَاهُ الْبَيْهَقِيُّ وَابْنُ سَعْدٍ وَابْنُ هِشَامٍ.

54/2. According to Ibn Isḥāq:

"A Christian delegation from Najrān came to meet Allah's Messenger ﷺ in Medina. Muhammad b. Jaʿfar b. al-Nadā b. al-Nadā said that they reached the Prophet's mosque after the ʿAṣr prayer. It was their prayer time so they stood up in the Prophet's mosque to perform their religious service. People tried to stop them but the Messenger of Allah ﷺ said: 'Leave them be.' They faced eastward and performed their rituals (prayers)."[1]

Reported by al-Bayhaqī, Ibn Saʿd and Ibn Hishām.

٣/٥٥. عَنْ عُبَيْدِ اللهِ ابْنِ أَبِي حُمَيْدٍ، عَنْ أَبِي الْمَلِيْحِ الْهُذَلِيِّ أَنَّ رَسُوْلَ اللهِ صَالَحَ أَهْلَ نَجْرَانَ وَكَتَبَ لَهُمْ كِتَابًا (فَمِنْهُ) وَلِنَجْرَانَ وَحَاشِيَتِهَا ذِمَّةُ اللهِ وَذِمَّةُ مُحَمَّدٍ النَّبِيِّ رَسُوْلِ اللهِ، عَلَى دِمَائِهِمْ وَأَنْفُسِهِمْ وَأَرْضِهِمْ وَأَمْوَالِهِمْ وَمِلَّتِهِمْ وَرَهْبَانِيَّتِهِمْ

---

*fay*ʾ [The Book on the Land Tax, Leadership and Spoils Acquired without Fighting], chapter: "Taking One Tenth from Non- Muslim Citizens When They Do Business," 3:170 §3052. •al-Bayhaqī in *al-Sunan al-kubrā*, 9:205 §18511. •al-Mundhirī in *al-Targhīb wa al-tarhīb*, 4:7 §4558. •al-ʿAjlūnī in *Kashf al-khafā*ʾ, 2:342.

[1] Set forth by •al-Bayhaqī in *Dalāʾil al-Nubuwwa*, 5:382. •Ibn Saʿd in *al-Ṭabaqāt al-kubrā*, 1:357. •Ibn Hishām in *al-Sīra al-Nabawiyya*, 2:239–240. •Ibn Kathīr in *al-Sīra*, 4:108. •Ibn Qayyim in *Zād al-maʿād*, 3:629.

وَأَسَاقِفَتِهِمْ وَغَائِبِهِمْ وَشَاهِدِهِمْ وَبَعْثِهِمْ وَأَمْثِلَتِهِمْ، لَا يُغَيَّرُ مَا كَانُوْا عَلَيْهِ، وَلَا يُغَيَّرُ حَقٌّ مِنْ حُقُوقِهِمْ وَأَمْثِلَتِهِمْ، لَا يُفْتَنُ أُسْقُفٌ مِنْ أُسْقُفِيَّتِهِ، وَلَا رَاهِبٌ مِنْ رَهْبَانِيَّتِهِ، وَلَا وَاقِفٌ مِنْ وَقَافِيَّتِهِ، عَلَى مَا تَحْتَ أَيْدِيْهِمْ مِنْ قَلِيْلٍ أَوْ كَثِيْرٍ، وَلَيْسَ عَلَيْهِمْ رَهَقٌ.

رَوَاهُ الْبَيْهَقِيُّ وَابْنُ سَعْدٍ وَذَكَرَهُ كَثِيْرٌ مِنَ الأَئِمَّةِ.

55/3. ʿUbayd Allah b. Abī Ḥumayd reported on the authority of Abū al-Malīḥ al-Hudhalī that when Allah's Messenger ﷺ reconciled with the people of Najrān, he concluded an agreement with them (in which it was written):

"Indeed, Najrān and her allies are under the guarantee and protection of Allah ﷻ and Allah's Messenger ﷺ in regard to their blood, lives, lands, assets and religion. This includes their priests, monks, those who are present amongst them and those who are absent, and others amongst them, and their delegations and the like. They shall not be forced to change their faith and no right of theirs shall be forfeited. No monk, priest or attendant amongst them should lose what is in his possession, be it plentiful or scarce, and no fear or danger should threaten them."[1]

Reported by al-Bayhaqī, Ibn Saʿd and cited by many imams.

٥٦/ ٤. عَنْ سَعِيدِ بْنِ الْمُسَيِّبِ أَنَّ أَبَا بَكْرٍ ﵁ لَمَّا بَعَثَ الْجُنُوْدَ نَحْوَ الشَّامِ يَزِيْدَ بْنَ أَبِي سُفْيَانَ وَعَمْرَو بْنَ الْعَاصِ وَشُرَحْبِيْلَ بْنَ حَسَنَةَ، جَعَلَ يُوْصِيهِمْ فَقَالَ: وَلَا تُغْرِقُنَّ نَخْلاً وَلَا تُحْرِقُنَّهَا وَلَا تَعْقِرُوْا بَهِيْمَةً وَلَا شَجَرَةً تُثْمِرُ وَلَا تَهْدِمُوْا بِيْعَةً وَلَا تَقْتُلُوْا الْوِلْدَانِ وَلَا الشُّيُوْخَ وَلَا النِّسَاءَ وَسَتَجِدُوْنَ أَقْوَامًا حَبَسُوا أَنْفُسَهُمْ فِي الصَّوَامِعِ فَدَعُوْهُمْ وَمَا حَبَسُوْا أَنْفُسَهُمْ لَهُ.

[1] Set forth by •al-Bayhaqī in *Dalāʾil al-Nubuwwa*, 5:359, 389. •Ibn Saʿd in *al-Ṭabaqāt al-kubrā*, 1:288, 358. •Abū Yūsuf in *Kitāb al-kharāj*, p. 78. •Abū ʿUbayd al-Qāsim b. Sallām in *Kitāb al-amwāl*, pp. 244–245 §503. •Ibn Zanjawayh in *Kitāb al-amwāl*, pp. 449–450 §732.

رَوَاهُ الْبَيْهَقِيُّ وَالطَّحَاوِيُّ وَابْنُ عَسَاكِرَ وَذَكَرَهُ الْهِنْدِيُّ.

56/4. According to Saʿīd b. al-Musayyab ﷺ, Abū Bakr al-Ṣiddīq ﷺ directed Yazīd b. Abī Sufyān, ʿAmr b. al-ʿĀṣ and Shuraḥbīl b. Ḥasana as he was sending them to Syria:

"Do not drown or burn date-palm trees. Do not kill any animal. Do not cut down a fruit-bearing tree. Do not demolish a church. Do not kill any children or old people or women. Soon you shall come upon people who have secluded themselves in cloisters; you must leave them to engage in that for which they have secluded themselves."[1]

Reported by al-Bayhaqī, al-Ṭaḥāwī, Ibn ʿAsākir and cited by al-Hindī.

٥٧/ ٥. وَرُوِيَ مِثْلُهُ لِعُمَرَ بْنِ الْـخَطَّابِ ﷺ كَمَا ذَكَرَهُ الطَّبَرِيُّ فِي تَارِيْخِهِ: هَذَا مَا أَعْطَى عَبْدُ اللهِ عُمَرُ أَمِيْرُ الْـمُؤْمِنِيْنَ أَهْلَ إِيْلِيَاءَ مِنَ الْأَمَانِ، أَعْطَاهُمْ أَمَانًا لِأَنْفُسِهِمْ وَأَمْوَالِـهِمْ وَلِكَنَائِسِهِمْ وَصُلْبَانِهِمْ، وَسَقِيْمِهَا وَبَرِيْئِهَا وَسَائِرِ مِلَّتِهَا، أَنَّهُ لَا تُسْكَنُ كَنَائِسُهُمْ وَلَا تُهْدَمُ وَلَا يُنْتَقَصُ مِنْهَا وَلَا مِنْ حَيِّزِهَا، وَلَا مِنْ صَلِيْبِهِمْ، وَلَا مِنْ شَيْءٍ مِنْ أَمْوَالِـهِمْ، وَلَا يُكْرَهُوْنَ عَلَى دِيْنِهِمْ، وَلَا يُضَارُّ أَحَدٌ مِنْهُمْ، وَلَا يُسْكَنُ بِإِيْلِيَاءَ مَعَهُمْ أَحَدٌ مِنَ الْيَهُوْدِ.

57/5. A similar report has been reported from ʿUmar b. al-Khaṭṭāb ﷺ as has been narrated by al-Ṭabarī in *Tārīkh al-umam wa al-mulūk*:

"This is the covenant of security and protection from the servant of Allah, ʿUmar, the Commander of the Faithful, to the people of Jerusalem. He grants them security in their lives, properties, churches, crucifixes and to their ill and their healthy and their entire religious community. Their churches are not to be occupied, demolished or decreased in number. Their churches or crucifixes should not be desecrated, or anything else of their property. They are not to be

[1] Set forth by •al-Bayhaqī in *al-Sunan al-kubrā*, 9:85 §17904. •al-Ṭaḥāwī in *Sharḥ Mushkil al-āthār*, 3:144. •Ibn ʿAsākir in *Tārīkh Madina Dimashq*, 2:75. Cited by •al-Hindī in *Kanz al-ʿummāl*, 4:203 §11408.

proselytized, and no one amongst them is to be harmed in any way. And none of the Jews are to reside with them in Jerusalem [due to the severe enmity between them in those days]."[1]

٦/٥٨. عَنْ عِكْرِمَةَ ﷺ، قَالَ: قِيْلَ لِابْنِ عَبَّاسٍ: أَلِلْعَجَمِ أَنْ يُحْدِثُوْا فِي أَمْصَارِ الْـمُسْلِمِيْنَ بِنَاءً أَوْ بِيْعَةً؟ فَقَالَ: أَيُّمَا مِصْرٍ مَصَرَتْهُ الْعَرَبُ فَلَيْسَ لِلْعَجَمِ أَنْ يَبْنُوْا فِيْهِ بِنَاءً، أَوْ قَالَ: بِيْعَةً، وَلَا يَضْرِبُوْا فِيْهِ نَاقُوْسًا، وَلَا يَشْرَبُوْا فِيْهِ خَمْرًا، وَلَا يَتَّخِذُوْا فِيْهِ خِنْزِيْرًا أَوْ يُدْخِلُوْا فِيْهِ، أَيُّمَا مِصْرٍ مَصَرَتْهُ الْعَجَمُ يَفْتَحُهُ اللهُ عَلَى الْعَرَبِ وَنَزَلُوْا يَعْنِي عَلَى حُكْمِهِمْ فَلِلْعَجَمِ مَا فِي عَهْدِهِمْ، وَلِلْعَجَمِ عَلَى الْعَرَبِ أَنْ يُوْفُوْا بِعَهْدِهِمْ وَلَا يُكَلِّفُوْهُمْ فَوْقَ طَاقَتِهِمْ.

رَوَاهُ ابْنُ أَبِي شَيْبَةَ وَالْبَيْهَقِيُّ وَابْنُ زَنْجَوَيْهِ وَذَكَرَهُ ابْنُ قُدَامَةَ وَالْـمَقْدِسِيُّ.

58/6. ʿIkrima related that (ʿAbd Allāh) b. ʿAbbās ﷺ was asked:

"Is it permissible for non-Muslim citizens to construct new houses and places of worship in Muslim cities?" He said: "The cities that are raised by Muslims, therein the non-Muslim citizens do not have the right to build a new house or a place of worship or to ring the bell (to summon the congregation) or drink alcohol or farm pigs. As for the rest of the cities raised by non-Muslims that Allah conquered at the hands of Muslims and they embraced obedience to (Arab) Muslims, there they have the same rights as settled in the covenant of protection. And it is binding on the Arabs to fulfil the rights of non-Arabs and the latter should also not be burdened beyond their capacity."[2]

Reported by Ibn Abī Shayba, al-Bayhaqī, Ibn Zanjawayh and

---

[1] •Al-Ṭabarī, *Tārīkh al-umam wa al-mulūk*, 2:449.

[2] Set forth by •Ibn Abī Shayba in *al-Muṣannaf*, 6:467 §32982. •al-Bayhaqī in *al-Sunan al-kubrā*, 9:202 §18496. •Ibn Zanjawayh in *Kitāb al-amwāl*, p. 328. •Ibn Qudāma in *al-Mughnī*, 9:283. •al-Maqdisī in *al-Furūʿ*, 6:250. •Ibn al-Qayyim in *Aḥkām ahl al-dhimma*, 3:1181, 1195, 1235. •Ibn Ḍawyān in *Manār al-sabīl*, 1:283.

cited by Ibn Qudāma and al-Maqdisī.

٥٩/ ٧. وَرُوِيَ مِثْلُهُ لِعُمَرَ بْنِ عَبْدِ الْعَزِيْزِ كَمَا ذَكَرَهُ الْبَلَاذِرِيُّ: فَلَمَّا اسْتَخْلَفَ عُمَرُ بْنُ عَبْدِ الْعَزِيْزِ ﷺ، شَكَى النَّصَارَى إِلَيْهِ مَا فَعَلَ الْوَلِيْدُ بِهِمْ فِي كَنِيْسَتِهِمْ، فَكَتَبَ إِلَى عَامِلِهِ يَأْمُرُهُ بِرَدِّ مَا زَادَهُ فِي الْمَسْجِدِ.

59/7. Al-Balādhurī related about ʿUmar b. ʿAbd al-ʿAzīz:

"When ʿUmar b. ʿAbd al-ʿAzīz ﷺ became the Caliph, the Christians complained to him about al-Walīd's seizure of church property. He dictated orders to his governor there, commanding him to return to them the portion of the church that was added to the mosque. [It was implemented.]"[1]

- قَالَ الْحَافِظُ ابْنُ كَثِيْرٍ فِي تَفْسِيْرِ الْآيَةِ ﴿لَآ إِكْرَاهَ فِي ٱلدِّينِ﴾: لَا تُكْرِهُوْا أَحَدًا عَلَى الدُّخُوْلِ فِي دِيْنِ الْإِسْلَامِ، فَإِنَّهُ بَيِّنٌ وَاضِحٌ جَلِيٌّ دَلَائِلُهُ وَبَرَاهِيْنُهُ. لَا يَحْتَاجُ إِلَى أَنْ يُكْرَهَ أَحَدٌ عَلَى الدُّخُوْلِ فِيْهِ.

Ibn Kathīr explained this Qurʾānic verse: ﴾*There is no compulsion in* Dīn *(Religion).*﴿[2] in the following words: "Do not coerce anyone to embrace the religion of Islam, for its proofs and evidence are clear, obvious and manifest. There is no need for anyone to be coerced into embracing it."[3]

- ذَكَرَ الْإِمَامُ أَبُوْ بَكْرٍ الْجَصَّاصُ فِي 'أَحْكَامِ الْقُرْآنِ' قَوْلَ الْإِمَامِ حَسَنِ الْبَصَرِيِّ فِي تَفْسِيْرِ الْآيَةِ: ﴿وَلَوْلَا دَفْعُ ٱللَّهِ ٱلنَّاسَ بَعْضَهُم بِبَعْضٍ لَّهُدِّمَتْ صَوَامِعُ وَبِيَعٌ وَصَلَوَاتٌ وَمَسَاجِدُ يُذْكَرُ فِيهَا ٱسْمُ ٱللَّهِ كَثِيرًا﴾. يَدْفَعُ عَنْ هَدْمِ مُصَلَّيَاتِ أَهْلِ الذِّمَّةِ بِالْمُؤْمِنِيْنَ.

---

[1] •Al-Balādhurī, *Futūḥ al-buldān*, p. 132.

[2] Qurʾān 2:256.

[3] •Ibn Kathīr, *Tafsīr al-Qurʾān al-ʿAẓīm*, 1:310.

In his commentary on the verse ﴿*And had Allah not been repelling one class of human society by the other (through progressive struggle and persistent toil), the cloisters, synagogues, churches and mosques (i.e., religious centres and places of worship of all religions) would have been ruined where Allah's Name is abundantly commemorated.*﴾[1], Imam Abū Bakr al-Jaṣṣāṣ quoted the words of Imam al-Ḥasan al-Baṣrī: "Allah uses the believers as a means to prevent the destruction of the places of worship belonging to the non-Muslim citizens."[2]

- وَيَزْدَادُ الْإِمَامُ أَبُوْ بَكْرٍ الْـجَصَّاصُ فِي تَفسِيْرِ الْآيَةِ السَّابِقَةِ: فِي الْآيَةِ دَلِيْلٌ عَلَى أَنَّ هَذِهِ الْـمَوَاضِعَ الْـمَذْكُوْرَةَ لَا يَجُوْزُ أَنْ تُهْدَمَ عَلَى مَنْ كَانَ لَهُ ذِمَّةٌ أَوْ عَهْدٌ مِنَ الْكُفَّارِ.

Imam Abū Bakr al-Jaṣṣāṣ continued: "Within this verse is a proof that it is impermissible to destroy the aforementioned places of worship belonging to those of the non-Muslims who are citizens or under a guarantee of protection."[3]

So in other words, it is the responsibility of the Islamic state to provide them complete protection in all circumstances. Every community safeguards its own values and culture and it is their right to do so. So the Muslims have been ordered to protect the places of worship belonging to the non-Muslims, despite religious differences.

- قَالَ الْعَلَّامَةُ ابْنُ الْقَيِّمِ فِي كِتَابِهِ 'أَحْكَامِ أَهْلِ الذِّمَّةِ': يَدْفَعُ عَنْ مَوَاضِعِ مُتَعَبَّدَاتِهِمْ بِالْـمُسْلِمِيْنَ. ... كَمَا يُحِبُّ الدَّفْعَ عَنْ أَرْبَابِهَا وَإِنْ كَانَ يُبْغِضُهُمْ، وَهَذَا الْقَوْلُ هُوَ الرَّاجِحُ، وَهُوَ مَذْهَبُ ابْنِ عَبَّاسٍ.

Ibn al-Qayyim writes in *Aḥkām ahl al-dhimma*: "Allah

---

[1] Qur'ān 22:40.

[2] •Abū Bakr al-Jaṣṣāṣ, *Aḥkām al-Qur'ān*, 5:83. •Ibn al-Qayyim, *Aḥkām ahl al-dhimma*, 3:1169.

[3] •Abū Bakr al-Jaṣṣāṣ, *Aḥkām al-Qur'ān*, 5:83.

uses the believers to defend their places of worship.... Moreover, it is obligatory for him [the believer] to defend their objects of worship, even though he detests them. This is the correct position and the view maintained by Ibn ʿAbbās."[1]

- فِي أَرْضِ الصُّلْحِ إِذَا صَارَتْ مِصْرًا لِلْمُسْلِمِيْنَ، لَمْ يُهْدَمْ مَا كَانَ فِيْهَا مِنْ بِيْعَةٍ أَوْ كَنِيْسَةٍ أَوْ بَيْتِ نَارٍ.

"When a territory under treaty becomes a territory of the Muslims, no church, sanctuary or Zoroastrian temple that was there before should be demolished."[2]

---

[1] •Ibn al-Qayyim, *Aḥkām ahl al-dhimma*, 3:1169.

[2] •Abū Bakr al-Jaṣṣāṣ, *Aḥkām al-Qurʾān*, 5:83.

اَلْبَابُ السَّادِسُ

اَلْعَدْلُ مَعَهُمْ فِي الْحُكْمِ وَالْقَضَاءِ

CHAPTER SIX

JUSTICE IN ALL JUDGMENTS AND RULINGS FOR NON-MUSLIMS

Qurʾān

١. ﴿فَمَنِ ٱعۡتَدَىٰ عَلَيۡكُمۡ فَٱعۡتَدُواْ عَلَيۡهِ بِمِثۡلِ مَا ٱعۡتَدَىٰ عَلَيۡكُمۡۚ
وَٱتَّقُواْ ٱللَّهَ وَٱعۡلَمُوٓاْ أَنَّ ٱللَّهَ مَعَ ٱلۡمُتَّقِينَ﴾

1. *﴿So if someone wrongs you, you may also respond in kind but proportional to his offence. And fear Allah. And remember that Allah is with those who fear Him.﴾*[1]

٢. ﴿يَٰٓأَيُّهَا ٱلَّذِينَ ءَامَنُواْ كُونُواْ قَوَّٰمِينَ لِلَّهِ شُهَدَآءَ بِٱلۡقِسۡطِۖ وَلَا
يَجۡرِمَنَّكُمۡ شَنَـَٔانُ قَوۡمٍ عَلَىٰٓ أَلَّا تَعۡدِلُواْۚ ٱعۡدِلُواْ هُوَ أَقۡرَبُ لِلتَّقۡوَىٰۖ وَٱتَّقُواْ
ٱللَّهَۚ إِنَّ ٱللَّهَ خَبِيرُۢ بِمَا تَعۡمَلُونَ﴾

2. *﴿O believers! Holding fast to the cause of Allah, bear witness based on justice. And let not (even) the extreme hostility against a people provoke you into abstaining from justice (in their case). Always do justice, (for) it is closer to piousness. And fear Allah. Indeed, Allah is Well Aware of your works.﴾*[2]

٣. ﴿وَلَا تَكۡسِبُ كُلُّ نَفۡسٍ إِلَّا عَلَيۡهَاۚ وَلَا تَزِرُ وَازِرَةٞ وِزۡرَ أُخۡرَىٰ﴾

3. *﴿And whatever (sin) each soul earns, (its evil outcome) falls back upon it. And no bearer of burden will bear another's burden.﴾*[3]

٤. ﴿لَقَدۡ أَرۡسَلۡنَا رُسُلَنَا بِٱلۡبَيِّنَٰتِ وَأَنزَلۡنَا مَعَهُمُ ٱلۡكِتَٰبَ وَٱلۡمِيزَانَ لِيَقُومَ

---

[1] Qurʾān 2:194.

[2] Ibid., 5:8.

[3] Ibid., 6:164.

﴿ٱلنَّاسُ بِٱلْقِسْطِ﴾

4. ﴾*Verily, We sent Our Messengers with clear signs, and We sent down with them the Book and the balance of justice so that people might grow firm and stable in justice.*﴿[1]

٥. ﴿لَّا يَنْهَىٰكُمُ ٱللَّهُ عَنِ ٱلَّذِينَ لَمْ يُقَٰتِلُوكُمْ فِى ٱلدِّينِ وَلَمْ يُخْرِجُوكُم مِّن دِيَٰرِكُمْ أَن تَبَرُّوهُمْ وَتُقْسِطُوٓا۟ إِلَيْهِمْ ۚ إِنَّ ٱللَّهَ يُحِبُّ ٱلْمُقْسِطِينَ﴾

5. ﴾*Allah does not forbid you to be good to them and treat them with equity and justice who did not fight against you on (the question of)* Dīn *(Religion), nor did they drive you out of your homes (i.e., homeland). Surely, Allah likes those who conduct themselves with equity and justice.*﴿[2]

Hadith

٦٠/ ١. عَنْ عَبْدِ الرَّحْمَنِ بْنِ الْبَيْلَمَانِيِّ ﷺ، أَنَّ رَجُلًا مِنَ الْمُسْلِمِيْنَ قَتَلَ رَجُلًا مِنْ أَهْلِ الْكِتَابِ، فَرُفِعَ إِلَى النَّبِيِّ ﷺ، فَقَالَ رَسُوْلُ اللهِ ﷺ: أَنَا أَحَقُّ مَنْ وَفَّى بِذِمَّتِهِ، ثُمَّ أَمَرَ بِهِ فَقُتِلَ.

رَوَاهُ الشَّافِعِيُّ وَالْبَيْهَقِيُّ وَالشَّيْبَانِيُّ وَالْقُرَشِيُّ.

60/1. According to ʿAbd al-Raḥmān b. Baylamānī ﷺ:

"There was a man from the Muslims who killed a non-Muslim with whom there was a peace treaty. The case was presented to the Prophet ﷺ and he said: 'I am the most responsible of all for fulfilling the rights of those under my care [non-Muslim citizens].' Then he

[1] Ibid., 57:25.

[2] Ibid., 60:8.

ordered [the killing of the Muslim killer by way of retribution] and he was executed."[1]

Reported by al-Shāfiʿī, al-Bayhaqī, al-Shaybanī and al-Qurashī.

٦١/ ٢. وَفِي رِوَايَةٍ عَنْهُ، قَالَ: إِنَّ رَجُلًا مِنْ أَهْلِ الذِّمَّةِ أَتَى رَسُولَ اللهِ ﷺ فَقَالَ: إِنَّا عَاهَدْنَاكَ وَبَايَعْنَاكَ عَلَى كَذَا وَكَذَا وقَدْ خترَ برَجُلٍ مِنَّا، فقُتِلَ. فقَالَ: أَنَا أَحَقُّ مَنْ أَوْفَى بِذِمَّتِهِ. فَأَمْكَنَهُ مِنْهُ فَضُرِبَتْ عُنُقُهُ.

رَوَاهُ الْبَيْهَقِيُّ وَالدَّارَقُطْنِيُّ وَالشَّافِعِيُّ.

61/2. In a similar report, ʿAbd al-Raḥmān b. Baylamānī ☙ related: "A man from among the non-Muslim citizens came to Allah's Messenger ﷺ and said: 'We have entered into a treaty with you on such and such issue. One of us was betrayed and murdered.' Allah's Messenger ﷺ said: 'I am most responsible of all for fulfilling the rights of those under my care [non-Muslim citizens].' Then he ordered [the killing of the Muslim killer by way of retribution] and he was killed."[2]

Reported by al-Bayhaqī, al-Dāraquṭnī and al-Shāfiʿī.

٦٢/ ٣. عَنْ أَبِي شُرَيْحٍ الْخُزَاعِيِّ أَنَّ النَّبِيَّ ﷺ قَالَ: مَنْ أُصِيبَ بِقَتْلٍ أَوْ خَبْلٍ، فَإِنَّهُ يَخْتَارُ إِحْدَى ثَلَاثٍ: إِمَّا أَنْ يَقْتَصَّ، وَإِمَّا أَنْ يَعْفُوَ، وَإِمَّا أَنْ يَأْخُذَ الدِّيَةَ. فَإِنْ أَرَادَ الرَّابِعَةَ فَخُذُوا عَلَى يَدَيْهِ ﴿فَمَنِ ٱعْتَدَىٰ بَعْدَ ذَٰلِكَ فَلَهُۥ عَذَابٌ أَلِيمٌ﴾.

رَوَاهُ أَبُو دَاوُدَ وَعَبْدُ الرَّزَّاقِ.

62/3. Abū Shurayḥ al-Khuzaʿī related that the Prophet ﷺ said:

---

[1] Set forth by •al-Shāfiʿī in *al-Musnad*, p. 343 and in *al-Umm*, 7:320. •Abū Nuʿaym in *Musnad Abī Ḥanīfa*, p. 104. •al-Bayhaqī in *al-Sunan al-kubrā*, 8:30 §15696. •al-Shaybānī in *al-Mabsūṭ*, 4:488 and in *al-Ḥujja*, 4:342-344. •al-Qurashī in *al-Kharāj*, p. 82 §238.

[2] Set forth by •al-Bayhaqī in *al-Sunan al-kubrā*, 8:30 §15697 and in *Maʿrifa al-sunan wa al-āthār*, 6:149 §4814. •al-Daraquṭunī in *al-Sunan*, 3:135 §167. •al-Shāfiʿī in *al-Musnad*, 1:443.

"If someone's relative is killed, or if one of his extremities is cut off, he may choose one of the three options: he may retaliate, forgive or receive compensation. But if he wishes a fourth [something that exceeds the bounds set by the Shariah], you must hold him back [for Allah says,] ﴾*So, anyone who transgresses after that, there is painful torment for him*﴿[1] ."[2]

Reported by Abū Dāwūd and ʿAbd al-Razzāq.

٦٣/ ٤. عَنْ عَلِيِّ بْنِ أَبِي طَالِبٍ ﷺ، إِذَا قَتَلَ الْـمُسْلِمُ النَّصْرَانِيَّ قُتِلَ بِهِ.

رَوَاهُ الشَّيْبَانِيُّ وَالشَّافِعِيُّ.

63/4. ʿAlī b. Abī Ṭālib ﷺ said:

"If a Muslim kills a Christian, he shall be killed in retribution."[3]

Reported by al-Shaybānī and al-Shāfiʿī.

٦٤/ ٥. عَنْ مُجَاهِدٍ، عَنِ ابْنِ مَسْعُودٍ ﷺ، قَالَ: كَانَ يَقُولُ: دِيَةُ أَهْلِ الْكِتَابِ مِثْلُ دِيَةِ الْـمُسْلِمِ.

رَوَاهُ ابْنُ أَبِي شَيْبَةَ.

64/5. According to Mujāhid, Ibn Masʿūd ﷺ said:

"The blood money for the people of the Book is equal to that of Muslims."[4]

Reported by Ibn Abī Shayba.

---

[1] Qurʾān 2:178.

[2] Set forth by •Abū Dāwūd in *al-Sunan*: *Kitāb al-diyāt* [The Book of Blood Money], chapter: "The Leader Should Urge Forgiveness in the Matter of Shedding Blood," 4:169 §4496. •ʿAbd al-Razzāq in *al-Muṣannaf*, 10:86 §18454.

[3] Cited by •al-Shāfiʿī in *al-Umm*, 7:320. •al-Shaybānī in *Kitāb al-ḥujja ʿalā ahl al-Madīna*, 4:347.

[4] Set forth by •Ibn Abī Shayba in *al-Muṣannaf*, 5:406 §27444.

٦٥/٦. عَنِ الْقَاسِمِ بْنِ عَبْدِ الرَّحْمَنِ، قَال: قَالَ عَبْدُ اللهِ: مَنْ كَانَ لَهُ عَهْدٌ، أَوْ ذِمَّةٌ فَدِيَتُهُ دِيَةُ الْـحُرِّ الْـمُسْلِمِ.

رَوَاهُ ابْنُ أَبِي شَيْبَةَ.

65/6. Al-Qāsim b. ʿAbd al-Raḥmān related that ʿAbd Allah b. Masʿūd said:

"The blood money of a non-Muslim who is under treaty (of protection of life and property) or is under guarantee is equal to that of a free Muslim."[1]

Reported by Ibn Abī Shayba.

• عَنْ إِبْرَاهِيمَ، عَنْ عَلْقَمَةَ، قَالَ: دِيَةُ الْـمُعَاهَدِ مِثْلُ دِيَةِ الْـمُسْلِمِ.

رَوَاهُ ابْنُ أَبِي شَيْبَةَ.

Ibrāhīm related that ʿAlqama said: "The blood money of a person under peace treaty [*muʿāhad*] is equal to that of a Muslim."[2]

Reported by Ibn Abī Shayba.

• عَنْ أَبِي حَنِيْفَةَ عَنِ الْـحَكَمِ بْنِ عُتَيْبَةَ أَنَّ عَلِيًّا ﷺ قَالَ: دِيَةُ الْيَهُوْدِيِّ وَالنَّصْرَانِيِّ وَكُلِّ ذِمِّيٍّ مِثْلُ دِيَةِ الْـمُسْلِمِ. قَالَ أَبُوْ حَنِيْفَةَ وَهُوَ قَوْلِي.

رَوَاهُ عَبْدُ الرَّزَّاقِ.

Imam Abū Ḥanīfa reported on the authority of ʿUtba that ʿAlī b. Abī Ṭālib ﷺ said: "The blood money for a [peaceful] Jew, Christian and every non-Muslim citizen is like that of the Muslim [i.e., their heirs receive the same amount of monetary compensation as a Muslim family does]." Imam

---

[1] Ibid., §27445.

[2] Ibid., §27446.

Abū Ḥanīfa said: "I support this statement."[1]

Reported by ʿAbd al-Razzāq.

- قَالَ بَعْضُ أَهْلِ الْعِلْمِ: دِيَةُ الْيَهُوْدِيِّ وَالنَّصْرَانِيِّ مِثْلُ دِيَةِ الْـمُسْلِمِ وَهُوَ قَوْلُ سُفْيَانَ الثَّوْرِيِّ وَأَهْلِ الْكُوْفَةِ.

رَوَاهُ التِّرْمِذِيُّ.

Some jurists said: "The blood money for a [peaceful] Jew or a Christian is like that of a Muslim. This is the position of Sufyān al-Thawrī and the people of Kufa."[2]

Reported by al-Tirmidhī.

- عَنِ الزُّهْرِيِّ قَالَ: دِيَةُ الْيَهُوْدِيِّ وَالنَّصْرَانِيِّ وَالْـمَجُوْسِيِّ وَكُلِّ ذِمِّيٍّ مِثْلُ دِيَةِ الْـمُسْلِمِ.

رَوَاهُ عَبْدُ الرَّزَّاقِ.

According to al-Zuhrī: "The blood money for a [peaceful] Jew, a Christian or a Zoroastrian and every non-Muslim citizen is like that of a Muslim [i.e., their heirs receive the same amount of monetary compensation as a Muslim family]."[3]

Reported by ʿAbd al-Razzāq.

- قَالَ ابْنُ شِهَابٍ الزُّهْرِيُّ: إِنَّ دِيَةَ الْـمُعَاهَدِ فِيْ عَهْدِ أَبِي بَكْرٍ وَعُمَرَ وَعُثْمَانَ ﷺ مِثْلُ دِيَةِ الْـحُرِّ الْـمُسْلِمِ.

---

[1] Set forth by •ʿAbd al-Razzāq in *al-Muṣannaf*, 10:97 §18494.

[2] Set forth by •al-Tirmidhī in *al-Sunan*: *Kitāb al-diyāt* [The Book of Blood Money], chapter: "What Has Come To Us Concerning The Blood Money Of Non-Muslims," 4:25 §1413.

[3] Set forth by •ʿAbd al-Razzāq in *al-Muṣannaf*, 10:95 §18491.

ذَكَرَهُ الشَّيْبَانِيُّ وَالشَّافِعِيُّ.

Imam Ibn Shihāb al-Zuhrī said: 'During the reigns of Abū Bakr, ʿUmar and ʿUthmān ﷺ, the blood money for a non-Muslim citizen was equal to that of a free Muslim."[1]

Cited by al-Shaybānī and al-Shāfiʿī.

The position of the Ḥanafī school of jurisprudence is that a Muslim should be killed in retribution for killing a non-Muslim citizen. This position is supported by the general import of the texts within the Qurʾān and hadith, which make retribution obligatory. Muslim and non-Muslim blood share an equal amount of inviolability and sanctity, without any discrimination. Imam al-Nakhaʿī, Ibn Abī Laylā, al-Shaʿbī and ʿUthmān al-Battī also share this view held by the Ḥanafī school.

A doubt may emerge pertaining to the saying of the Prophet ﷺ,

وَلَا يُقْتَلُ مُسْلِمٌ بِكَافِرٍ.

"A Muslim is not to be killed in retaliation for murdering a disbeliever."[2]

What does that mean? The jurists explained this and said that here the word "disbeliever" does not refer to a peaceful citizen; it rather signifies a combatant who is killed. There is to be no retribution in this case. This is an international law in effect in all countries of the world and there is no difference of opinion about it.

٦٦/٧. عَنْ إِبْرَاهِيْمَ أَنَّ رَجُلًا مِنْ بَنِي بَكْرِ بْنِ وَائِلٍ قَتَلَ رَجُلًا مِنْ أَهْلِ الْحِيْرَةِ، فَكَتَبَ فِيْهِ عُمَرُ بْنُ الْخَطَّابِ ﷺ أَنْ يَّدْفَعَ إِلَى أَوْلِيَاءِ الْمَقْتُوْلِ. فَإِنْ شَاؤُوْا قَتَلُوْا وَإِنْ شَاؤُوْا عَفَوْا. فَدَفَعَ الرَّجُلُ إِلَى وَلِيِّ الْمَقْتُوْلِ إِلَى رَجُلٍ يُقَالُ لَهُ حُنَيْنٌ مِنْ أَهْلِ الْحِيْرَةِ، فَقَتَلَهُ.

---

[1] Cited by •al-Shāfiʿī in *al-Umm*, 7:321. •al-Shaybānī in *al-Ḥujja*, 4:351.

[2] Set forth by •al-Bukhārī in *al-Ṣaḥīḥ*: *Kitāb al-ʿilm* [The Book of Knowledge], chapter: "On Writing Down Knowledge," 1:53 §111.

رَوَاهُ الشَّافِعِيُّ وَالْبَيْهَقِيُّ.

66/7. Ibrāhīm related: "During the Caliphate of ʿUmar ◉, a person from the tribe of Banū Bakr b. Wāʾil killed a non-Muslim citizen of Ḥira. On this, ʿUmar b. al-Khaṭṭāb wrote the judgment to hand the killer over to the guardian of the victim, who had the choice of either killing or pardoning him. Hence, the killer was handed over to the guardian of the victim named Ḥunayn, who killed him."[1]

Reported by al-Shāfiʿī and al-Bayhaqī.

٨ / ٦٧. عَنْ أَبِي الْجُنُوبِ الْأَسَدِيِّ قَالَ: أُتِيَ عَلِيُّ بْنُ أَبِي طَالِبٍ ◉ بِرَجُلٍ مِنَ الْـمُسْلِمِينَ قَتَلَ رَجُلًا مِنْ أَهْلِ الذِّمَّةِ. قَالَ: فَقَامَتْ عَلَيْهِ الْبَيِّنَةُ، فَأَمَرَ بِقَتْلِهِ، فَجَاءَ أَخُوهُ فَقَالَ: إِنِّي قَدْ عَفَوْتُ عَنْهُ. قَالَ: فَلَعَلَّهُمْ هَدَّدُوكَ أَوْ فَرَّقُوكَ أَوْ فَزَّعُوكَ. قَالَ: لَا، وَلَـكِنَّ قَتْلَهُ لَا يَرُدُّ عَلَيَّ أَخِي، وَعَوَّضُونِي فَرَضِيْتُ. قَالَ: أَنْتَ أَعْلَمُ. مَنْ كَانَ لَهُ ذِمَّتُنَا فَدَمُهُ كَدَمِنَا وَدِيَتُهُ كَدِيَتِنَا.

رَوَاهُ الشَّافِعِيُّ وَأَبُوْ يُوْسُفَ وَالْبَيْهَقِيُّ.

67/8. Abū Junūb al-Asadī related:

"A Muslim who had killed a non-Muslim citizen was presented in the court of ʿAlī ◉. The proof of his crime was found valid, and for that, ʿAlī ◉ ordered him to be killed in retribution. The brother of the victim came to ʿAlī and said: 'I have forgiven him.' ʿAlī said: 'Perhaps they [the heirs of the killer] scared you or threatened you.' He replied in the negative and said: 'My brother would not come back, even if the killer was killed in retribution, and they (the heirs of the killer) paid me the blood money; therefore, I am content.' On this, ʿAlī said: 'You know better (but this is the principle of our government). When someone comes under the guarantee of our protection, his blood

---

[1] Set forth by •al-Shāfiʿī in *al-Umm*, 7:321. •al-Bayhaqī in *al-Sunan al-kubrā*, 8:32 §15706. •al-Shaybānī in *al-Ḥujja*, 4:335. •al-Zaylaʿī in *Naṣb al-rāya*, 4:337.

becomes like our blood, and the blood money due to him is like the blood money due to us.'"[1]

Reported by Shāfiʿī, Abū Yūsuf and al-Bayhaqī.

٦٨/ ٩. وَفِي رِوَايَةٍ عَنْ أَنَسٍ أَنَّ رَجُلاً مِنْ أَهْلِ مِصْرَ أَتَى عُمَرَ بْنَ الْـخَطَّابِ فَقَالَ: يَا أَمِيْرَ الْـمُؤْمِنِيْنَ، عَائِذٌ بِكَ مِنَ الظُّلْمِ. قَالَ: عُذْتَ مَعَاذًا. قَالَ: سَابَقْتُ ابْنَ عَمْرِو بْنِ الْعَاصِ، فَسَبَقْتُهُ، فَجَعَلَ يَضْرِبُنِي بِالسَّوْطِ وَيَقُوْلُ: أَنَا ابْنُ الْأَكْرَمِيْنَ. فَكَتَبَ عُمَرُ إِلَى عَمْرٍو يَأْمُرُهُ بِالْقُدُوْمِ وَيَقْدَمُ بِابْنِهِ مَعَهُ، فَقَدِمَ، فَقَالَ عُمَرُ: أَيْنَ الْـمِصْرِيُّ؟ خُذِ السَّوْطَ فَاضْرِبْ. فَجَعَلَ يَضْرِبُهُ بِالسَّوْطِ وَيَقُوْلُ عُمَرُ: اضْرِبِ ابْنَ الْأَكْرَمِيْنَ. قَالَ أَنَسٌ: فَضَرَبَ، فَوَاللهِ، لَقَدْ ضَرَبَهُ وَنَحْنُ نُحِبُّ ضَرْبَهُ. فَمَا أَقْلَعَ عَنْهُ حَتَّى تَمَنَّيْنَا أَنَّهُ يَرْفَعُ عَنْهُ. ثُمَّ قَالَ عُمَرُ لِلْمِصْرِيِّ: ضَعِ السَّوْطَ عَلَى صُلْعَةِ عَمْرٍو، فَقَالَ: يَا أَمِيْرَ الْـمُؤْمِنِيْنَ، إِنَّمَا ابْنُهُ الَّذِي ضَرَبَنِي وَقَدِ اسْتَقَدْتُ مِنْهُ. فَقَالَ عُمَرُ لِعَمْرٍو: مُذْ كَمْ تَعَبَّدْتُمُ النَّاسَ وَقَدْ وَلَدَتْهُمْ أُمَّهَاتُهُمْ أَحْرَارًا؟ قَالَ: يَا أَمِيْرَ الْـمُؤْمِنِيْنَ، لَـمْ أَعْلَمْ وَلَـمْ يَأْتِنِي.

ذَكَرَهُ الْهِنْدِيُّ.

68/9. Anas b. Mālik ﷺ related:

"A person from Egypt came to ʿUmar b. al-Khaṭṭāb and said: 'O Commander of the faithful! I beg your refuge from wrongdoing.' He said: 'You are granted total refuge.' He said: 'I had a race with the son of ʿAmr b. al-ʿĀṣ and I beat him, then he whipped me, saying: 'I am the son of the noble!' ʿUmar wrote to ʿAmr b. al-ʿĀṣ and ordered him to present his son in his court. ʿAmr b. al-ʿĀṣ followed the command and submitted. ʿUmar called that Egyptian and said: 'Take this whip and flog (the son of ʿAmr b. al-ʿĀṣ).' He was flogged while ʿUmar b. al-

[1] Set forth by •al-Shāfiʿī in *al-Musnad* p. 344. •Abū Yūsuf in *Kitāb al-kharāj*, p. 187. •al-Bayhaqī in *al-Sunan al-kubrā*, 8:34 §15712. •al-ʿAsqalānī in *al-Dirāya fī takhrīj aḥādīth al-Hidāya*, 2:263. •al-Zaylaʿī in *Naṣb al-rāya*, 4:336.

Khaṭṭāb was saying: 'Flog the son of the noble!'" Anas reported: "By Allah! He flogged him vigorously and we appreciated it (the justice of ᶜUmar). He did not stop flogging him until we felt that he must stop. Then ᶜUmar said to the Egyptian to put the whip on the head of ᶜAmr b. al-ᶜĀṣ. He said: 'O Commander of the faithful! I took revenge from his son who whipped me.' ᶜUmar said to ᶜAmr b. al-ᶜĀṣ: 'Since when have you regarded people as your slaves, while their mothers gave birth to them as free men?' ᶜAmr b. al-ᶜĀṣ said: 'O Commander of the faithful! I was unaware of this incident and this man did not come to me.'"[1]

Cited by al-Hindī.

[1] Set forth by •Ibn ᶜAbd al-Ḥakam in *Futūḥ Miṣr wa akhbaru-hā*, p. 114–115. •al-Hindī in *Kanz al-ᶜummāl*, 12:294 §36010.

اَلْبَابُ السَّابِعُ

اَلْبِرُّ وَحُسْنُ التَّعَامُلِ مَعَهُمْ

CHAPTER SEVEN

TREATING NON-MUSLIMS WITH PIETY AND EXCELLENCE

Qur'ān

١. ﴿ٱدۡعُ إِلَىٰ سَبِيلِ رَبِّكَ بِٱلۡحِكۡمَةِ وَٱلۡمَوۡعِظَةِ ٱلۡحَسَنَةِۖ وَجَٰدِلۡهُم بِٱلَّتِي هِيَ أَحۡسَنُۚ إِنَّ رَبَّكَ هُوَ أَعۡلَمُ بِمَن ضَلَّ عَن سَبِيلِهِۦ وَهُوَ أَعۡلَمُ بِٱلۡمُهۡتَدِينَ﴾

1. ﴾*(O Glorious Messenger!) Invite towards the path of your Lord with wisdom and refined exhortation and (also) argue with them in a most decent manner. Surely, your Lord knows well the one who strayed away from His path, and He also knows well the rightly guided.*﴿[1]

٢. ﴿وَلَا تُجَٰدِلُوٓاْ أَهۡلَ ٱلۡكِتَٰبِ إِلَّا بِٱلَّتِي هِيَ أَحۡسَنُ إِلَّا ٱلَّذِينَ ظَلَمُواْ مِنۡهُمۡۖ وَقُولُوٓاْ ءَامَنَّا بِٱلَّذِيٓ أُنزِلَ إِلَيۡنَا وَأُنزِلَ إِلَيۡكُمۡ وَإِلَٰهُنَا وَإِلَٰهُكُمۡ وَٰحِدٞ وَنَحۡنُ لَهُۥ مُسۡلِمُونَ﴾

2. ﴾*And, (O believers,) do not argue with the People of the Book but in a suitable and decent way, except those of them who did injustice. And say (to them): "We believe in that (Book) which has been revealed to us and which was sent down to you, and our God and your God is but One and we obey Him alone."*﴿[2]

Hadith

٦٩/ ١. عَنْ أَسْمَاءَ بِنْتِ أَبِي بَكْرٍ رضي الله عنهما قَالَتْ: قَدِمَتْ عَلَيَّ أُمِّي وَهِيَ مُشْرِكَةٌ فِي عَهْدِ

---

[1] Qur'ān 16:125.

[2] Ibid., 29:46.

رَسُوْلِ الله ﷺ، فَاسْتَفْتَيْتُ رَسُوْلَ الله ﷺ قُلْتُ: وَهِيَ رَاغِبَةٌ أَفَأَصِلُ أُمِّي؟ قَالَ: نَعَمْ،

صِلِي أُمَّكِ.

مُتَّفَقٌ عَلَيْهِ.

69/1. Asmā’, daughter of Abū Bakr &, narrated:

"My mother came to me during the period of Allah's Messenger ﷺ when she was still a polytheist. I asked about the ruling from Allah's Messenger ﷺ: 'She desires (a gift from me); shall I keep kinship with her?' He said: 'Yes, keep good relations with your (polytheist) mother.'"[1]

Agreed upon by al-Bukhārī and Muslim.

٧٠ / ٢. عَنْ جَابِرِ بْنِ عَبْدِ الله ﷺ قَالَ: مَرَّتْ بِنَا جَنَازَةٌ فَقَامَ لَهَا النَّبِيُّ ﷺ وَقُمْنَا لَهُ، فَقُلْنَا: يَا رَسُوْلَ الله، إِنَّهَا جِنَازَةٌ يَهُوْدِيٍّ! قَالَ: إِذَا رَأَيْتُمُ الْجِنَازَةَ فَقُوْمُوْا.

مُتَّفَقٌ عَلَيْهِ.

70/2. Jābir b. ʿAbd Allah & related:

"A funeral procession passed in front of us and the Prophet ﷺ stood up and we too stood up." We said, 'O Messenger of Allah ﷺ, this is the funeral procession of a Jew!' He said: 'If you catch sight of the bier (the funeral procession), you must stand up.'"[2]

---

[1] Set forth by •al-Bukhārī in al-Ṣaḥīḥ: Kitāb al-hiba wa faḍlu-hā [The Book of Gifts and their Excellence], chapter: "Gifts to idolaters," 2:924 §2477 and in Kitāb al-Jizya [The Book of Annual Security Tax for non-Muslims], chapter: The sin committed by someone who promises and then betrays, 3:1162 §3012. •Muslim in al-Ṣaḥīḥ: Kitāb al-Zakāt [The book of the Alms-due], chapter: "The excellence of spending on and giving alms to relatives, to spouse, to children, and parents even if they are polytheists," 2:696 §1003. •Aḥmad b. Ḥanbal in al-Musnad, 6:347 §26985. •Abū Dāwūd in al-Sunan: Kitāb al-Zakāt [The book of the Alms-due], chapter: "Bestowing charity upon the non-Muslim citizens of a Muslim country," 2:127 §1668. •al-Ṭabarānī in al-Muʿjam al-kabīr, 24:78 §203. •ʿAbd al-Razzāq in al-Muṣannaf, 6:38 §9932.

[2] Set forth by •al-Bukhārī in al-Ṣaḥīḥ: Kitāb al-Janāʾiz [The Book of Funeral

Agreed upon by al-Bukhārī and Muslim.

٧١/ ٣. وَفِي رِوَايَةٍ عَنْ عَبْدِ الرَّحْمَنِ بْنِ أَبِي لَيْلَى ﷺ قَالَ: كَانَ سَهْلُ بْنُ حُنَيْفٍ وَقَيْسُ بْنُ سَعْدٍ ﷺ قَاعِدَيْنِ بِالْقَادِسِيَّةِ. فَمَرُّوْا عَلَيْهِمَا بِجِنَازَةٍ، فَقَامَا. فَقِيْلَ لَهُمَا: إِنَّهَا مِنْ أَهْلِ الْأَرْضِ أَيْ مِنْ أَهْلِ الذِّمَّةِ. فَقَالَا: إِنَّ النَّبِيَّ ﷺ مَرَّتْ بِهِ جِنَازَةٌ، فَقَامَ، فَقِيْلَ لَهُ: إِنَّهَا جِنَازَةُ يَهُوْدِيٍّ. فَقَالَ: أَلَيْسَتْ نَفْسًا؟

مُتَّفَقٌ عَلَيْهِ.

71/3. ʿAbd al-Raḥmān b. Abī Layla ﷺ related:

"Sahl b. Ḥunayf and Qays b. Saʿd ﷺ were sitting in the city of al-Qādisīyya. A funeral procession passed in front of them and they both stood up. They were told that the funeral procession was of one of the inhabitants of the land (i.e., of a non-believer). They both said: '(Once) a funeral procession passed in front of the Prophet ﷺ and he stood up. When he was told that it was the funeral of a Jew, he said: 'Is it not a soul?'"[1]

Agreed upon by al-Bukhārī and Muslim.

Ceremonies], chapter: "Someone standing up for a Jewish funeral procession," 1:441 §1249. •Muslim in *al-Ṣaḥīḥ*: *Kitāb al-Janāʾiz* [The Book of Funeral Ceremonies], chapter: "Someone standing up for a funeral procession," 2:660 §960. •Aḥmad b. Ḥanbal in *al-Musnad*, 3:319 §14467. •al-Nasāʾī in *al-Sunan*: *Kitāb al-Janāʾiz* [The Book of Funeral Ceremonies], chapter: "Someone standing up for the funeral procession of the people who associate partners with Allah," 4:45 §1922 and in *al-Sunan al-kubrā*, 1:626 §2049.

[1] Set forth by •al-Bukhārī in *al-Ṣaḥīḥ*: *Kitāb al-Janāʾiz* [The Book of Funeral Ceremonies], chapter: "Someone standing up for a Jewish funeral procession," 1:441 §1250. •Muslim in *al-Ṣaḥīḥ*: *Kitāb al-Janāʾiz* [The Book of Funeral Ceremonies], chapter: "Someone getting to his feet for a funeral procession," 2:661 §961. •Aḥmad b. Ḥanbal in *al-Musnad*, 6:6 §23893. •al-Nasāʾī in *al-Sunan*: *Kitāb al-Janāʾiz* [The Book of Funeral Ceremonies], chapter: "Someone standing up for the funeral procession of the people who associate partners with Allah," 4:45 §1921 and in *al-Sunan al-Kubrā*, 1:626 §2048. •Ibn Abī Shayba in *al-Muṣannaf*, 3:39 §11918. •Ibn al-Jaʿd in *al-Musnad*, p. 27 §70. •al-Ṭabarānī in *al-Muʿjam al-Kabīr*, 6:90 §5606. •al-Bayhaqī in *al-Sunan al-Kubrā*, 4:27 §6672.

٧٢/ ٤. عَنْ هِشَامِ بْنِ حَكِيمِ بْنِ حِزَامٍ قَالَ: مَرَّ بِالشَّامِ عَلَى أُنَاسٍ وَقَدْ أُقِيمُوا فِي الشَّمْسِ وَصُبَّ عَلَى رُؤُوسِهِمُ الزَّيْتُ. فَقَالَ: مَا هَذَا؟ قِيلَ: يُعَذَّبُونَ فِي الْـخَرَاجِ. فَقَالَ: أَمَا إِنِّي سَمِعْتُ رَسُولَ اللهِ ﷺ يَقُولُ: إِنَّ اللهَ يُعَذِّبُ الَّذِينَ يُعَذِّبُونَ فِي الدُّنْيَا.

رَوَاهُ مُسْلِمٌ وَأَحْمَدُ وَأَبُو دَاوُدَ وَالنَّسَائِيُّ.

72/4. Hishām b. Ḥakīm b. Ḥizām reported:

"Once he passed by some people in Syria who were made to stand in the sun, and olive oil was poured on their heads. He asked: 'Why are they getting punished?' He was told that they were being punished for not paying the land tax. Ḥakīm b. Hizām said that he heard Allah's Messenger ﷺ say: 'Indeed, Allah shall torment those who torment others in the life of this world.'"[1]

Reported by Muslim and Aḥmad, Abū Dāwūd and al-Nasāʾī.

٧٣/ ٥. وَفِي رِوَايَةٍ عَنْ عُرْوَةَ بْنِ الزُّبَيْرِ أَنَّ هِشَامَ بْنَ حَكِيمٍ وَجَدَ رَجُلًا وَهُوَ عَلَى حِمْصَ يُشَمِّسُ نَاسًا مِنَ النَّبَطِ فِي أَدَاءِ الْجِزْيَةِ فَقَالَ: مَا هَذَا؟ إِنِّي سَمِعْتُ رَسُولَ اللهِ ﷺ يَقُولُ: إِنَّ اللهَ يُعَذِّبُ الَّذِينَ يُعَذِّبُونَ النَّاسَ فِي الدُّنْيَا.

رَوَاهُ مُسْلِمٌ وَأَحْمَدُ وَأَبُو دَاوُدَ وَالنَّسَائِيُّ.

73/5. ʿUrwa b. al-Zubayr reported:

"Hishām b. Ḥakīm found that the ruler of Homs made some Nabateans (a nation in Iraq) stand in the sun, for not paying their annual security tax *(jizya)*. He said: 'What is this? I heard Allah's

---

[1] Set forth by •Muslim in *al-Ṣaḥīḥ*: *Kitāb al-birr wa al-ṣila wa al-ādāb* [The Book of Piety, Filial Duty and Good Manners], chapter: "The Severe Divine Threat to the One Who Punishes People Unjustly," 4:2018 § 2613. •Aḥmad b. Ḥanbal in *al-Musnad*, 3:403, 404, 468. •Abū Dāwūd in *al-Sunan*: *Kitāb al-kharāj* [The Book of Land Taxation], chapter: "On Being Harsh," 3:106 §3045. •al-Nasāʾī in *al-Sunan al-kubrā*, 5:236 §8771.

Messenger ﷺ say: "Allah Most High will torment those who torture people in this world."'"[1]

Reported by Muslim and Aḥmad, Abū Dāwūd and al-Nasāʾī.

٧٤/ ٦. عَنْ أَبِي قَتَادَةَ قَالَ: قَدِمَ وَفْدُ النَّجَاشِيِّ عَلَى النَّبِيِّ ﷺ فَقَامَ يَخْدُمُهُمْ. فَقَالَ أَصْحَابُهُ: نَحْنُ نَكْفِيْكَ، يَا رَسُوْلَ اللهِ. قَالَ: إِنَّهُمْ كَانُوْا لِأَصْحَابِ مُكْرِمِيْنَ، فَإِنِّي أُحِبُّ أَنْ أُكَافِئَهُمْ.

رَوَاهُ الْبَيْهَقِيُّ وَالصَّيْدَاوِيُّ وَذَكَرَهُ ابْنُ كَثِيْرٍ وَالْحَلَبِيُّ.

74/6. Abū Qatāda related:

"A delegation of King Negus of Abyssinia [*Ḥabasha*] came to the Prophet ﷺ and he served them (very well). His Companions said: 'O Messenger of Allah! We are here to serve them.' Allah's Messenger ﷺ replied: 'These people paid respect to my Companions; therefore, I like that I myself pay back their generosity.'"[2]

Reported by al-Bayhaqī, al-Ṣaydāwī and cited by Ibn Kathīr and al-Ḥalabī.

٧٥/ ٧. عَنْ جُبَيْرِ بْنِ نُفَيْرٍ رضي الله عنه أَنَّ عُمَرَ بْنَ الْخَطَّابِ رضي الله عنه أُتِيَ بِمَالٍ كَثِيْرٍ، قَالَ أَبُوْ عُبَيْدٍ: أَحْسِبُ قَالَ: مِنَ الْجِزْيَةِ، فَقَالَ: إِنِّي لَأَظُنُّكُمْ قَدْ أَهْلَكْتُمُ النَّاسَ. قَالُوْا: لَا، وَاللهِ، مَا أَخَذْنَا إِلَّا عَفْوًا صَفْوًا. قَالَ: بِلَا سَوْطٍ وَلَا نَوْطٍ؟ قَالُوْا: نَعَمْ. قَالَ: اَلْحَمْدُ

---

[1] Narrated by •Muslim in *al-Ṣaḥīḥ*: *Kitāb al-birr wa al-ṣila wa al-ādāb* [The Book of Piety, Filial Duty and Good Manners], chapter: "The Severe Divine Threat for Someone Who Punishes People Unjustly," 4:2018 §2613. •Aḥmad b. Ḥanbal in *al-Musnad*, 3:404 §5612. •Abū Dāwūd in *al-Sunan*: *al-Kharāj wa al-Imāra wa al-Fay*ʾ [The Book of the Land Tax, Imperial Authority and the Bestowal of Booty], chapter: "Recovering the Capitation Tax Forcibly," 3:169 §3045. •al-Nasāʾī in *al-Sunan al-Kubrā*, 5:236 §8771.

[2] Set forth by •al-Bayhaqī in *Shuʿab al-īmān*, 6:518 §9125 and in *Dalāʾil al-Nubuwwa*, 2:307. •al-Ṣaydāwī in *Muʿjam al-shūyūkh*, 1:97. •al-Ḥalabī in *al-Sīra al-Ḥalabiyya*, 2:758. •Ibn Kathīr in *al-Sīra*, 2:31.

لله الَّذِي لَـمْ يَجْعَلْ ذَالِكَ عَلَى يَدَيَّ وَلَا فِي سُلْطَانِي.

رَوَاهُ أَبُوْ عُبَيْدٍ وَذَكَرَهُ ابْنُ قُدَامَةَ فِي الْـمُغْنِي.

75/7. According to Jubayr b. Nufayr ﷺ:

"A large amount of wealth was brought to ʿUmar b. al-Khaṭṭāb ﷺ. Abū ʿUbayd said: 'I believe it was the money collected from tax.' ʿUmar said: 'For certain, you have destroyed the people!' They [the tax collectors] said: 'No, by Allah! We have only taken with tenderness and ease what was surplus to their needs.' ʿUmar inquired, 'Was it acquired without recourse to a whip or coercion?' They replied: 'Yes.' He said: 'All praise is due to Allah, Who did not put that (oppression and injustice) on my hands or during my rule.'"[1]

Reported by Abū ʿUbayd al-Qāsim b. Sallām and cited by Ibn Qudāma in *al-Mughnī*.

TRADITIONS OF PIOUS SCHOLARS OF EARLY TIMES

- وَفِي الدُّرِّ الْـمُخْتَارِ: وَيَجِبُ كَفُّ الْأَذَى عَنْهُ وَتَحْرُمُ غِيبَتُهُ كَالْـمُسْلِمِ.

  In *al-Durr al-mukhtār* it is stated: "It is mandatory to keep him [the non-Muslim citizen] from agony and torture. Backbiting him is forbidden, just as it is forbidden to backbite a Muslim."[2]

- وَقَالَ الْإِمَامُ شِهَابُ الدِّيْنِ الْقَرَافِيُّ الْـمَالِكِيُّ فِي كِتَابِهِ 'الْفُرُوْقِ' عَنْ حُقُوْقِ غَيْرِ الْـمُسْلِمِيْنَ:

  إِنَّ عَقْدَ الذِّمَّةِ يُوْجِبُ لَهُمْ حُقُوْقًا عَلَيْنَا، لِأَنَّهُمْ فِي جَوَارِنَا وَفِي خِفَارَتِنَا (حِمَايَتِنَا) وَذِمَّتِنَا وَذِمَّةِ اللهِ تَعَالَى، وَذِمَّةِ رَسُوْلِ اللهِ ﷺ، وَدِيْنِ الإِسْلَامِ.

---

[1] Cited by •Abū ʿUbayd al-Qāsim b. Sallām in *Kitāb al-amwāl*, p. 54 §114. •Ibn Qudāma in *al-Mughnī*, 9:290.

[2] •Al-Ḥaṣkafī, *al-Durr al-mukhtār*, 2:223. •Ibn ʿĀbidīn al-Shāmī, *Radd al-muḥtār*, 3:273–274.

فَمَنِ اعْتَدَى عَلَيْهِمْ وَلَو بِكَلِمَةِ سُوءٍ أَوْ غِيْبَةٍ، فَقَدْ ضَيَّعَ ذِمَّةَ اللهِ، وَذِمَّةَ رَسُوْلِهِ ﷺ وَذِمَّةَ دِينِ الإِسْلَامِ.

Imam Shihāb al-Dīn al-Qurāfī, the famous Mālikī jurist, wrote in his book *al-Furūq* about the rights of non-Muslim citizens: "The *dhimma* contract for non-Muslims establishes certain rights that they have upon us because they live in proximity to us and are under our protection and care and the care of Allah and His Messenger ﷺ and the religion of Islam. So whoever transgresses against them—even by an evil word or through backbiting—has lost the guarantee of Allah, His Messenger ﷺ and the religion of Islam [i.e., did not fulfil the rights and duties owed to them, and has acted sinfully].[1]

- قَالَ ابْنُ عَابِدِيْنَ الشَّامِيُّ فِي حُقُوْقِ غَيْرِ الْمُسْلِمِيْنَ: لِأَنَّهُ بِعَقْدِ الذِّمَّةِ وَجَبَ لَهُ مَا لَنَا، فَإِذَا حَرُمَتْ غِيْبَةُ الْمُسْلِمِ حَرُمَتْ غِيْبَتُهُ، بَلْ قَالُوْا: إِنَّ ظُلْمَ الذِّمِّيِّ أَشَدُّ.

Ibn ʿĀbidīn al-Shāmī writes about the rights of non-Muslim citizens: "For due to the contract of *dhimma* he [a non-Muslim] enjoys the same rights as we do. Backbiting a non-Muslim is forbidden the same way as it is for Muslims. Nay, they [the jurists] have said that oppression meted out to a non-Muslim citizen is even severer [in sin]."[2]

- قَدْ حَقَّقَ الْإِمَامُ الْكَاسَانِيُّ فِي كِتَابِهِ 'بَدَائِعُ الصَّنَائِعِ' الْمُسَاوَاةَ فِي الْحُقُوْقِ بَيْنَ الْمَسْلِمِيْنَ وغَيْرِ الْمُسْلِمِيْنَ: لَهُمْ مَا لَنَا وَعَلَيْهِمْ مَا عَلَيْنَا.

Al-Kāsānī, in his book *Badāʾiʿ al-ṣanāʾiʿ*, has regarded

---

[1] •Al-Qurāfī, *al-Furūq*, 3:14.

[2] •Ibn ʿĀbidīn al-Shāmī, *Radd al-muḥtār*, 3:273–274.

the rights of Muslims and non-Muslims as equal: "Non-Muslim citizens enjoy the same rights that are enjoyed by us (Muslims), and they have the same responsibilities as we do."[1]

---

[1] •Al-Kāsānī, *Badāʾiʿ al-ṣanāʾiʿ*, 7:111.

اَلْبَابُ الثَّامِنُ

اَلتَّعَامُلُ مَعَهُمْ بِالصَّبْرِ وَعَدَمُ الْاِنْتِقَامِ مِنْهُمْ

Chapter Eight

Non-Revengeful, Forbearing and Tolerant Behaviour towards Non-Muslims

٧٦/ ١. عَنْ عَبْدِ اللهِ ﵁ قَالَ: كَأَنِّي أَنْظُرُ إِلَى النَّبِيِّ ﷺ يَحْكِي نَبِيًّا مِنَ الأَنْبِيَاءِ، ضَرَبَهُ قَوْمُهُ فَأَدْمَوْهُ وَهُوَ يَمْسَحُ الدَّمَ عَنْ وَجْهِهِ وَيَقُوْلُ: اَللَّهُمَّ، اغْفِرْ لِقَوْمِي فَإِنَّهُمْ لَا يَعْلَمُوْنَ.

مُتَّفَقٌ عَلَيْهِ.

76/1. ʿAbd Allah b. Masʿūd ﵁ related:

"I saw the Prophet ﷺ in a state, as though he was talking about one of the Prophets whose nation had beaten him and caused him to bleed, and while he was wiping his face, he supplicated: 'O Allah! Forgive my people, for they do not know.'"[1]

Agreed upon by al-Bukhārī and Muslim.

٧٧/ ٢. وَفِي رِوَايَةِ عَائِشَةَ زَوْجِ النَّبِيِّ ﷺ أَنَّهَا قَالَتْ لِرَسُوْلِ اللهِ ﷺ: يَا رَسُوْلَ اللهِ، هَلْ أَتَى عَلَيْكَ يَوْمٌ كَانَ أَشَدَّ مِنْ يَوْمِ أُحُدٍ؟ فَقَالَ: لَقَدْ لَقِيتُ مِنْ قَوْمِكِ وَكَانَ أَشَدَّ مَا لَقِيْتُ مِنْهُمْ يَوْمَ الْعَقَبَةِ. إِذْ عَرَضْتُ نَفْسِي عَلَى ابْنِ عَبْدِ يَالِيْلَ بْنِ عَبْدِ كُلَالٍ فَلَمْ يُجِبْنِي إِلَى مَا أَرَدْتُ، فَانْطَلَقْتُ وَأَنَا مَهْمُوْمٌ عَلَى وَجْهِي. فَلَمْ أَسْتَفِقْ إِلَّا بِقَرْنِ الثَّعَالِبِ.

[1] Set forth by •al-Bukhārī in *al-Ṣaḥīḥ*, *Kitāb al-Anbiyā*ʾ [The Book of the Prophets], chapter: The Narration of the Cave, 3:1282 §3290 and in *Kitāb istitāba al-murtaddīn wa al-muʿānidīn wa qitālihim* [The Book on Demanding the Repentance of the Apostates and Reprobates, and Fighting Them], chapter: "What is to be Done When a Non-Muslim Citizen or Anyone Else Presents Himself," 6:2539 §6530. •Muslim in *al-Ṣaḥīḥ*, *Kitāb al-jihād wa al-siyar* [The Book of Struggle and Military Expeditions], chapter: "The Battle of Uḥud," 3:1417 §1792. •Aḥmad b. Ḥanbal in *al-Musnad*, 1:453 §4331. •Ibn Mājah in *al-Sunan*, 2:1335 §4025. •Ibn Ḥibbān in *al-Ṣaḥīḥ*, 14:537 §6576. •Abū Yaʿlā in *al-Musnad*, 9:131 §5205. •al-Bazzār in *al-Musnad*, 5:106–107 §1686. •Abū ʿAwāna in *al-Musnad*, 4:329 §6869.

فَرَفَعْتُ رَأْسِي فَإِذَا أَنَا بِسَحَابَةٍ قَدْ أَظَلَّتْنِي. فَنَظَرْتُ فَإِذَا فِيهَا جِبْرِيْلُ فَنَادَانِي، فَقَالَ: إِنَّ اللهَ ﷻ قَدْ سَمِعَ قَوْلَ قَوْمِكَ لَكَ، وَمَا رَدُّوا عَلَيْكَ، وَقَدْ بَعَثَ إِلَيْكَ مَلَكَ الْجِبَالِ لِتَأْمُرَهُ بِمَا شِئْتَ فِيهِمْ. قَالَ: فَنَادَانِي مَلَكُ الْجِبَالِ، وَسَلَّمَ عَلَيَّ، ثُمَّ قَالَ: يَا مُحَمَّدُ، إِنَّ اللهَ قَدْ سَمِعَ قَوْلَ قَوْمِكَ لَكَ، وَأَنَا مَلَكُ الْجِبَالِ وَقَدْ بَعَثَنِي رَبُّكَ إِلَيْكَ لِتَأْمُرَنِي بِأَمْرِكَ فَمَا شِئْتَ. إِنْ شِئْتَ أَنْ أُطْبِقَ عَلَيْهِمُ الْأَخْشَبَيْنِ؟ فَقَالَ لَهُ رَسُوْلُ اللهِ ﷺ: بَلْ أَرْجُو أَنْ يُخْرِجَ اللهُ مِنْ أَصْلَابِهِمْ مَنْ يَعْبُدُ اللهَ وَحْدَهُ لَا يُشْرِكُ بِهِ شَيْئًا.

مُتَّفَقٌ عَلَيْهِ وَاللَّفْظُ لِمُسْلِمٍ.

77/2. And in a similar narration, ʿA'isha, the wife of Allah's Messenger ﷺ, reported that she asked him:

"O Messenger of Allah! Have you endured a day more hurtful than the Day of Uḥud?" He said: "Indeed, I experienced a great deal at the hands of your people [the Quraysh]. The hardest treatment I met from them was on the Day of ʿAqaba when I presented myself to Ibn ʿAbd Yālīl b. ʿAbd Kulāl [one of the chiefs of Ṭāif]. He did not respond [to my call], so I departed with deep distress and I did not recover until I arrived at Qarn al-Thaʿālib. There, I raised my head and suddenly I was under a cloud that cast its shadow on me. I looked at it and saw Jibrīl inside it and he called out to me, saying: 'Indeed, Allah Most High heard what your people said to you and He heard their response to you, and He has sent you the angel in charge of the mountains that you may command him with what you wish.' Then the angel of the mountains called me, greeted me with salutations of peace, and said: 'O Muhammad! I will do as you wish; if you like, I will bring together the two mountains [that stand opposite to each other at the extremities of Mecca] to crush them in between.' But I said: 'Nay, rather I hope that Allah will bring forth from among their descendants people who will worship Allah alone and associate no partners with Him.'"[1]

---

[1] Set forth by •al-Bukhārī in *al-Ṣaḥīḥ*: *Kitāb bad'u al-khalq* [The Beginning of Creation], chapter: "When one of you says, "Amen," as do the angels in the heaven, and they coincide with one another, he will be forgiven his past wrong actions," 3:1180 §3059. •Muslim in *al-Ṣaḥīḥ*: *Kitāb al-jihād wa al-siyar* [The

Agreed upon by al-Bukhārī and Muslim and the wording is his.

٧٨/ ٣. وَفِي رِوَايَةِ أَنَسٍ ﷺ أَنَّ امْرَأَةً يَهُوْدِيَّةً أَتَتْ رَسُوْلَ اللهِ ﷺ بِشَاةٍ مَسْمُوْمَةٍ، فَأَكَلَ مِنْهَا، فَجِيءَ بِهَا إِلَى رَسُوْلِ اللهِ ﷺ، فَسَأَلَـهَا عَنْ ذَلِكَ. فَقَالَتْ: أَرَدْتُ لِأَقْتُلَكَ. قَالَ: مَا كَانَ اللهُ لِيُسَلِّطَكِ عَلَى ذَاكِ، قَالَ: أَوْ قَالَ: عَلَيَّ، قَالَ: قَالُوْا: أَلَا نَقْتُلُهَا؟ قَالَ: لَا. قَالَ: فَمَا زِلْتُ أَعْرِفُهَا فِي لَـهَوَاتِ رَسُوْلِ اللهِ ﷺ.

مُتَّفَقٌ عَلَيْهِ وَاللَّفْظُ لِـمُسْلِمٍ.

78/3. Anas b. Mālik ﷺ related:

"A Jewish woman brought a poisoned cooked goat to the Allah's Messenger ﷺ. He ate some from it (then the meat spoke out, saying that it was poisoned). Then the woman was brought to him and he asked her about the meat. She said: 'I planned to kill you.' He said: 'Allah ﷻ will not enable you to do it.' The narrator said: 'Or he said: "He will not give you authority over me."' The Companions submitted: '(O Messenger of Allah!) Shall we not kill her?' He said: 'No (I have forgiven her).' The narrator said: 'The effect of the poison was always felt in his blessed mouth.'"[1]

Agreed upon by al-Bukhārī and Muslim and the wording is his.

٧٩/ ٤. عَنْ جَابِرِ بْنِ عَبْدِ اللهِ ﷺ قَالَ: غَزَوْنَا مَعَ رَسُوْلِ اللهِ ﷺ غَزْوَةً قِبَلَ نَجْدٍ،

Book of Jihad and Military Expeditions], chapter: "On the Harm Experienced by the Prophet ﷺ at the Hands of the Pagans and Hypocrites," 3:1420 §1795. •al-Nasā'ī in *al-Sunan al-kubrā*, 4:405 §7706. •al-Ṭabarānī in *al-Muʿjam al-awsaṭ*, 8:370 §8902.

[1] Set forth by •al-Bukhārī in *al-Ṣaḥīḥ*: *Kitāb al-hiba wa faḍlu-hā* [The Book of Gifts and their Excellence], chapter: "Accepting a gift from the idolaters," 2:923 §2474. •Muslim in *al-Ṣaḥīḥ*: *Kitāb al-salām* [The salutation of peace], chapter: "On Poison," 4:1721 §2190. •Aḥmad b. Ḥanbal in *al-Musnad*, 3:218 §13309. •Abū Dāwūd in *al-Sunan*: *Kitāb al-jihād wa al-siyar* [The Book of Struggle and Military Expeditions], chapter: "Someone hanging his sword on a tree in a journey at midday," 4:173 §4508. •al-Ṭabarānī in *al-Muʿjam al-awsaṭ*, 3:43 §2417. •al-Bayhaqī in *al-Sunan al-kubrā*, 10:11 §19500.

فَأَدْرَكَنَا رَسُوْلُ اللهِ ﷺ فِي وَادٍ كَثِيْرِ الْعِضَاهِ، فَنَزَلَ رَسُوْلُ اللهِ ﷺ تَحْتَ شَجَرَةٍ، فَعَلَّقَ سَيْفَهُ بِغُصْنٍ مِنْ أَغْصَانِهَا، قَالَ: وَتَفَرَّقَ النَّاسُ فِي الْوَادِي يَسْتَظِلُّوْنَ بِالشَّجَرِ، قَالَ: فَقَالَ رَسُوْلُ اللهِ ﷺ: إِنَّ رَجُلًا أَتَانِي وَأَنَا نَائِمٌ، فَأَخَذَ السَّيْفَ، فَاسْتَيْقَظْتُ، وَهُوَ قَائِمٌ عَلَى رَأْسِي، فَلَمْ أَشْعُرْ، إِلَّا وَالسَّيْفُ صَلْتًا فِي يَدِهِ، فَقَالَ لِي: مَنْ يَمْنَعُكَ مِنِّي؟ قَالَ: قُلْتُ: اَللهُ، ثُمَّ قَالَ فِي الثَّانِيَةِ: مَنْ يَمْنَعُكَ مِنِّي؟ قَالَ: قُلْتُ: اَللهُ. قَالَ: فَشَامَ السَّيْفَ، فَهَا هُوَ ذَا جَالِسٌ، ثُمَّ لَمْ يَعْرِضْ لَهُ رَسُوْلُ اللهِ ﷺ.

مُتَّفَقٌ عَلَيْهِ وَاللَّفْظُ لِمُسْلِمٍ.

79/4. Jābir b. ʿAbd Allah ﷺ related:

"We went with Allah's Messenger toward Najd in order to participate in a battle. Allah's Messenger found us in a valley filled with thorny trees. So Allah's Messenger ﷺ disembarked and settled under a tree, hanging his sword on one of its branches. Afterwards the people took their own spots here and there in the valley, seeking shade under the trees. Later on Allah's Messenger ﷺ informed us, saying, 'When I was taking a nap, a man came to me, took my sword, and I woke up to find him standing over my head, and did not sense him coming although the sword was unsheathed and in his hand. He said to me, "Who will protect you from me now?" I replied, "Allah will." He said to me a second time, "Who will protect you from me now? And I replied once more, "Allah will." Then (afraid) he cast down the sword and here he is sitting down'—and Allah's Messenger did not do anything to him to avenge."[1]

---

[1] Set forth by •al-Bukhārī in *al-Ṣaḥīḥ: Kitāb al-jihād wa al-siyar* [The Book of Struggle and Military Expeditions], chapter: "Someone hanging his sword on a tree in a journey at midday," 3:1065–1066 §2753–2756 and in *Kitāb al-Maghāzī* [The Book of Military Expeditions], chapter: "The expedition of Dhāt al-Riqāʿ," 4:515 §3905. •Muslim in *al-Ṣaḥīḥ: Kitāb al-Faḍāʾil* [The Book of Excellent Merits], chapter: "The reliance of the Prophet on Allah, exalted is He, and how Allah protected the Messenger from the people," 4:1786 §843. •Aḥmad b. Ḥanbal in *al-Musnad*, 3:311 §14374. •al-Nasāʾī in *al-Sunan al-Kubrā*, 5:236, 267 §8772, 8852. •al-Bayhaqī in *al-Sunan al-Kubrā*, 6:319

Agreed upon by al-Bukhārī and Muslim (the wording is his).

٨٠/ ٥. عَنْ عَائِشَةَ ﵂ قَالَتْ: اسْتَأْذَنَ رَهْطٌ مِنَ الْيَهُوْدِ عَلَى النَّبِيِّ ﷺ فَقَالُوْا: اَلسَّامُ عَلَيْكَ، فَقُلْتُ: بَلْ عَلَيْكُمُ السَّامُ وَاللَّعْنَةُ، فَقَالَ: يَا عَائِشَةُ، إِنَّ اللهَ رَفِيْقٌ يُحِبُّ الرِّفْقَ فِي الْأَمْرِ كُلِّهِ، قُلْتُ: أَوَ لَمْ تَسْمَعْ مَا قَالُوا؟ قَالَ: قُلْتُ: وَعَلَيْكُمْ.

مُتَّفَقٌ عَلَيْهِ.

80/5. ʿĀʾisha ﵂, the wife of the Prophet ﷺ, reported:

"A few Jews asked permission of the Prophet ﷺ and then said: "Assāmu ʿalayka (death be upon you)." I said: "And may death and curses be upon you!" He said: "O ʿĀʾisha! Indeed, Allah Most High is lenient and likes leniency in every matter." I submitted: "(O Messenger of Allah!) Have you not heard what they said?" He said: "I said: 'And upon you (wa ʿalaykum).'"[1]

Agreed upon by al-Bukhārī and Muslim.

٨١/ ٦. وَفِي رِوَايَةِ أَنَسِ بْنِ مَالِكٍ ﵁ قَالَ: مَرَّ يَهُوْدِيٌّ بِرَسُوْلِ اللهِ ﷺ فَقَالَ: اَلسَّامُ عَلَيْكَ، فَقَالَ رَسُوْلُ اللهِ ﷺ: وَعَلَيْكَ، فَقَالَ رَسُوْلُ اللهِ ﷺ: أَتَدْرُوْنَ مَا يَقُوْلُ؟ قَالَ: اَلسَّامُ عَلَيْكَ، قَالُوا: يَا رَسُوْلَ اللهِ، أَلَا نَقْتُلُهُ؟ قَالَ: لَا، إِذَا سَلَّمَ عَلَيْكُمْ أَهْلُ الْكِتَابِ فَقُوْلُوا: وَعَلَيْكُمْ.

---

§12613. •al-Ṭabarānī in Musnad al-Shāmiyyīn, 3:66 §1815.

[1] Set forth by •al-Bukhārī in al-Ṣaḥīḥ: Kitāb istitāba al-murtaddīn wa al-muʿānidīn wa qitālihim [The Book on Demanding the Repentance of the Apostates and Reprobates, and Fighting Them], chapter: "What is to be Done When a Non-Muslim Citizen or Anyone Else Presents Himself," 6:2539 §6528. •Muslim in al-Ṣaḥīḥ: Kitāb al-birr wa al-ṣila wa al-ādāb [The Book of Piety, Filial Duty and Good Manners], chapter: "The Virtue of Gentleness," 4:2003 §2593. •Aḥmad b. Ḥanbal in al-Musnad, 1:112 §902. •Abū Dāwūd in al-Sunan: Kitāb al-adab [The Book of Good Manners], chapter: "On Gentleness," 4:254 §4807. •Ibn Mājah in al-Sunan: Kitāb al-adab [The Book of Good Manners], chapter: "On Gentleness," 2:1216 §3688.

مُتَّفَقٌ عَلَيْهِ.

81/6. Anas b. Mālik ﷺ related:

"A Jew passed by Allah's Messenger ﷺ and said: '*Assāmu ʿalayka* (death be upon you).' The Messenger of Allah ﷺ said: '*Wa ʿalayka* (and upon you).' The Messenger of Allah ﷺ inquired of his Companions: 'Do you know what he has said? He said: "Death be upon you."' The people submitted: 'O Messenger of Allah! Shall we not kill him?' He said: 'No. When the People of the Book invoke peace upon you, say: "And upon you!"'"[1]

Agreed upon by al-Bukhārī and Muslim.

٨٢/ ٧. عَنْ أَنَسِ بْنِ مَالِكٍ ﷺ أَنَّ ثَمَانِيْنَ رَجُلًا مِنْ أَهْلِ مَكَّةَ هَبَطُوْا عَلَى رَسُوْلِ اللهِ ﷺ مِنْ جَبَلِ التَّنْعِيْمِ مُتَسَلِّحِيْنَ، يُرِيْدُوْنَ غِرَّةَ النَّبِيِّ ﷺ وَأَصْحَابِهِ، فَأَخَذَهُمْ سِلْمًا، فَاسْتَحْيَاهُمْ، فَأَنْزَلَ اللهُ ﷻ: ﴿وَهُوَ ٱلَّذِى كَفَّ أَيْدِيَهُمْ عَنكُمْ وَأَيْدِيَكُمْ عَنْهُم بِبَطْنِ مَكَّةَ مِنۢ بَعْدِ أَنْ أَظْفَرَكُمْ عَلَيْهِمْ﴾.

رَوَاهُ مُسْلِمٌ وَأَحْمَدُ وَأَبُوْ دَاوُدَ وَالتِّرْمِذِيُّ وَالنَّسَائِيُّ. وَقَالَ التِّرْمِذِيُّ: هَذَا حَدِيْثٌ حَسَنٌ صَحِيْحٌ.

82/7. Anas b. Mālik ﷺ related:

"(On the occasion of the treaty of Ḥudaybiya) eighty armed people came down from Mount Tanʿīm with a plan to attack the Prophet ﷺ and his Companions through a ruse. He captured them and later freed

[1] Set forth by •al-Bukhārī in *al-Ṣaḥīḥ*: *Kitāb istitāba al-murtaddīn wa al-muʿānidīn wa qitālihim* [The Book on Demanding the Repentance of the Apostates and Reprobates, and Fighting Them], chapter: "What is to be Done When a Non-Muslim Citizen or Anyone Else Presents Himself," 6:2538 §6527. •Muslim in *al-Ṣaḥīḥ*: *Kitāb al-salām* [The salutation of peace], chapter: "The Prohibition of the People of the Scripture [Jews and Christians] from beginning with the salutation of peace, and how to respond to them," 4:1705 §2163. •Aḥmd b. Ḥanbal in *al-Musnad*, 3:218 §13308. •Abū Yaʿlā in *al-Musnad*, 5:445 §3153.

them, allowing them to live. Then, Allah Most High revealed the verse ﴾*And He is the One Who held back the hands of those (disbelievers) from you and your hands from them on the frontier of Mecca (near Ḥudaybiya) after giving you the upper hand over their (party)*﴿[1] .[2]

Reported by Muslim, Aḥmad, Abū Dāwūd, al-Tirmidhī and al-Nasāʾī. Accroding to al-Tirmidhī: This is a fine authentic tradition.

٨٣/ ٨. وَفِي رِوَايَةِ أَبِي هُرَيْرَةَ ﷺ قَالَ: قِيْلَ: يَا رَسُوْلَ اللهِ، ادْعُ عَلَى الْـمُشْرِكِيْنَ، قَالَ: إِنِّي لَـمْ أُبْعَثْ لَعَّانًا، وَإِنَّمَا بُعِثْتُ رَحْمَةً.

رَوَاهُ مُسْلِمٌ وَأَبُوْ يَعْلَى وَالْبُخَارِيُّ فِي الْأَدَبِ.

83/8. And in the narration of Abū Hurayra ﷺ:

"It was submitted to the Messenger of Allah ﷺ: 'Invoke a curse upon the polytheists!' He said: 'I was not sent as a curser; I have been sent only as mercy.'"[3]

Reported by Muslim, Abū Yaʿlā and al-Bukhārī in *al-Adab al-mufrad*.

٨٤/ ٩. وَفِي رِوَايَةٍ عَنْهُ: قَالَ: إِنَّمَا بُعِثْتُ رَحْمَةً وَلَـمْ أُبْعَثْ عَذَابًا.

---

[1] Qurʾān 48:24.

[2] Set forth by •Muslim in *al-Ṣaḥīḥ*, 3:1442 §1808. •Aḥmad b. Ḥanbal in *al-Musnad*, 3:124, 290 §12276, 14122. •Abū Dāwūd in *al-Sunan*: *Kitāb al-jihād* [The Book of Striving], chapter: "Freeing Captives without Ransom," 3:61 §2688. •al-Tirmidhī in *al-Sunan*: *Kitāb al-Tafsīr* [The Book of Interpretation], "From Sūra al-Fatḥ," 5:386 §3264. •al-Nasāʾī in *al-Sunan al-kubrā*, 5:202, 6:464 §§8667, 11510. •Ibn Abī Shayba in *al-Muṣannaf*, 7:405 §36916. •Abū ʿAwāna in *al-Musnad*, 4:291 §6782–6783. •ʿAbd b. Ḥumayd in *al-Musnad*, 1:363 §1208.

[3] Set forth by •Muslim in *al-Ṣaḥīḥ*: *Kitāb al-birr wa al-ṣila wa al-ādāb* [The Book of Piety, Filial Duty and Good Manners], chapter: "The Prohibition of Invoking Curses on Creatures and Other Things," 4:2006 §2599. •al-Bukhārī in *al-Adab al-mufrad*, p. 119 §321. •Abū Yaʿlā in *al-Musnad*, 11:35 §6174. •al-Ḥusaynī in *al-Bayān wa al-taʿrīf*, 1:283 §754. •Ibn Kathīr in *Tafsīr al-Qurʾān al-ʿAẓīm*, 3:202.

رَوَاهُ الْبَيْهَقِيُّ وَابْنُ عَسَاكِرَ.

84/9. In one tradition, Allah's Messenger ﷺ said:
"I have been sent as mercy incarnate and not as a torment."[1]

Reported by al-Bayhaqī and Ibn ʿAsākir.

٨٥/ ١٠. وَفِي رِوَايَةٍ عَنْهُ: إِنَّمَا بُعِثْتُ نِعْمَةً، وَلَمْ أُبْعَثْ عَذَابًا.

رَوَاهُ أَبُوْ نُعَيْمٍ.

85/10. In one tradition, Allah's Messenger ﷺ said:
"I have been sent as bounty incarnate and not as a torment."[2]

Reported by Abu Nuʿaym.

٨٦/ ١١. وَفِي رِوَايَةِ سَهْلِ بْنِ سَعْدٍ السَّاعِدِيِّ رضي الله عنه قَالَ: قَالَ رَسُوْلُ اللهِ ﷺ: اَللَّهُمَّ، اغْفِرْ لِقَوْمِي فَإِنَّهُمْ لَا يَعْلَمُوْنَ.

رَوَاهُ ابْنُ حِبَّانَ وَابْنُ أَبِي عَاصِمٍ وَالطَّبَرَانِيُّ وَالْبَيْهَقِيُّ، وَقَالَ الْهَيْثَمِيُّ: وَرِجَالُهُ رِجَالُ الصَّحِيْحِ.

86/11. Sahl b. Saʿd al-Sāʿidī رضي الله عنه related:

"The Messenger of Allah ﷺ said: 'O Allah! Forgive my nation, for they do not know.'"[3]

Reported by Ibn Ḥibbān, Ibn Abī ʿĀṣim and al-Bayhaqī. Al-Haythamī said: "Its sources are reliable."

---

[1] Set forth by •al-Bayhaqī in *Shuʿab al-īmān*, 2:144 §1403. •Ibn ʿAsākir in *Tārīkh Madīna Dimashq*, 4:92.

[2] Set forth by •Abū Nuʿaym in *Dalāʾil al-Nubuwwa*, 1:40 §2.

[3] Set forth by •Ibn Ḥibbān in *al-Ṣaḥīḥ*, 3:254 §973. •Ibn ʿĀṣim in *al-Āḥād wa al-mathānī*, 4:123 §2096. •al-Ṭabarānī in *al-Muʿjam al-kabīr*, 6:120 §5694. •al-Bayhaqī in *Shuʿab al-īmān*, 2:164 §1448. •al-Daylamī in *Musnad al-firdaws*, 1:500 §2042. Cited by •al-Haythamī in *Majmaʿ al-zawāʾid*, 6:117.

٨٧/ ١٢ . عَنِ الْإِمَامِ أَبِي يُوْسُفَ قَالَ: إِنَّ رَسُوْلَ اللهِ ﷺ عَفَا عَنْ مَكَّةَ وَأَهْلِهَا وَقَالَ: مَنْ أَغْلَقَ عَلَيْهِ بَابَهُ فَهُوَ آمِنٌ وَمَنْ دَخَلَ الْمَسْجِدَ فَهُوَ آمِنٌ وَمَنْ دَخَلَ دَارَ أَبِي سُفْيَانَ فَهُوَ آمِنٌ. وَنَهَى عَنِ الْقَتْلِ إِلَّا نَفَرًا قَدْ سَمَّاهُمْ إِلَّا أَنْ يُقَاتِلَ أَحَدًا فَيُقْتَلَ وَقَالَ لَهُمْ حِيْنَ اجْتَمَعُوْا فِي الْمَسْجِدِ: مَا تَرَوْنَ أَنِّي صَانِعٌ بِكُمْ؟ قَالُوْا: خَيْرًا أَخٌ كَرِيْمٌ وَابْنُ أَخٍ كَرِيْمٍ. قَالَ: اذْهَبُوْا فَأَنْتُمُ الطُّلَقَاءُ.

رَوَاهُ الشَّافِعِيُّ وَابْنُ حِبَّانَ وَالرَّبِيْعُ.

87/12. Imam Abū Yūsuf said:

"Allah's Messenger ﷺ forgave the people of Mecca and said: 'The one who shuts his door is safe; the one who enters the Sacred Mosque is safe; and the one who enters the house of Abū Sufyān is safe.' He forbade killing, except for a few (blasphemous) people whose names were declared. He commanded to kill the polytheists who wage war against any Muslim. When people [among Quraysh] gathered in the Sacred Mosque, he said: 'Do you know how I am going to treat you?' They said: 'We expect the well-wishing for us as you are an esteemed brother and a son of an esteemed brother!' He said: 'Leave, for you are all free.'"[1]

Reported by al-Shafiʿī, Ibn Ḥibbān and al-Rabīʿ.

[1] Recorded by •al-Shāfiʿī in *al-Umm*, 7:361. •Ibn Ḥibbān in *al-Thiqāt*, 2:56. •al-Rabīʿ in *al-Musnad*, p. 170 §419. •al-Bayhaqī in *al-Sunan al-kubrā*, 9:118 §18055.

اَلْبَابُ التَّاسِعُ

وَفَاءُ الْعَهْدِ وَالْعَمَلُ بِالْمَوَاثِيْقِ مَعَهُمْ

Chapter Nine

Fulfilment of Agreements and Covenants with Non-Muslims

٨٨/ ١. عَنْ عُمَرَ بْنِ الْـخَطَّابِ ﷺ قَالَ: وَأُوْصِيْهِ بِذِمَّةِ اللهِ وَذِمَّةِ رَسُوْلِهِ ﷺ أَنْ يُوْفَى لَهُمْ بِعَهْدِهِمْ وَأَنْ يُقَاتَلَ مِنْ وَرَائِهِمْ وَلَا يُكَلَّفُوْا إِلَّا طَاقَتَهُمْ.

رَوَاهُ الْبُخَارِيُّ وَابْنُ أَبِي شَيْبَةَ وَابْنُ حِبَّانَ وَالْقُرَشِيُّ.

88/1. ʿUmar b. al-Khaṭṭāb ﷺ stated (the following legacy before his martyrdom):

"I counsel him [the ruler] to uphold the guarantee of Allah and His Messenger ﷺ, and to fulfil the terms of their treaty, and to fight in their defence. I also counsel him not to overburden them with more than they can bear."[1]

Reported by al-Bukhārī and Ibn Abī Shayba, Ibn Ḥibbān and al-Qurashī.

٨٩/ ٢. عَنْ سُلَيْمِ بْنِ عَامِرٍ يَقُولُ: كَانَ بَيْنَ مُعَاوِيَةَ وَبَيْنَ أَهْلِ الرُّومِ عَهْدٌ وَكَانَ يَسِيرُ فِي بِلَادِهِمْ حَتَّى إِذَا انْقَضَى الْعَهْدُ أَغَارَ عَلَيْهِمْ. فَإِذَا رَجُلٌ عَلَى دَابَّةٍ أَوْ عَلَى فَرَسٍ وَهُوَ يَقُولُ: اللهُ أَكْبَرُ وَفَاءٌ لَا غَدْرٌ، وَإِذَا هُوَ عَمْرُو بْنُ عَبَسَةَ. فَسَأَلَهُ مُعَاوِيَةُ عَنْ ذٰلِكَ فَقَالَ: سَمِعْتُ رَسُولَ اللهِ ﷺ يَقُولُ: مَنْ كَانَ بَيْنَهُ وَبَيْنَ قَوْمٍ عَهْدٌ فَلَا يَحُلَّنَّ عَهْدًا وَلَا يَشُدَّنَّهُ حَتَّى يَمْضِيَ أَمَدُهُ أَوْ يَنْبِذَ إِلَيْهِمْ عَلَى سَوَاءٍ. قَالَ: فَرَجَعَ مُعَاوِيَةُ بِالنَّاسِ.

رَوَاهُ أَحْمَدُ وَالتِّرْمِذِيُّ وَاللَّفْظُ لَهُ وَالطَّيَالِسِيُّ. وَقَالَ التِّرْمِذِيُّ: هٰذَا حَدِيثٌ حَسَنٌ صَحِيحٌ.

89/2. Sulaym b. ʿĀmir related:

[1] Set forth by •al-Bukhārī in *al-Ṣaḥīḥ*, 3:1111 §2887 and 1:469 §1328. •Ibn Abī Shayba in *al-Muṣannaf*, 7:436 §37059. •Ibn Ḥibbān in *al-Ṣaḥīḥ*, 15:354 §6917. •al-Qurashī in *al-Kharāj*, p. 80 §232.

"There was a treaty between Muʿāwiya and the Byzantines, and he (Muʿāwiya) approached their land so he could attack them when the treaty would end. Suddenly, he saw a man on a horse, saying: 'Allah is the Greatest! Fulfil the promise; do not break it!' And when they looked, they found that he was ʿAmr b. ʿAbasa. Muʿāwiya questioned him (about that), and ʿAmr said: 'I heard Allah's Messenger ﷺ say: "When one has a treaty with a people, he must not breach it until its term comes to an end or they openly declare the cancellation of the treaty equally in retribution."' Upon hearing that, Muʿāwiya returned with his troops."[1]

> Reported by Aḥmad b. Ḥanbal, al-Tirmidhī (the wording is his) and al-Ṭayālisī. Al-Tirmidhī said: "This is a fine authentic tradition."

[1] Set forth by •Aḥmad b. Ḥanbal in *al-Musnad*, 4:111 §17056. •al-Tirmidhī in *al-Sunan*, 4:143 §1580. •al-Ṭayalisī in *al-Musnad*, 1:157 §1155.

اَلْبَابُ الْعَاشِرُ

إِعَانَةُ شُيُوْخِهِمْ وَضُعَفَائِهِمُ الْمَالِيَّةُ

Chapter Ten

Financial Support for the Elderly, Infirm and Feeble amongst the Non-Muslims

٩٠/١. عَنْ عَبدِ اللهِ بْنِ حَدْرَدٍ الْأَسْلَمِيِّ قَالَ: لَـمَّا قَدِمْنَا مَعَ عُمَرَ بْنِ الْـخَطَّابِ الْـجَابِيَةَ، إِذَا هُوَ بِشَيْخٍ مِنْ أَهْلِ الذِّمَّةِ يَسْتَطْعِمُ. فَسَأَلَ عَنْهُ، فَقُلْنَا: يَا أَمِيرَ الْـمُؤْمِنِيْنَ، هَذَا رَجُلٌ مِنْ أَهْلِ الذِّمَّةِ كَبُرَ وَضَعُفَ. فَوَضَعَ عَنْهُ عُمَرُ الْجِزْيَةَ الَّتِي فِي رَقَبَتِهِ. وَقَالَ: كَلَّفْتُمُوْهُ الْجِزْيَةَ حَتَّى إِذَا ضَعُفَ تَرَكْتُمُوهُ يَسْتَطْعِمُ. فَأَجْرَى عَلَيْهِ مِنْ بَيْتِ الْـمَالِ عَشْرَةَ دَرَاهِمَ، وَكَانَ لَهُ عِيَالٌ.

رَوَاهُ ابْنُ عَسَاكِرَ.

90/1. ʿAbd Allāh b. Ḥadrad al-Aslamī said:

"When we reached al-Jābiya with ʿUmar b. al-Khaṭṭāb ﷺ, there was an elderly man from the non-Muslim citizens who was begging of others and asking for food. ʿUmar inquired about him and we said: 'O Commander of the Faithful! This is a man from the non-Muslim citizens. He is elderly and weak.' Upon learning of this, ʿUmar exempted him from the tax that was due from him and said: 'You burdened him with the payment of the tax and when he became weak you left him to beg!' Then ʿUmar provided him with ten dirhams [monthly] from the public treasury because he had his family."[1]

Reported by Ibn ʿAsākir.

٩١/٢. إِنَّ أَمِيرَ الْـمُؤْمِنِيْنَ عُمَرَ ﷺ مَرَّ بِشَيْخٍ مِّنْ أَهْلِ الذِّمَّةِ، يَسْأَلُ عَلَى أَبْوَابِ النَّاسِ. فَقَالَ: مَا أَنْصَفْنَاكَ أَنْ كُنَّا أَخَذْنَا مِنْكَ الْـجِزْيَةَ فِى شَبِيْبَتِكَ، ثُمَّ ضَيَّعْنَاكَ فِي كِبْرِكَ. قَالَ: ثُمَّ أَجْرَى عَلَيْهِ مِنْ بَيْتِ الْـمَالِ مَا يَصْلُحُهُ.

رَوَاهُ أَبُو عُبَيْدٍ الْقَاسِمُ بْنُ سَلَامٍ فِي الْأَمْوَالِ.

---

[1] Set forth by •Ibn ʿAsākir in *Tārīkh Dimashq al-kabīr*, 27:334.

91/2. Abū ʿUbayd al-Qāsim b. Salām mentioned in *Kitāb al-Amwāl*:

"The Commander of the faithful, ʿUmar ﵁, passed by an elderly man amongst the non-Muslim citizens who was begging at people's doors. ʿUmar said to him: 'We have not been fair to you, as we have taken the tax from you when you were younger but left you in helplessness in your old age.' After that, ʿUmar issued instructions for the man to receive enough money from the public treasury that would take care of his needs."[1]

Reported by Abū ʿUbayd al-Qāsim b. Sallām in *al-Amwāl*.

٣/٩٢. مَرَّ عُمَرُ بْنُ الْخَطَّابِ ﵁ بِبَابِ قَوْمٍ وَعَلَيْهِ سَائِلٌ يَسْأَلُ، شَيْخٌ كَبِيرٌ ضَرِيْرُ الْبَصَرِ، فَضَرَبَ عَضُدَهُ مِنْ خَلْفِهِ، وَقَالَ: مِنْ أَيِّ أَهْلِ الْكِتَابِ أَنْتَ؟ فَقَالَ: يَهُوْدِيٌّ. قَالَ: فَمَا أَلْجَاكَ إِلَى مَا أَرَى؟ قَال أَسْأَلُ الْجِزْيَةَ وَالْحَاجَةَ وَالسِّنَّ. قَالَ: فَأَخَذَ عُمَرُ بِيَدِهِ وَذَهَبَ إِلَى مَنْزِلِهِ فَرَضَخَ لَهُ بِشَيْءٍ مِنَ الْمَنْزِلِ. ثُمَّ أَرْسَلَ إِلَى خَازِنِ بَيتِ الْمَالِ، فَقَالَ: انْظُرْ إِلَى هَذَا وَضُرَبَائِهِ، فَوَاللهِ، مَا أَنْصَفْنَاهُ أَنْ أَكَلْنَا شَبِيْبَتَهُ، ثُمَّ نَخْذُلُهُ عِنْدَ الْهَرَمِ ﴿إِنَّمَا ٱلصَّدَقَٰتُ لِلْفُقَرَآءِ وَٱلْمَسَٰكِينِ﴾ وَالفُقَرَآءُ هُمُ الْمُسْلِمُوْنَ، وَهَذَا مِنَ الْمَسَاكِيْنِ مِن أَهلِ الْكِتَابِ. وَوَضَعَ عَنْهُ الْجِزْيَةَ وَعَنْ ضُرَبَائِهِ.

رَوَاهُ أَبُوْ يُوسُفَ.

92/3. Imam Abū Yūsuf described the same report in *Kitāb al-kharāj* in the following words:

"ʿUmar b. al-Khaṭṭāb ﵁ passed by the door of some people and there was an elderly blind man there, begging. ʿUmar put his hand on his arm from behind and asked: 'To which group amongst the People of the Book do you belong?' The man replied: 'I am a Jew.' ʿUmar then asked him: 'So why are you begging?' 'I am begging for money,' the man said, 'so I can pay the tax and fulfil my needs, because I am too old to earn money.' ʿUmar took him by the hand and led him to his home and gave him a few things, then he sent him to the treasurer

---

[1] Set forth by •Abū ʿUbayd al-Qāsim b. Sallām in *Kitāb al-amwāl*, p. 57 §119.

of the public treasury and said: 'Take care of him and those like him, for by Allah, we have not treated him fairly if we benefited from him in his younger days but left him helpless in his old age!' [Then he recited the verse] ﴾*Indeed, alms (Zakāt) are meant for the poor and the indigent*﴿[1] and the poor are amongst the Muslims and this one is from the indigent amongst the People of the Book. So ʿUmar exempted him and those like him from the payment of taxes."[2]

Reported by Abū Yūsuf.

• قَالَ مَالِكٌ: مَضَتِ السُّنَّةُ أَنْ لَا جِزْيَةَ عَلَى نِسَاءِ أَهْلِ الْكِتَابِ، وَلَا عَلَى صِبْيَانِهِمْ، وَأَنَّ الْجِزْيَةَ لَا تُؤْخَذُ إِلَّا مِنَ الرِّجَالِ الَّذِينَ قَدْ بَلَغُوْا الْـحُلُمَ.

Imam Mālik said: "It was the rule (in Muslim states) that the women and children of the People of the Book were not liable to pay the security tax; it was collected only from the adults."[3]

٩٣/ ٤. وَقَدْ رُوِيَ عَنِ النَّبِيِّ ﷺ أَنَّهُ قَالَ: لَا جِزْيَةَ عَلَى عَبْدٍ وَفِي رَفْعِهِ نَظَرٌ وَهُوَ ثَابِتٌ عَنِ ابْنِ عُمَرَ.

93/4. It is related that Allah's Messenger ﷺ said:
"The security tax is not obligatory for the hired servants."[4]

• قَالَ ابْنُ الْـمُنْذِرِ: أَجْمَعَ كُلُّ مَنْ نَحْفَظُ عَنْهُ مِنْ أَهْلِ الْعِلْمِ عَلَى أَنَّهُ لَا جِزْيَةَ عَلَى الْعَبْدِ.

Ibn al-Mundhir said: "All of the jurists from whom we

---

[1] Qurʾān 9:60.

[2] Set forth by •Abū Yūsuf in *Kitāb al-kharāj*, p. 136.

[3] Set forth by •Mālik in *al-Muwaṭṭā*ʾ, 2:280.

[4] •Ibn al-Qayyim, *Aḥkām ahl al-Dhimma*, 1:172. This tradition is considered as *marfū*ʿ but the same is proved from the authority of Ibn ʿUmar ﷺ.

learned concur that the security tax is not obligatory for the (hired house) servant."[1]

- عَنْ أَسْلَمَ مَوْلَى عُمَرَ إِنَّ عُمَرَ كَتَبَ إِلَى أُمَرَاءِ الْأَجْنَادِ: أَنْ لَّا يَضْرِبُوْا الْـجِزْيَةَ عَلَى النِّسَاءِ، وَلَا عَلَى الصِّبْيَانِ.

رَوَاهُ عَبْدُ الرَّزَّاقِ وَالْبَيْهَقِيُّ.

According to Aslam, a freed slave of ʿUmar ﷺ: "ʿUmar ﷺ wrote a letter to the military commanders stating that they should not impose taxes on non-Muslim women or children."[2]

Reported by ʿAbd al-Razzāq and al-Bayhaqī.

---

[1] Cited by •Ibn al-Qayyim in *Aḥkām ahl al-Dhimma*, 1:172.

[2] Set forth by •ʿAbd al-Razzāq in *al-Muṣannaf*, 6:85 §10090. •al-Bayhaqī in *al-Sunan al-kubrā*, 9:195 §18463.

اَلْبَابُ الْحَادِي عَشَرَ

اَلْأَحْكَامُ الْمَأْخُوْذَةُ مِنْ أَحْكَامِ أَهْلِ الذِّمَّةِ لِابْنِ الْقَيِّمِ

CHAPTER ELEVEN

EXTRACTS FROM IBN AL-QAYYIM'S *AḤKĀM AHL AL-DHIMMA*

The preceding chapters of the book have expressly demonstrated in the light of proofs from the Quran, books on hadith, exegesis, jurisprudence and beliefs what commands Islam has issued to establish pleasant and peaceful relations with the non-Muslims. Ibn al-Qayyim, the honourable disciple of Ibn Taymiyya, has written a voluminous book titled *Aḥkām Ahl al-Dhimma* that has taken a detailed account of commands with regard to relations with non-Muslims. In view of the significance and utility of the book, the important rulings about non-Muslims have been reproduced here for our readers.

11.1 Entrance of non-Muslims in the Sacred Mosque

Describing his point of view about non-Muslims entering the mosque, Ibn al-Qayyim writes:

إِنْ دَخَلُوهَا بِإِذْنِ مُسْلِمٍ فَفِيهِ قَوْلَانِ لِلْفُقَهَاءِ، هُمَا رِوَايَتَانِ عَنْ أَحْمَدَ.

> Regarding the case where non-Muslim citizens enter the Precincts of the Sacred Mosque with the permission of a Muslim, the jurists have two opinions, both of which are reported positions from [Imam] Aḥmad.

11.1.1 First Report

وَوَجْهُ الْجَوَازِ أَنَّ رَسُولَ اللهِ ﷺ أَنْزَلَ الْوُفُودَ مِنَ الْكُفَّارِ فِي مَسْجِدِهِ، فَأَنْزَلَ فِيهِ وَفْدَ نَجْرَانَ وَوَفْدَ ثَقِيفٍ وَغَيْرَهُمْ.

> The angle by which it is judged permissible is the fact that the Messenger of Allah ﷺ received delegations of disbelievers inside his mosque. He received the delegation of Najrān and Thaqīf and others.[1]

[1] •Ibn al-Qayyim, *Aḥkām ahl al-Dhimma*, 1:406.

It is reported by Aḥmad b. Ḥanbal and Abū Dāwūd from ʿUthmān b. Abī al-ʿĀṣ ﷺ:

إِنَّ وَفْدَ ثَقِيفٍ قَدِمُوا عَلَى رَسُولِ اللهِ ﷺ فَأَنْزَلَهُمُ الْمَسْجِدَ.

"The delegation of Thaqīf went to see Allah's Messenger ﷺ, and he hosted them in the mosque."[1]

Reported by Aḥmad and Abū Dāwūd, and its sources are reliable.

ʿAbd al-Razzāq has narrated on the authority of Ibn Jurayj:

أَنْزَلَ النَّبِيُّ ﷺ وَفْدَ ثَقِيفٍ فِي الْمَسْجِدِ، وَبَنَى لَهُمْ فِيهِ الْخِيَامَ، يَرَوْنَ النَّاسَ حِيْنَ يُصَلُّوْنَ وَيَسْمَعُوْنَ الْقُرْآنَ.

"The Prophet ﷺ received the delegation of Thaqīf inside the mosque and pitched a tent for them inside of it. They would see the people as they came for prayer and would hear them recite the Qurʾān."[2]

Reported by ʿAbd al-Razzāq.

According to al-Bayhaqī, Ibn Saʿd and Ibn al-Qayyim, Muḥammad b. Jaʿfar said:

لَـمَّـا قَدِمَ وَفْدُ نَجْرَانَ عَلَى رَسُوْلِ اللهِ ﷺ دَخَلُوْا عَلَيْهِ مَسْجِدَهُ بَعْدَ الْعَصْرِ.

"When the Najrān delegation came to see Allah's Messenger ﷺ, they entered in upon him in his mosque after the late

[1] Set forth by •Aḥmad b. Ḥanbal in *al-Musnad*, 4:218 §17942. •Abū Dāwūd in *al-Sunan*, *Kitāb al-kharāj wa al-imāra wa al-fay*ʾ [The Book of Land Tax, Leadership, and War Spoils Captured without Fighting], chapter: "What has been Reported about Ṭāʾif," 3:163 §3026. •al-Ṭabarānī in *al-Muʿjam al-Kabīr*, 9:54 §8372. •al-Bayhaqī in *al-Sunan al-kubrā*, 2:444 §4131. •Ibn Khuzayma in *al-Ṣaḥīḥ*, 2:285 §1328. The narrators of the above hadith are authentic.

[2] Narrated by •ʿAbd al-Razzāq in *al-Muṣannaf*, 1:414 §1622.

noon [ʿAṣr] prayer."[1]

Reported by al-Bayhaqī.

Ibn al-Qayyim states about Najrān delegation's stay in the Prophetic mosque:

وَقَدْ مَكَّنَ النَّبِيُّ ﷺ وَفْدَ نَصَارَى نَجْرَانَ مِنْ صَلَاتِهِمْ فِي مَسْجِدِهِ إِلَى قِبْلَتِهِمْ.

"The Prophet ﷺ enabled the Christian delegation of Najrān to offer their prayers and face their direction of prayer [*qibla*] in his mosque."[2]

11.1.2 SECOND REPORT

قَالَ سَعِيدُ بْنُ الْـمُسَيِّبِ: كَانَ أَبُو سُفْيَانَ يَدْخُلُ مَسْجِدَ الْـمَدِينَةِ وَهُوَ عَلَى شِرْكِهِ.

Saʿīd b. al-Musayyib said: "Abū Sufyān would enter the mosque of Medina during his time as an idolater."[3]

When, before the conquest of Mecca, the idolaters of Mecca supported Banū Bakr against Banū Khuzāʿah, the Ḥudaybiya Treaty between the believers and the idolaters became void. To revive this peace treaty, Abū Sufyān (who had not yet embraced faith) came to the Prophet ﷺ in Medina and entered the Mosque. Ibn Hishām furnishes its details:

فَقَامَ أَبُو سُفْيَانَ فِي الْـمَسْجِدِ، فَقَالَ: أَيُّهَا النَّاسُ، إِنِّي قَدْ أُجِرْتُ بَيْنَ

---

[1] Narrated by •al-Bayhaqī in *Dalāʾil al-Nubuwwa*, 5:382. •Ibn Saʿd in *al-Ṭabaqāt al-kubrā*, 1:357. •Ibn al-Qayyim in *Zād al-maʿād*, 3:629. •al-Dhahabī in *Tārīkh al-Islām*, 2:695.

[2] •Ibn al-Qayyim, *Aḥkām ahl al-dhimma*, 2:822.

[3] Ibid, 1:406.

النَّاسِ. ثُمَّ رَكِبَ بَعِيْرَهُ فَانْطَلَقَ.

There, he stood up and said: 'I have received a guarantee of protection among the people!' Then he mounted his camel and departed."[1]

11.1.3 Third Report

وَقَدِمَ عُمَيْرُ بْنُ وَهْبٍ - وَهُوَ مُشْرِكٌ - فَدَخَلَ الْـمَسْجِدَ وَالنَّبِيُّ ﷺ فِيهِ، لِيَفْتِكَ بِهِ، فَرَزَقَهُ اللهُ تَعَالَى الإِسْلَامَ.

ʿUmayr b. Wahb—who at the time was an idolater—arrived in Medina and entered the mosque while the Prophet ﷺ was inside in order to assassinate him, but Allah blessed him with Islam.[2]

The books on history and *sīra* have expanded upon the entrance of ʿUmayr b. Wahb who was yet an idolater. His son, Wahb b. ʿUmayr was a prisoner of the battle of Badr and he came to Medina to seek his freedom while the Prophet ﷺ was inside the Mosque. When ʿUmar stopped him, the Prophet ﷺ said: "ʿUmar! Leave him", and said to him: "ʿUmayr! Get closer." ʿUmayr b. Wahb then professed Islam. Al-Ṭabarānī has narrated it in *al-Muʿjam al-kabīr*. Ibn al-Athīr, Ibn Kathīr and other books on history have related this incident in detail.[3]

Concluding the discussion, Ibn al-Qayyim describes the reason of non-Muslims' entrance in the Prophetic Mosque:

وَأَمَّا دُخُولُ الْكُفَّارِ مَسْجِدَ النَّبِيِّ ﷺ فَكَانَ ذَلِكَ لِـمَا كَانَ بِالْـمُسْلِمِينَ حَاجَةٌ إِلَى ذَلِكَ، وَلِأَنَّهُمْ كَانُوا يُخَاطِبُونَ النَّبِيَّ ﷺ فِي عُهُودِهِمْ، وَيُؤَدُّونَ

[1] •Ibn Hishām, *al-Sīra al-Nabawiyya*, 5:49–51. •Ibn Kathīr, *al-Bidāya wa al-nihāya*, 4:280. •al-Ḥalabī, *al-Sīra al-Ḥalabiyya*, 3:6–8.

[2] •Ibn al-Qayyim, *Aḥkām ahl al-dhimma*, 1:406.

[3] Narrated by •al-Ṭabarānī in *al-Muʿjam al-kabīr*, 17:58 §118. •Ibn al-Athīr in *al-Kāmil fī al-tārīkh*, 2:30–31. •Ibn Kathīr in *al-Bidāya wa al-nihāya*, 3:313–314. •al-Haythamī in *Majmaʿ al-zawāʾid*, 8:284–285.

إِلَيْهِ الرَّسَائِلَ، وَيَحْمِلُونَ مِنْهُ الْأَجْوِبَةَ وَيَسْمَعُونَ مِنْهُ الدَّعْوَةَ، وَلَـمْ يَكُنِ النَّبِيُّ ﷺ لِيَخْرُجَ مِنَ الْـمَسْجِدِ لِكُلِّ مَنْ قَصَدَهُ مِنَ الْكُفَّارِ، فَكَانَتِ الْـمَصْلَحَةُ فِي دُخُولِـهِمْ.

As for disbelievers entering the Prophet's mosque ﷺ, such was done when the Muslims were in need of that, and was also because those disbelievers [who entered it] were addressing the Prophet ﷺ in their peace treaties and delivering official messages as emissaries and bringing back [his replies], and were also hearing his invitation [to Islam]. The Prophet ﷺ did not make it his habit to go out of the mosque to meet with those disbelievers who came to see him, and thus their entering the mosque to see him was a Shariah countenanced benefit.[1]

11.2 Visiting the non-Muslims when They Are Sick

The non-Muslims should be visited when they fall sick out of human sentiments. Ibn al-Qayyim has narrated different reports and incidents in this regard, which are described here in detail.

١. قَالَ الْـمَرْوَزِيُّ: بَلَغَنِي أَنَّ أَبَا عَبْدِ اللهِ سُئِلَ عَنْ رَجُلٍ لَهُ قَرَابَةٌ نَصْرَانِيٌّ يَعُودُهُ؟ قَالَ: نَعَمْ.

1. Al-Marwadhī said: "It has reached me that Abū ʿAbd Allāh [Imam Aḥmad b. Ḥanbal] was asked about a man who had close relatives who were Christian and if he should visit them when they are ill. He replied: 'Yes.'"

٢. قَالَ الْأَثْرَمُ: وَسَمِعْتُ أَبَا عَبْدِ اللهِ يُسْأَلُ عَنِ الرَّجُلِ لَهُ قَرَابَةٌ نَصْرَانِيٌّ يَعُودُهُ؟ قَالَ: نَعَمْ، قِيلَ لَهُ: نَصْرَانِيٌّ. قَالَ: أَرْجُو أَلَا تَضِيقَ الْعِيَادَةُ.

2. Al-Athram said: "I heard Abū ʿAbd Allāh being asked

[1] Narrated by •al-Ṭabarānī in *al-Muʿjam al-kabīr*, 17:58 §118. •Ibn Kathīr in *al-Bidāya wa al-nihāya*, 3:313–314. •Ibn al-Athīr in *al-Kāmil fī al-tārīkh*, 2:30–31. •al-Haythamī in *Majmaʿ al-zawāʾid*, 8:284–285.

about a man who had close relatives who were Christian, and whether he should visit them when they are ill. He replied: 'Yes.' It was asked: '[Should they be visited] even though they are Christians?' and he said: 'Hopefully, visits to the sick are not constrictive as such.'"

٣. قَالَ الْأَثْرَمُ: وَقُلْتُ لَهُ مَرَّةً أُخْرَى يَعُودُ الرَّجُلُ الْيَهُودَ وَالنَّصَارَى؟ قَالَ: أَلَيْسَ عَادَ النَّبِيُّ ﷺ الْيَهُودِيَّ وَدَعَاهُ إِلَى الْإِسْلَامِ؟

3. Al-Athram also said: "On another occasion I asked him if a person is allowed to visit a sick Jew or a Christian, and he replied: 'Did the Prophet ﷺ not visit a Jewish man and call him to Islam?'"[1]

٤. قَالَ أَبُو مَسْعُودٍ الأَصْبَهَانِيُّ: سَأَلْتُ أَحْمَدَ بْنَ حَنْبَلٍ عَنْ عِيَادَةِ الْقَرَابَةِ وَالْـجَارِ النَّصْرَانِيِّ. قَالَ: نَعَمْ.

4. Abū Masʿūd al-Aṣbahānī said: "I asked Aḥmad b. Ḥanbal if it was allowed to visit a close relative and neighbour who was Christian, and he replied: 'Yes.'"[2]

٥. وَثَبَتَ عَنِ النَّبِيِّ ﷺ أَنَّهُ عَادَ عَبْدَ اللهِ بْنَ أُبَيٍّ ابْنِ سَلُولٍ رَأْسَ الْـمُنَافِقِينَ.

5. It is recorded that the Prophet ﷺ visited ʿAbd Allāh b. Ubayy b. Salūl, the chief of the hypocrites, when the latter was ill.[3]

After these reports from Ibn al-Qayyim, it seems worthwhile to

[1] Narrated by •al-Khallāl in *Aḥkām ahl al-milal*, p. 212 §597. •Ibn al-Qayyim in *Aḥkām ahl al-dhimma*, 1:427.

[2] Narrated by •al-Khallāl in *Aḥkām ahl al-milal*, p. 212 §598. •Ibn al-Qayyim in *Aḥkām ahl al-dhimma*, 1:427.

[3] •Ibn al-Qayyim, *Aḥkām ahl al-dhimma*, 1:430.

mention a few hadiths on the subject.

1. Narrated from Anas b. Mālik ﵁ in *Ṣaḥīḥ al-Bukhārī*, *Musnad Aḥmad* and *Sunan Abī Dāwūd*, the Prophet ﷺ said:

كَانَ غُلَامٌ يَهُوْدِيٌّ يَخْدُمُ النَّبِيَّ ﷺ فَمَرِضَ، فَأَتَاهُ النَّبِيُّ ﷺ يَعُوْدُهُ، فَقَعَدَ عِنْدَ رَأْسِهِ، فَقَالَ لَهُ: أَسْلِمْ. فَنَظَرَ إِلَى أَبِيْهِ وَهُوَ عِنْدَهُ، فَقَالَ لَهُ: أَطِعْ أَبَا الْقَاسِمِ ﷺ. فَأَسْلَمَ، فَخَرَجَ النَّبِيُّ ﷺ وَهُوَ يَقُوْلُ: اَلْـحَمْدُ لله الَّذِي أَنْقَذَهُ مِنَ النَّارِ.

It is reported that Anas ﵁ said: "There was a young Jewish boy who used to serve the Prophet ﷺ. When he fell ill, the Prophet went to visit him. He sat by his side and said to him: 'Embrace Islam.' Then, the boy looked at his father, who was by his side, and his father said to him: 'Obey Abū al-Qāsim [the Prophet ﷺ],' and so the boy embraced Islam. As the Prophet ﷺ left, he said: 'All praise is due to Allah who delivered him from Hellfire!'"[1]

In another narration of this report, from Aḥmad and Abū Dāwūd, it is mentioned:

فَخَرَجَ النَّبِيُّ ﷺ وَهُوَ يَقُوْلُ: اَلْـحَمْدُ لله الَّذِي أَنْقَذَهُ بِي مِنَ النَّارِ.

"As the Prophet ﷺ left he said: 'All praise is due to Allah who, through me, delivered him from Hellfire!'"[2]

2. According to *Musnad Aḥmad* and *Sunan Abī Dāwūd*, Usāma b. Zayd ﵁ narrates:

---

[1] Narrated by •al-Bukhārī in *al-Ṣaḥīḥ*: *Kitāb al-janāza* [The Book of the Funeral Prayer], chapter: "When a Young Boy Embraces Islam and Dies, should He be Prayed over, and should He be Invited to Islam?" 1:455 §1290, and also in *al-Adab al-mufrad*, 1:185 §524. •Abū Yaʿlā in *al-Musnad*, 6:93 §3350. •al-Bayhaqī in *al-Sunan al-kubrā*, 3:383 §6389.

[2] Narrated by •Aḥmad b. Ḥanbal in *al-Musnad*, 3:280 §§14009,14010. •Abū Dāwūd in *al-Sunan*: *Kitāb al-janāʾiz* [The Book of Funeral Rites], chapter: "On Visiting a Non-Muslim Citizen," 3:185 §3095.

خَرَجَ رَسُولُ اللهِ ﷺ يَعُودُ عَبْدَ اللهِ بْنَ أُبَيٍّ فِي مَرَضِهِ الَّذِي مَاتَ فِيهِ.

"The Prophet ﷺ went out to visit ʿAbd Allāh b. Ubayy when the latter was in the throes of his sickness of which he was to die."[1]

Reported by Aḥmad, Abū Dāwūd (the wording is his), and al-Ḥākim. Al-Ḥākim said: "This is an authentic tradition in conformity with the stipulation of al-Bukhārī and Muslim."

11.3 Attending the Funerals of non-Muslims

The funerals of the People of the Book or idolaters can be attended for condolence. Ibn al-Qayyim serves in detail different episodes as evidence.

١. قَالَ مُحَمَّدُ بْنُ مُوسَى: قُلْتُ لِأَبِي عَبْدِ اللهِ: يُشَيِّعُ الْمُسْلِمُ جِنَازَةَ الْمُشْرِكِ؟ قَالَ: نَعَمْ.

1. Muḥammad b. Mūsā said: "I asked Abū ʿAbd Allāh [Imam Aḥmad]: 'Can a Muslim follow the funeral procession of an idolater?' He said: 'Yes.'"[2]

٢. وَقَالَ مُحَمَّدُ بْنُ الْحَسَنِ بْنِ هَارُوْنَ: قِيلَ لِأَبِي عَبْدِ اللهِ: وَيَشْهَدُ جِنَازَتَهُ؟ قَالَ: نَعَمْ، نَحْوُ مَا صَنَعَ الْحَارِثُ بْنُ أَبِي رَبِيعَةَ؛ كَانَ شَهِدَ جِنَازَةَ أُمِّهِ.

2. Muḥammad b. al-Ḥasan b. Hārūn said: "Abū ʿAbd Allāh [Imam Aḥmad] was asked: 'May one attend his [the

[1] Narrated by •Aḥmad b. Ḥanbal in *al-Musnad*, 5:201 §21806. •Abū Dāwūd in *al-Sunan*: *Kitāb al-janāʾiz* [The Book of Funeral Rites], chapter: "On Visiting the Sick," 3:184 §3094. •al-Ḥākim in *al-Mustadrak*, 1:491 §1262. •al-Ṭabarānī in *al-Muʿjam al-kabīr*, 1:163 §390. •al-Maqdisī in *al-Aḥādīth al-mukhtāra*, 4:117 §1328. The narrators of this chain of transmission are all reliable.

[2] Narrated by •al-Khallāl in *Aḥkām ahl al-milal*, p. 218 §619. •Ibn al-Qayyim in *Aḥkām ahl al-dhimma*, 1:432.

idolater's] funeral?' He replied: 'Yes, that is what al-Ḥārith b. Abī Rabīʿa did when he attended his mother's funeral.'"[1]

٣. قَالَ أَبُو طَالِبٍ: سَأَلْتُ أَبَا عَبْدِ اللهِ عَنِ الرَّجُلِ يَمُوتُ وَهُوَ يَهُودِيٌّ، وَلَهُ وَلَدٌ مُسْلِمٌ كَيْفَ يَصْنَعُ؟ قَالَ: يَرْكَبُ دَابَّتَهُ وَيَسِيرُ أَمَامَ الْجِنَازَةِ.

3. Abū Ṭālib said: "I asked Abū ʿAbd Allah [Imam Aḥmad] about what one should do if a Jewish man dies and he has a son who is Muslim. He replied: 'He should mount his animal and lead the funeral procession.'"[2]

٤. عَنْ عَامِرِ بْنِ شَقِيقٍ، عَنْ أَبِي وَائِلٍ، قَالَ: مَاتَتْ أُمِّي نَصْرَانِيَّةً، فَأَتَيْتُ عُمَرَ فَسَأَلْتُهُ، فَقَالَ: ارْكَبْ فِي جِنَازَتِهَا وَسِرْ أَمَامَهَا.

4. It is reported on the authority of ʿĀmir b. Shaqīq, on the authority of Abū Wāʾil, who said: "My mother, who was a Christian, died so I went to ʿUmar and asked him about the matter. He said: 'Mount your animal, join her funeral procession and travel at the head of it.'"[3]

٥. قَالَ الْخَلَّالُ: عَنْ عَبْدِ اللهِ بْنِ كَعْبِ بْنِ مَالِكٍ عَنْ أَبِيهِ، قَالَ: جَاءَ قَيْسُ بْنُ شَمَّاسٍ إِلَى النَّبِيِّ ﷺ، فَقَالَ: إِنَّ أُمَّهُ تُوُفِّيَتْ وَهِيَ نَصْرَانِيَّةٌ، وَهُوَ يُحِبُّ أَنْ يَحْضُرَهَا. فَقَالَ لَهُ النَّبِيُّ ﷺ: ارْكَبْ دَابَّتَكَ وَسِرْ أَمَامَهَا.

5. Al-Khallāl said: "It is reported on the authority of ʿAbd Allah b. Kaʿb b. Mālik, on the authority of his father, who said: 'Qays b. Shammās went to the Prophet ﷺ and informed

[1] Narrated by •al-Khallāl in *Aḥkām ahl al-milal*, p. 218 §620. •Ibn al-Qayyim in *Aḥkām ahl al-dhimma*, 1:432.

[2] Narrated by •al-Khallāl in *Aḥkām ahl al-milal*, p. 218 §621. •Ibn al-Qayyim in *Aḥkām ahl al-dhimma*, 1:433.

[3] Narrated by •al-Khallāl in *Aḥkām ahl al-milal*, p. 218 §622. •Ibn al-Qayyim in *Aḥkām ahl al-dhimma*, 1:433.

him that his mother, who was a Christian, had died, and that he wished to attend her funeral. The Prophet ﷺ said to him: "Mount your animal and travel at the head of the procession.'"[1]

٦. وَقَالَ حَنْبَلٌ: سَأَلْتُ أَبَا عَبْدِ اللهِ عَنِ الْمُسْلِمِ تَمُوتُ لَهُ أُمٌّ نَصْرَانِيَّةٌ أَوْ أَبُوهُ أَوْ أَخُوهُ أَوْ ذُو قَرَابَتِهِ، وَتَرَى أَنْ يَلِيَ شَيْئًا مِنْ أَمْرِهِ حَتَّى يُوَارِيَهُ؟ قَالَ: إِنْ كَانَ أَبًا أَوْ أُمًّا أَوْ أَخًا أَوْ قَرَابَةً قَرِيبَةً وَحَضَرَهُ فَلَا بَأْسَ.

6. Ḥanbal said: "I asked Abū ʿAbd Allah [Imam Aḥmad] about a Muslim whose mother, father, brother, or other close relative dies as a Christian. He replied: 'If it is a father or mother or brother or close relative, then there is no harm if he attends the funeral.'"[2]

٧. إِنَّ عَبْدَ اللهِ بْنَ رَبِيعَةَ قَالَ لِعَبْدِ اللهِ بْنِ عُمَرَ رضي الله عنهما: إِنَّ أُمِّي مَاتَتْ، وَقَدْ عَلِمْتَ الَّذِي كَانَتْ عَلَيْهِ مِنَ النَّصْرَانِيَّةِ. قَالَ: أَحْسِنْ وِلَايَتَهَا، وَكَفِّنْهَا، وَلَا تَقُمْ عَلَى قَبْرِهَا.

7. ʿAbd Allāh b. Rabīʿa said to ʿAbd Allāh b. ʿUmar رضي الله عنهما: "My mother has died and, as you know, she was a Christian." ʿAbd Allāh b. ʿUmar said: "Take care of what she has entrusted to you and shroud her—but do not stand at her grave."[3]

---

[1] Narrated by •al-Khallāl in *Aḥkām ahl al-milal*, p. 219 §623. •al-Dāraquṭnī in *al-Sunan*: *Kitāb al-janāʾiz* [The Book of Funeral Rites], chapter: "On Placing the Right Hand over the Left Hand and Raising the Hands During the Opening *Takbīr*," 2:75 §6. •al-Zaylaʿī in *Naṣb al-rāya*, 2:292. •Ibn al-Qayyim in *Aḥkām ahl al-dhimma*, 1:434.

[2] Narrated by •al-Khallāl in *Aḥkām ahl al-milal*, p. 219 §624. •Ibn al-Qayyim in *Aḥkām ahl al-dhimma*, 1:435.

[3] Narrated by •al-Khallāl in *Aḥkām ahl al-milal*, p. 219 §624. •Ibn al-Qayyim in *Aḥkām ahl al-dhimma*, 1:436.

٨. عَنْ سَعِيدِ بْنِ جُبَيْرٍ، قَالَ: سَأَلْتُ ابْنَ عَبَّاسٍ ﵄ عَنْ رَجُلٍ مَاتَ أَبُوهُ نَصْرَانِيًّا. قَالَ: يَشْهَدُهُ وَيَدْفِنُهُ.

8. It is related on the authority of Saʿīd b. Jubayr that he said: "I asked Ibn ʿAbbās ﵄ about a man whose father dies as a Christian. He replied: 'He should attend his funeral and bury him.'"[1]

11.4 GIVING CONDOLENCES TO NON-MUSLIMS

Islam permits to offer condolence to the dependents of the deceased People of the Book and share their pain and grief. Ibn al-Qayyim serves some arguments as proofs.

١. عَنْ مَنْصُورٍ عَنْ إِبْرَاهِيمَ، قَالَ: إِذَا أَرَدْتَ أَنْ تُعَزِّيَ رَجُلًا مِنْ أَهْلِ الْكِتَابِ فَقُلْ: أَكْثَرَ اللهُ مَالَكَ وَوَلَدَكَ وَأَطَالَ حَيَاتَكَ أَوْ عُمُرَكَ.

1. It is related on the authority of Manṣūr b. Ibrāhīm: "When you want to express your condolences to a person from the People of the Book, say: 'May Allah increase your wealth and offspring and lengthen your life.'"[2]

٢. قَالَ الْحَسَنُ: إِذَا عَزَّيْتَ الذِّمِّيَّ، فَقُلْ: لَا يُصِيبُكَ إِلَّا خَيْرٌ.

2. Al-Ḥasan said: "When you offer your condolences to a non-Muslim citizen, say: 'May you be touched by naught save goodness.'"[3]

[1] Narrated by •al-Khallāl in *Aḥkām ahl al-milal*, p. 220 §628. •Ibn al-Qayyim, in*Aḥkām ahl al-dhimma*, 1:437.

[2] Narrated by •al-Khallāl in *Aḥkām ahl al-milal*, p. 224 §636. •Ibn al-Qayyim in *Aḥkām ahl al-dhimma*, 1:438–439.

[3] Narrated by •al-Khallāl in *Aḥkām ahl al-milal*, p. 224 §638. •Ibn al-Qayyim in *Aḥkām ahl al-dhimma*, 1:439.

11.5 The Slaughtered Animals of the People of the Book

Ibn al-Qayyim related some arguments in this regard:

قَالَ تَعَالَى: ﴿وَطَعَامُ ٱلَّذِينَ أُوتُوا۟ ٱلْكِتَـٰبَ حِلٌّ لَّكُمْ وَطَعَامُكُمْ حِلٌّ لَّهُمْ﴾ [المائدة، ٥:٥].

Allah Most High says:

﴾*And the food of those who were given the Scripture is permissible for you, and your food is permissible for them.*﴿[1]

وَلَـمْ يَخْتَلِفِ السَّلَفُ أَنَّ الْـمُرَادَ بِذَلِكَ الذَّبَائِحُ.

The early forebears (*salaf*) were in unanimous agreement that this [verse] pertains to the slaughtered animals of the People of the Book.[2]

Then Ibn al-Qayyim presents different quotes:

١. قَالَ الْبُخَارِيُّ: قَالَ ابْنُ عَبَّاسٍ: طَعَامُهُمْ ذَبَائِحُهُمْ.

1. Al-Bukhārī said: "Ibn ʿAbbās said: 'Their food here refers to their slaughtered animals.'"[3]

٢. وَكَذَلِكَ قَالَ ابْنُ مَسْعُودٍ وَمُجَاهِدٌ وَإِبْرَاهِيمُ وَقَتَادَةُ وَالْحَسَنُ وَغَيْرُهُمْ.

2. This was also the position of Ibn Masʿūd, Mujāhid, Ibrāhīm, Qatāda, al-Ḥasan and others.[4]

---

[1] Qur'ān, 5:5.

[2] •Ibn al-Qayyim, *Aḥkām ahl al-dhimma*, 1:502.

[3] Narrated by •al-Bukhārī in *al-Ṣaḥīḥ*, *Kitāb al-dhabāʾiḥ wa al-ṣayd* [The Book of Slaughtered Animals and Hunting], chapter: "The Slaughtered Animals and Fat of the People of the Book and the People of War, and Others," 5:2097. •al-Bayhaqī in *al-Sunan al-kubrā*, 9:282 §18934. •Ibn al-Qayyim in *Aḥkām ahl al-dhimma*, 1:502.

[4] •Ibn al-Qayyim, *Aḥkām ahl al-dhimma*, 1:502.

٣. وَقَالَ أَحْمَدُ بْنُ الْـحَسَنِ التِّرْمِذِيُّ: سَأَلْتُ أَبَا عَبْدِ اللهِ عَنْ ذَبَائِحِ أَهْلِ الْكِتَابِ؛ فَقَالَ: لَا بَأْسَ بِهَا.

3. Aḥmad b. al-Ḥasan al-Tirmidhī said: "I asked Abū ʿAbd Allāh [Imam Aḥmad] about the slaughtered animals of the People of the Book, and he replied: 'There is no harm in them.'"[1]

٤. وَقَالَ حَنْبَلٌ: سَمِعْتُ أَبَا عَبْدِ اللهِ يَقُوْلُ: تُؤْكَلُ ذَبِيْحَةُ الْيَهُودِيِّ وَالنَّصْرَانِيِّ.

4. Ḥanbal said: "I heard Abū ʿAbd Allāh [Imam Aḥmad] say: 'The meat slaughtered by a Jew or a Christian may be eaten.'"[2]

٥. وَقَالَ إِسْحَاقُ بْنُ مَنْصُورٍ: قَالَ أَبُو عَبْدِ اللهِ: لَا بَأْسَ أَنْ يَذْبَحَ أَهْلُ الْكِتَابِ لِلْمُسْلِمِينَ غَيْرَ النَّسِيكَةِ.

5. Isḥāq b. Manṣūr said: "Abū ʿAbd Allāh [Imam Aḥmad] said: 'There is no harm in someone from the People of the Book slaughtering an animal for the Muslims, so long as it is not a specific ritual offering [done in the name of ʿĪsa ﷺ].'"[3]

٦. وَقَالَ حَنْبَلٌ: سَمِعْتُ أَبَا عَبْدِ اللهِ قَالَ: لَا بَأْسَ بِذَبِيحَةِ أَهْلِ الْكِتَابِ إِذَا أَهَلُّوا للهِ وَسَمَّوْا عَلَيْهِ، قَالَ تَعَالَى: ﴿وَلَا تَأْكُلُوا۟ مِمَّا لَمْ يُذْكَرِ ٱسْمُ ٱللَّهِ عَلَيْهِ﴾ [الأنعام، ٦:١٢١]، وَالْـمُسْلِمُ فِي قَلْبِهِ اسْمُ اللهِ، وَمَا أُهِلَّ لِغَيْرِ اللهِ بِهِ مِـمَّـا ذَبَحُوا لِكَنَائِسِهِمْ وَأَعْيَادِهِمْ يُجْتَنَبُ ذَلِكَ، وَأَهْلُ الْكِتَابِ

[1] Ibid., 1:503.

[2] Narrated by •al-Khallāl in *Aḥkām ahl al-milal*, p. 362 §1007. •Ibn al-Qayyim in *Aḥkām ahl al-dhimma*, 1:503–504.

[3] Narrated by •al-Khallāl in *Aḥkām ahl al-milal*, p. 362 §1008. •Ibn al-Qayyim in *Aḥkām ahl al-dhimma*, 1: 504.

يُسَمُّونَ عَلَى ذَبَائِحِهِمْ أَحَبُّ إِلَيَّ.

6. Ḥanbal said: "I heard Abū ʿAbd Allāh [Imam Aḥmad] say: 'There is no harm in [eating from] the meat slaughtered by the People of the Book if they slaughter it for Allah's sake and in His Name. Allah Most High says: "*And do not eat of that over which Allah's Name has not been pronounced.*"[1] The Name of Allah is ever in the heart of the Muslims. The meat that they [the Christians] slaughter for other than Allah, such as for their churches and festivals, should be avoided. It is more beloved to me that the People of the Book pronounce Allah's Name as they slaughter their animals.'"[2]

٧. وَقَالَ مُهَنَّا بْنُ يَحْيَى: سَأَلْتُ أَبَا عَبْدِ اللهِ عَنْ ذَبَائِحِ السَّامِرَةِ. قَالَ: تُؤْكَلُ، هُمْ مِنْ أَهْلِ الْكِتَابِ.

7. Muhannā b. Yaḥyā said: "I asked Abū ʿAbd Allāh [Imam Aḥmad] about the meat of the Samaritans and he said: 'It may be eaten since they are from the People of the Book.'"[3]

٨. قَالَ عَبْدُ اللهِ بْنُ أَحْمَدَ: قَالَ أَبِي: لَا بَأْسَ بِذَبَائِحِ أَهْلِ الْحَرْبِ إِذَا كَانُوا مِنْ أَهْلِ الْكِتَابِ.

8. ʿAbd Allāh, the son of Imam Aḥmad, said: "My father said: 'There is no harm in eating the meat of those with whom we are at war, so long as they are from the People of the Book.'"[4]

---

[1] Qurʾān 6:121.

[2] Narrated by •al-Khallāl in *Aḥkām ahl al-milal*, pp. 362–363 §1009. •Ibn al-Qayyim in *Aḥkām ahl al-dhimma*, 1:504–505.

[3] Narrated by •al-Khallāl in *Aḥkām ahl al-milal*, pp. 364 §1016. •Ibn al-Qayyim in *Aḥkām ahl al-dhimma*, 1:505.

[4] Narrated by •al-Khallāl in *Aḥkām ahl al-milal*, pp. 365–366 §1018. •Ibn al-Qayyim in *Aḥkām ahl al-dhimma*, 1:505.

٩. قَالَ ابْنُ الْـمُنْذِرِ: أَجْمَعَ عَلَى هَذَا كُلُّ مَنْ يُحْفَظُ عَنْهُ مِنْ أَهْلِ الْعِلْمِ.

9. Ibn al-Mundhir said: "All of the scholars whose positions are recorded agree with this."[1]

Presenting the preceding quotes about the slaughtered animals of the People of the Book, Ibn al-Qayyim writes:

وَأَمَّا قَوْلُـهُمْ: إِنَّ التَّسْمِيَةَ شَرْطٌ فِي الْـحِلِّ، فَلَعَمْرُ اللهِ! إِنَّهَا لَشَرْطٌ بِكِتَابِ اللهِ وَسُنَّةِ رَسُولِهِ ﷺ، وَأَهْلُ الْكِتَابِ وَغَيْرُهُمْ فِيهَا سَوَاءٌ، فَـلَا يُؤْكَلُ مَتْرُوكُ التَّسْمِيَةِ سَوَاءٌ ذَبَحَهُ مُسْلِمٌ أَوْ كِتَابِيٌّ، لِبِضْعَةَ عَشَرَ دَلِيلًا.

As for their [the scholars'] judgment that the pronouncement of Allah's Name is a condition for the meat to be lawful, then by Allah it is the truth, for it is established as a condition in the Book of Allah and the Sunna of His Messenger—and the People of the Book and others share in this condition, since the meat over which Allah's Name has not been pronounced should not be eaten, whether it was killed by a Muslim or someone from the People of the Book. This is established through over ten legal proofs.[2]

11.5.1 Rulings about Meat are the same for the People of Treaty and People at War

Advancing the argument, Ibn al-Qayyim, loud and clear, states that rulings about meat are the same for the People of Treaty and People at War; that ruling about the People of the Book at war or in truce is the same. He states:

إِذَا ثَبَتَ هَذَا فَلَا فَرْقَ بَيْنَ الْـحَرْبِيِّ وَالْـمُعَاهَدِ لِدُخُولِـهِمْ جَمِيعًا فِي أَهْلِ الْكِتَابِ.

Thus, with respect to the rulings of slaughtered animals,

[1] •Ibn al-Qayyim, *Aḥkām ahl al-dhimma*, 1:505.

[2] Ibid., 1:510.

there is no difference between the non-Muslim with whom we have a treaty of peace and the non-Muslim with whom we are at war, as both are subsumed under the term the "People of the Book."[1]

11.5.2 ISSUES PERTAINING TO THE ANIMALS' MEAT OF THE PEOPLE OF THE BOOK

Ibn al-Qayyim elaborates the issues pertaining to the meat of the slaughtered animals of the People of the Book. He writes:

فَأَمَّا الْـمَسْأَلَةُ الأُولَى: فَمَنْ أَبَاحَ مَتْرُوكَ التَّسْمِيَةِ إِذَا ذَبَحَهُ الْـمُسْلِمُ، اخْتَلَفُوا: هَلْ يُبَاحُ إِذَا ذَبَحَهُ الْكِتَابِيُّ؟ فَقَالَتْ طَائِفَةٌ: يُبَاحُ، لِأَنَّ التَّسْمِيَةَ إِذَا لَـمْ تَكُنْ شَرْطًا فِي ذَبِيحَةِ الْـمُسْلِمِ لَـمْ تَكُنْ شَرْطًا فِي ذَبِيحَةِ الْكِتَابِيِّ.

وَقَالَتْ طَائِفَةٌ: لَا يُبَاحُ وَإِنْ أُبِيحَ مِنَ الْـمُسْلِمِ، وَفَرَّقُوا بَيْنَهُمَا بِأَنَّ اسْمَ اللهِ فِي قَلْبِ الْـمُسْلِمِ وَإِنْ تَرَكَ ذِكْرَهُ بِلِسَانِهِ، وَهَذَا مُقْتَضَى الْـمَنْقُولِ عَنِ ابْنِ عَبَّاسٍ رضي الله عنهما، وَهُوَ ظَاهِرُ نَصِّ أَحْمَدَ. فَإِنَّ أَحْمَدَ قَالَ فِي رِوَايَةِ حَنْبَلٍ: لَا بَأْسَ بِذَبِيحَةِ أَهْلِ الْكِتَابِ إِذَا أَهَلُّوا بِهَا للهِ وَسَمَّوْا عَلَيْهَا. قَالَ تَعَالَى: ﴿وَلَا تَأْكُلُوا مِمَّا لَمْ يُذْكَرِ اسْمُ اللَّهِ عَلَيْهِ﴾ [الأنعام، ٦/ ١٢١]، وَالْـمُسْلِمُ فِي قَلْبِهِ اسْمُ اللهِ، فَقَدْ خَرَجَ بِالْفَرْقِ كَمَا تَرَى.

THE FOREMOST ISSUE: As for those who allowed [eating from] an animal slaughtered by a Muslim but over which Allah's Name was not pronounced, they disagreed if it is allowed if the same is done by someone from the People of the Book.

One group of scholars maintained that it is allowed since they reasoned, if it is not a condition for eating an animal slaughtered by a Muslim, it is not a condition for eating meat slaughtered by someone from the People of the Book, either.

---

[1] Ibid., 1:513.

Another group maintained that it is not allowed, even if it is allowed when coming from a Muslim. They distinguished between the two by saying that the Name of Allah is always in the heart of the Muslim, even if he omits it with his tongue [at the time of slaughter]. This view corresponds to what is transmitted on the authority of Ibn ʿAbbās ﵄, and it is the most apparent view of Aḥmad [b. Ḥanbal], for he said in the narration of Ḥanbal: "There is no harm in [eating from] the meat slaughtered by the People of the Book if they slaughter it for Allah's sake and in His Name. Allah Most High says: '*And do not eat of that over which Allah's Name has not been pronounced*.'[1] The Name of Allah is ever in the heart of the Muslim."[2] So as you can see, Imam Aḥmad resolved the difference between the two standpoints.[3]

اَلْـمَسْأَلَةُ الثَّانِيَةُ: قَالَ الْـمَيْمُونِيُّ: سَأَلْتُ أَبَا عَبْدِ اللهِ عَمَّنْ يَذْبَحُ مِنْ أَهْلِ الْكِتَابِ وَلَـمْ يُسَمِّ؟ فَقَالَ: إِنْ كَانَ مِـمَّـا يَذْبَحُونَ لِكَنَائِسِهِمْ يَدَعُونَ التَّسْمِيَةَ فِيهِ عَلَى عَمْدٍ، إِنَّمَـا يُذْبَحُ لِلْمَسِيحِ فَقَدْ كَرِهَهُ ابْنُ عُمَرَ ﵄، إِلَّا أَنَّ أَبَا الدَّرْدَاءِ ﵁ يَتَأَوَّلُ أَنَّ طَعَامَهُمْ حِلٌّ، وَأَكْثَرُ مَا رَأَيْتُ مِنْهُ الْكَرَاهِيَةُ لِأَكْلِ مَا ذُبِحَ لِكَنَائِسِهِمْ.

THE SECOND ISSUE: Al-Maymūnī said: "I asked Abū ʿAbd Allāh [Imam Aḥmad] about someone from the People of the Book who slaughtered an animal and failed to mention Allah's Name over it. He replied: 'If he is of those who slaughter animals for their churches and purposely omits Allah's Name during the time of slaughter, then in reality he is only slaughtering it in the name of the Messiah [Prophet ʿĪsā ﵇]. Ibn ʿUmar found this reprehensible; however, Abū al-Darḍāʾ applied [a general] interpretation and argued that

---

[1] Qurʾān 6:121.

[2] Narrated by •al-Khallāl in *Aḥkām ahl al-milal*, p. 362–363 §1009.

[3] •Ibn al-Qayyim, *Aḥkām ahl al-dhimma*, 1:514.

their food is permissible. The most I have seen is that he found it detestable to eat of the meat that was slaughtered for their church services.'"[1]

قَالَ الْـمَيْمُونِيُّ أَيْضًا: سَأَلْتُ أَبَا عَبْدِ اللهِ عَنْ ذَبِيحَةِ الْـمَرْأَةِ مِنْ أَهْلِ الْكِتَابِ وَلَـمْ تُسَمِّ، قَالَ: إِنْ كَانَتْ نَاسِيَةً فَلَا بَأْسَ، وَإِنْ كَانَ مِـمَّا يَذْبَحُونَ لِكَنَائِسِهِمْ قَدْ يَدَعُونَ التَّسْمِيَةَ عَلَى عَمْدٍ.

Al-Maymūnī also said: "I asked Abū ʿAbd Allāh [Imam Aḥmad] about the meat slaughtered by a woman from the People of the Book, but who failed to mention Allah's Name over it. He replied: 'If she forgot to mention it then there is no harm, but if she is of those who slaughter for their church services, then there is a chance that she purposely omitted it.'"[2]

قَالَ فِي رِوَايَةِ ابْنِهِ عَبْدِ اللهِ: مَا ذُبِحَ 'لِلزُّهْرَةِ' فَلَا يُعْجِبُنِي أَكْلُهُ، قِيلَ لَهُ: أَحَرَامٌ أَكْلُهُ؟ قَالَ: لَا أَقُولُ حَرَامٌ، وَلَكِنْ لَا يُعْجِبُنِي.

Imam Aḥmad said in a narration reported by his son, ʿAbd Allāh: "I disapprove of eating from the meat that is slaughtered for al-Zuhra." He was asked: "Is it unlawful (*ḥarām*)?" He replied: "I am not saying that it is unlawful, however I disapprove of it."[3]

قَالَ فِي رِوَايَةِ حَنْبَلٍ: يُجْتَنَبُ مَا ذُبِحَ لِكَنَائِسِهِمْ وَأَعْيَادِهِمْ.

Imam Aḥmad said in a narration reported by Ḥanbal: "The meat that is slaughtered for the sake of their church services

[1] Narrated by •al-Khallāl in *Aḥkām ahl al-milal*, p. 367 §1028. •Ibn al-Qayyim in *Aḥkām ahl al-dhimma*, 1:515.

[2] Narrated by •al-Khallāl in *Aḥkām ahl al-milal*, p. 367 §1029. •Ibn al-Qayyim in *Aḥkām ahl al-dhimma*, 1:515–516.

[3] •Ibn al-Qayyim, *Aḥkām ahl al-dhimma*, 1:516

and festivals should be avoided."[1]

وَقَالَ أَبُو الْبَرَكَاتِ فِي 'مُحَرَّرِهِ': وَإِنْ ذَكَرُوا عَلَيْهِ اسْمَ غَيْرِ اللهِ فَفِيهِ رِوَايَتَانِ مَنْصُوصَتَانِ، أَصَحُّهُمَا عِنْدِي تَحْرِيمُهُ.

Abū al-Barakāt said in *al-Muḥarrar*: "And if they mention other than Allah's Name [over the animal at the time of slaughter], then there are two transmitted opinions concerning its ruling. The soundest of them in my view is that it is forbidden."[2]

اِخْتَلَفَ النَّاسُ فِيمَا ذَبَحَ النَّصَارَى لِأَعْيَادِهِمْ أَوْ ذَبَحُوا بِاسْمِ الْمَسِيحِ، فَكَرِهَهُ قَوْمٌ لِأَنَّهُمْ أَخْلَصُوا الْكُفْرَ عِنْدَ تِلْكَ الذَّبِيحَةِ، فَصَارَتْ مِمَّا أُهِلَّ بِهِ لِغَيْرِ اللهِ، وَرَخَّصَ فِي ذَلِكَ قَوْمٌ عَلَى الأَصْلِ الَّذِي أُبِيحَ مِنْ ذَبَائِحِهِمْ.

People differ over [the ruling on] meat slaughtered by Christians for their religious festivals, or which they slaughter in the name of the Messiah. Some consider it reprehensible (*makrūh*) because they [the Christians] bring forth unmitigated disbelief (*kufr*) at the moment of slaughter, with the animal therefore becoming something slaughtered for other than Allah. Others, however, gave a dispensation and allowed eating this kind of meat on the verdict that allowed to eat their permissible slaughtered animals.[3]

فَأَمَّا مَنْ بَلَغَنَا عَنْهُ الرُّخْصَةُ فِي ذَلِكَ. فَحَدَّثَنَا عَلِيُّ بْنُ عَبْدِ اللهِ، ثَنَا عَبْدُ الرَّحْمَنِ بْنُ مَهْدِيٍّ، ثَنَا مُعَاوِيَةُ بْنُ صَالِحٍ عَنْ أَبِي الزَّاهِرِيَّةِ عَنْ عُمَيْرِ بْنِ

[1] Narrated by •al-Khallāl in *Aḥkām ahl al-milal*, pp. 363–364 §1009. •Ibn al-Qayyim in *Aḥkām ahl al-dhimma*, 1:516.

[2] •Ibn Taymiyya, *al-Muḥarrar fī al-fiqh ʿalā madhab al-Imām Aḥmad b. Ḥanbal*, 2:192. •Ibn al-Qayyim, *Aḥkām ahl al-dhimma*, 1:516.

[3] •Ibn al-Qayyim, *Aḥkām ahl al-dhimma*, 1:517.

الْأَسْوَدِ السُّكُونِيِّ. قَالَ: أَتَيْتُ أَهْلِي فَإِذَا كَتِفُ شَاةٍ مَطْبُوخَةٌ، قُلْتُ: مِنْ أَيْنَ هَذَا؟ قَالُوا: جِيرَانُنَا مِنَ النَّصَارَى ذَبَحُوا كَبْشًا لِكَنِيسَةِ جِرْجِسَ، قَلَّدُوهُ عِمَامَةً وَتَلَقَّوْا دَمَهُ فِي طَسْتٍ، ثُمَّ طَبَخُوا وَأَهْدَوْا إِلَيْنَا وَإِلَى جِيرَانِنَا. قَالَ: قُلْتُ: ارْفَعُوا هَذَا. ثُمَّ هَبَطْتُ إِلَى أَبِي الدَّرْدَاءِ فَسَأَلْتُهُ، وَذَكَرْتُ ذَلِكَ لَهُ، فَقَالَ: اَللَّهُمَّ، غُفْرًا، هُمْ أَهْلُ الْكِتَابِ؛ طَعَامُهُمْ لَنَا حِلٌّ وَطَعَامُنَا لَهُمْ حِلٌّ.

As for those scholars from whom it has reached us that they permitted it, we have the following: ʿAlī b. ʿAbd Allāh narrated to us via ʿAbd al-Raḥmān b. Mahdī › Muʿāwiya b. Ṣāliḥ › Abū al-Zāhiriyya › on the authority of ʿUmayr b. al-Aswad al-Sukūnī who said: "I came home to my family and found that a shoulder of lamb had been cooked. I asked: 'Where is this from?' and one of my family members said: 'Our Christian neighbour slaughtered a sheep for Church of [Saint] George. They wrapped it up and drained its blood into a bowl and then cooked it and gave it to us and our other neighbours as a gift.' I said: 'Hold on,' and went to Abū al-Dardāʾ and asked him about it. He said: 'O Allah, forgive us! They are the People of the Book; their food is lawful for us, and our food is lawful for them!'"[1]

Imam al-Bukhārī writes in *al-Tārīkh al-kabīr*:

عَنْ جَرِيرِ بْنِ عُتْبَةَ – أَوْ عُتْبَةَ بْنِ جَرِيرٍ – قَالَ: سَأَلْتُ عُبَادَةَ بْنَ الصَّامِتِ عَنْ ذَبَائِحِ النَّصَارَى لِمَوْتَاهُمْ. قَالَ: لَا بَأْسَ بِهِ.

It is reported on the authority of Jarīr b. ʿUtba—or ʿUtba b. Jarīr—that he said: "I asked ʿUbāda b. al-Ṣāmit about the meat of the People of the Book that they slaughter when one

[1] •Ibn ʿAbd al-Barr, *al-Istidhkār*, 5:258. •Ibn al-Qayyim, *Aḥkām ahl al-dhimma*, 1:517. The chain of this narration is rigorously authentic and its narrators are all reliable.

of them dies. He said: 'There is no harm in it.'"[1]

عَنِ الْأَوْزَاعِيِّ عَنْ مَكْحُولٍ، فِيمَا ذَبَحَتِ النَّصَارَى لِأَعْيَادِ كَذَا. قَالَ: كُلْهُ، قَدْ عَلِمَ اللهُ مَا يَقُولُونَ وَأَحَلَّ ذَبَائِحَهُمْ.

Al-Awzāʿī related on the authority of Makḥūl who said about the meat slaughtered by Christians for their religious celebrations: "Eat of it; Allah knows what they say [when they slaughter the animal] and [yet] he permitted their meat."[2]

11.5.3 An Important Point

وَإِلَى هَذَا ذَهَبَ الْفُقَهَاءُ الشَّامِيُّوْنَ مَكْحُوْلٌ وَالْقَاسِمُ بْنُ مُخَيْمِرَةَ وَعَبْدُ الرَّحْمَنِ بْنُ يَزِيْدَ بْنِ جَابِرٍ وَسَعِيْدُ بْنُ عَبْدِ الْعَزِيْزِ وَالْأَوْزَاعِيُّ؛ وَقَالُوْا: سَوَاءٌ سَمَّى النَّصْرَانِيُّ الْمَسِيْحَ عَلَى ذَبِيْحَتِهِ أَوْ سَمَّى جِرْجِسَ أَوْ ذَبَحَ لِعِيْدِهِ أَوْ لِكَنِيْسَتِهِ كُلُّ ذَلِكَ حَلَالٌ لِأَنَّهُ كِتَابِيٌّ، ذَبَحَ بِدِيْنِهِ وَقَدْ أَحَلَّ اللهُ ذَبَائِحَهُمْ فِي كِتَابِهِ.

The aforementioned view is shared by the Levantine jurists: Makḥūl, al-Qāsim b. Mukhaymira, ʿAbd al-Raḥmān b. Yazīd b. Jābir, Saʿīd b. ʿAbd al-ʿAzīz and al-Awzāʿī. They opine that such meat is lawful even if a Christian slaughters it in the name of the Messiah, or in the name of [Saint] George, or slaughters it for their festival or church—all of it, they maintain, is lawful, because the one who slaughters it is from the People of the Book who killed it according to the dictates of his own religion, and Allah, in His Book [the Qurʾān], has

---

[1] Narrated by •al-Bukhārī in *al-Tārīkh al-kabīr*, 2:214 §2236. •Ibn ʿAbd al-Barr in *al-Istidhkār*, 5:258. •Ibn al-Qayyim in *Aḥkām ahl al-dhimma*, 1:519.

[2] •Ibn al-Qayyim, *Aḥkām ahl al-dhimma*, 1:517. •al-Shāṭibī, *al-Muwāfaqāt*, 1:173–174. •al-Qurāfī in *al-Furūq*, 1:304. The narrators in this chain of transmission are all reliable.

declared their meat lawful for consumption.[1]

١. قَالَ الْإِمَامُ أَبُوْ بَكْرٍ الْكَاسَانِيُّ الْـحَنَفِيُّ فِي 'بَدَائِعِ الصَّنَائِعِ': وَقَدْ رُوِيَ عَنْ سَيِّدِنَا عَلِيٍّ ﷺ أَنَّهُ سُئِلَ عَنْ ذَبَائِحِ أَهْلِ الْكِتَابِ، وَهُمْ يَقُوْلُوْنَ مَا يَقُوْلُوْنَ. فَقَالَ ﷺ: قَدْ أَحَلَّ اللهُ ذَبَائِحَهُمْ وَهُوَ يَعْلَمُ بِمَا يَقُوْلُوْنَ. فَأَمَّا إِذَا سُمِعَ مِنْهُ أَنَّهُ سَمَّى الْـمَسِيْحَ ﷺ وَحْدَهُ، أَوْ سَمَّى اللهَ ﷻ وَسَمَّى الْـمَسِيْحَ، لَا تُؤْكَلُ ذَبِيْحَتُهُ.

كَذَا رُوِيَ عَنْ سَيِّدِنَا عَلِيٍّ ﷺ وَلَـمْ يُرْوَ عَنْ غَيْرِهِ خِلَافُهُ، فَيَكُوْنُ إِجْمَاعًا.

1. Imam Abū Bakr al-Kāsānī al-Ḥanafī said in *Badāʾiʿ al-ṣanāʾiʿ*: "It is reported that our master ʿAlī ﷺ was asked about the slaughtered meat of the People of the Book who say what they say [slaughtering the animals in the name of ʿĪsā ﷺ]. He replied: 'Allah permitted their meat knowing full well what they say [at the time of slaughter].'"

On the other hand, if a Muslim hears a Christian utter the Messiah's name alone [at the time of the slaughter], or hears him mention Allah's Name and the Messiah's name together, his meat should not be eaten. This is what has been reported by our master ʿAlī, and nothing contrary to it has been reported, so it is a form of consensus on the issue.[2]

٢. عَنْ عَبْدِ الرَّحْمَنِ بْنِ يَزِيدَ بْنِ جَابِرٍ يَقُولُ: سَمِعْتُ الْقَاسِمَ بْنَ مُخَيْمِرَةَ، قَالَ: كُلْهَا، وَلَوْ سَمِعْتُهُ يَقُولُ: عَلَى اسْمِ جِرْجِسَ لَأَكَلْتُهَا.

2. It is reported that ʿAbd al-Raḥmān b. Yazīd b. Jābir said: "I heard al-Qāsim b. Mukhaymira say: 'Eat of it [the meat of the People of the Book]; but if you hear him [the Christian] say "In the name of [Saint] George", do not eat from it.'"[3]

---

[1] •Ibn ʿAbd al-Barr in *al-Istidhkār*, 5:258.

[2] •Al-Kāsānī, *Badāʾiʿ al-ṣanāʾiʿ fī tartīb al-sharāʾiʿ*, 6:230.

[3] •Ibn al-Qayyim, *Aḥkām ahl al-dhimma*, 1:520. •Ibn ʿAbd al-Barr, *al-*

٣. عَنْ عَبْدِ الرَّحْمَنِ بْنِ جُبَيْرِ بْنِ نُفَيْرٍ عَنْ أَبِيهِ، قَالَ: كُلْهَا.

3. ʿAbd al-Raḥmān b. Jubayr b. Nufayr, on the authority of his father [Jubayr b. Nufayr], said: "Eat of it."[1]

٤. وَبِهِ إِلَى أَبِي بَكْرٍ عَنْ حَبِيبِ بْنِ عُبَيْدٍ: أَنَّ الْعِرْبَاضَ بْنَ سَارِيَةَ قَالَ: كُلْهُ.

4. It is also related from Abū Bakr on the authority of Ḥabīb b. ʿUbayd, who said that al-ʿIrbāḍ b. Sāriya said: "Eat of it."[2]

٥. عَنْ عَبْدِ الْمَلِكِ عَنْ عَطَاءٍ فِي النَّصْرَانِيِّ يَذْبَحُ وَيَذْكُرُ اسْمَ الْمَسِيحِ، قَالَ: كُلْهُ، قَدْ أَحَلَّ اللهُ ذَبَائِحَهُمْ، وَقَدْ عَلِمَ مَا يَقُولُونَ.

5. Regarding a Christian who slaughters an animal in the name of the Messiah, it is reported on the authority of ʿAbd al-Malik, on the authority of ʿAṭāʾ who said: "Eat of it; Allah permitted their meat knowing full well what they say."[3]

٦. ذُكِرَ عَنْ عَطَاءٍ أَيْضًا أَنَّهُ سُئِلَ عَنِ النَّصْرَانِيِّ يَذْبَحُ، وَيَقُولُ: بِاسْمِ الْمَسِيحِ. فَقَالَ: كُلْ.

6. It is also recorded that ʿAṭāʾ was asked about the meat of a Christian who slaughtered in the name of the Messiah. He said: "Eat of it."

٧. قَالَ إِبْرَاهِيمُ فِي الذِّمِّيِّ يَذْبَحُ وَيَقُولُ: بِاسْمِ الْمَسِيحِ. فَقَالَ: إِذَا تَوَارَى عَنْكَ فَكُلْ.

Istidhkār, 5:258. The chain of this narration is rigorously authentic and its narrators are all reliable.

[1] •Ibn al-Qayyim, *Aḥkām ahl al-dhimma*, 1:521.

[2] Ibid.

[3] Ibid. The narrators of this chain are all reliable.

7. On the same question, Ibrāhīm [al-Nakhaᶜī] said: "If he conceals it from you [uttering it inaudibly] then eat of it."

٨. وَقَالَ عَبْدُ اللهِ بْنُ وَهْبٍ: حَدَّثَنِي حَيْوَةُ بْنُ شُرَيْحٍ عَنْ عُقْبَةَ بْنِ مُسْلِمٍ التُّجِيبِيِّ وَقَيْسِ بْنِ رَافِعٍ الأَشْجَعِيِّ أَنَّهُمَا قَالَا: حَلَّ لَنَا مَا يُذْبَحُ لِعِيدِ الْكَنَائِسِ، وَمَا أُهْدِيَ مِنْ خُبْزٍ أَوْ لَحْمٍ، وَإِنَّمَا هُوَ طَعَامُ أَهْلِ الْكِتَابِ.

8. ᶜAbd Allāh b. Wahb said: "Ḥaywat b. Shurayḥ narrated to me that ᶜUqba b. Muslim al-Tujībī and Qays b. Rāfiᶜ al-Ashjaᶜī both said: 'Permitted for us [to eat] are the meat and bread prepared for their Church festivals and given as gifts, for they are the food of the People of the Book.'"[1]

٩. وَقَالَ أَيُّوبُ بْنُ نَجِيحٍ: سَأَلْتُ الشَّعْبِيَّ عَنْ ذَبَائِحِ نَصَارَى الْعَرَبِ، فَقُلْتُ: مِنْهُمْ مَنْ يَذْكُرُ اللهَ، وَمِنْهُمْ مَنْ يَذْكُرُ الْمَسِيحَ، فَقَالَ: كُلْ وَأَطْعِمْنِي.

9. Ayyūb b. Najīh said: "I asked al-Shaᶜbī about the meat slaughtered by the Christian Arabs and said: 'Some of them utter Allah's Name [at the time of slaughter] while others utter the Messiah's name.' He replied: 'Eat of it and feed me some!'"[2]

١٠. قَالَ الْقَاضِي إِسْمَاعِيلُ: وَأَمَّا مَنْ بَلَغَنَا عَنْهُ أَنَّهُ كَرِهَ ذَلِكَ، فَحَدَّثَنَا مُحَمَّدُ بْنُ أَبِي بَكْرٍ، ثَنَا ابْنُ مَهْدِيٍّ عَنْ قَيْسٍ عَنْ عَطَاءِ بْنِ السَّائِبِ عَنْ زَاذَانَ عَنْ عَلِيٍّ قَالَ: إِذَا سَمِعْتَ النَّصْرَانِيَّ يَقُولُ: بِاسْمِ الْمَسِيحِ فَلَا تَأْكُلْ وَإِذَا لَمْ تَسْمَعْ فَكُلْ، فَقَدْ أُحِلَّتْ لَنَا ذَبَائِحُهُمْ.

10. Al-Qāḍī Ismāᶜīl said: "As for those scholars from whom

---

[1] Ibid.

[2] Ibid., 1:523.

it has reached us that they disliked eating of their meat, we have the following: Muḥammad b. Abī Bakr narrated to us via Ibn Mahdī › Qays › ʿAṭāʾ b. al-Sāʾib › Zādhān on the authority of ʿAlī, who said: 'If you hear a Christian say [at the time of slaughter]: "In the name of the Messiah," then do not eat [his meat], and if you do not hear him say that then eat of it, for their meat has been permitted for us.'"[1]

١١. وَقَالَ حَمَّادٌ: كُلْ مَا لَـمْ تَسْمَعْهُمْ أَهَلُّوا بِهِ لِغَيْرِ اللهِ.

11. Ḥammād said: "Eat [their meat] so long as you do not hear them kill it in the name of other than Allah."[2]

١٢. وَكَرِهَهُ مُجَاهِدٌ وَطَاوُسٌ، وَكَرِهَهُ مَيْمُونُ بْنُ مِهْرَانَ. وَقَالَ الْقَاضِي إِسْمَاعِيلُ: وَكَانَ مَالِكٌ يَكْرَهُ ذَلِكَ مِنْ غَيْرِ أَنْ يُوجِبَ فِيهِ تَحْرِيمًا.

12. This was considered reprehensible (*makrūh*) by Mujāhid, Ṭāwūs, and Maymūn b. Mihrān. Al-Qāḍī Ismāʿīl said: "Mālik would consider it detestable, but without declaring it unlawful."[3]

١٣. قَالَ الْـمُبِيحُونَ: هَذَا مِنْ طَعَامِهِمْ، وَقَدْ أَبَاحَ اللهُ لَنَا طَعَامَهُمْ مِنْ غَيْرِ تَخْصِيصٍ، وَقَدْ عَلِمَ سُبْحَانَهُ أَنَّهُمْ يُسَمُّونَ غَيْرَ اسْمِهِ.

13. As for those who permitted it, they argued that such meat is "*from their food*," and that Allah has permitted us to eat their food without qualification (*takhṣīṣ*), even though He knew that they would slaughter their animals in other than His Name.[4]

---

[1] •Ibn ʿAbd al-Barr, *al-Istidhkār*, 5:259. •Ibn al-Qayyim, *Aḥkām ahl al-dhimma*, 1:523–524.

[2] •Ibn al-Qayyim, *Aḥkām ahl al-dhimma*, 1:525.

[3] •Ibn ʿAbd al-Barr, *al-Istidhkār*, 5:259. •Ibn al-Qayyim, *Aḥkām ahl al-dhimma*, 1:526.

[4] •Ibn al-Qayyim, *Aḥkām ahl al-dhimma*, 1:526.

١٤. قَالَ الْـمُحَرِّمُونَ: قَدْ صَرَّحَ الْقُرْآنُ بِتَحْرِيمِ مَا أُهِلَّ بِهِ لِغَيْرِ اللهِ، وَهَذَا عَامٌّ فِي ذَبِيحَةِ الْوَثَنِيِّ وَالْكِتَابِيِّ إِذَا أُهِلَّ بِهَا لِغَيْرِ اللهِ، وَإِبَاحَةُ ذَبَائِحِهِمْ - وَإِنْ كَانَتْ مُطْلَقَةً - لَكِنَّهَا مُقَيَّدَةٌ بِمَا لَـمْ يُهِلُّوا بِهِ لِغَيْرِهِ، فَلَا يَجُوزُ تَعْطِيلُ الْـمُقَيَّدِ وَإِلْغَاؤُهُ بَلْ يُحْمَلُ الْـمُطْلَقُ عَلَى الْـمُقَيَّدِ.

14. As for those who declared it unlawful, they argued that the Qurʾān expressly forbids eating of that which is slaughtered in other than Allah's Name. This, they maintain, is generally applicable to the idolater or the Christian or the Jew who slaughters an animal in other than Allah's Name. Though it is true that the allowance to eat their meat is open-ended, it is limited by the condition that it should not be slaughtered in other than Allah's Name. Therefore, it is not permitted to cancel out and void the restricted [and follow the unqualified text]; rather, the open-ended must be interpreted in the light of the restricted.[1]

11.6. THE PERMISSIBILITY OF MARRYING A WOMAN FROM THE PEOPLE OF THE BOOK

Let us evaluate Ibn al-Qayyim's standpoint about the permissibility of marrying a woman from the People of the Book. He opines:

وَيَجُوزُ نِكَاحُ الْكِتَابِيَّةِ بِنَصِّ الْقُرْآنِ، قَالَ تَعَالَى: ﴿وَٱلْمُحْصَنَٰتُ مِنَ ٱلْمُؤْمِنَٰتِ وَٱلْمُحْصَنَٰتُ مِنَ ٱلَّذِينَ أُوتُوا۟ ٱلْكِتَٰبَ مِن قَبْلِكُمْ﴾ [المائدة، ٥/ ٥]، وَالْـمُحْصَنَاتُ هُنَا هُنَّ الْعَفَايِفُ، وَأَمَّا الْـمُحْصَنَاتُ الْـمُحَرَّمَاتُ فِي 'سُورَةِ النِّسَاءِ' فَهُنَّ الْـمُزَوَّجَاتُ.

وَقِيلَ: الْـمُحْصَنَاتُ اللَّاتِي أُبِحْنَ هُنَّ الْـحَرَائِرُ، وَلِهَذَا لَـمْ تَحِلَّ إِمَاءُ أَهْلِ الْكِتَابِ، وَالصَّحِيحُ الْأَوَّلُ لِوُجُوهٍ:

[1] Ibid.

أَحَدُهَا: أَنَّ الْـحُرِّيَّةَ لَيْسَتْ شَرْطًا فِي نِكَاحِ الْـمُسْلِمَةِ.

الثَّانِي: أَنَّهُ ذَكَرَ الْإِحْصَانَ فِي جَانِبِ الرَّجُلِ كَمَا ذَكَرَهُ فِي جَانِبِ الْـمَرْأَةِ، فَقَالَ: ﴿إِذَآ ءَاتَيْتُمُوهُنَّ أُجُورَهُنَّ مُحْصِنِينَ﴾ [المائدة، ٥/ ٥]، وَهَذَا إِحْصَانٌ عِفَّةٌ بِلَا شَكٍّ، فَكَذَلِكَ الإِحْصَانُ الْـمَذْكُورُ فِي جَانِبِ الْـمَرْأَةِ.

الثَّالِثُ: أَنَّهُ سُبْحَانَهُ ذَكَرَ الطَّيِّبَاتِ مِنَ الْـمَطَاعِمِ، وَالطَّيِّبَاتِ مِنَ الْـمَنَاكِحِ، فَقَالَ تَعَالَى: ﴿ٱلْيَوْمَ أُحِلَّ لَكُمُ ٱلطَّيِّبَٰتُ ۖ وَطَعَامُ ٱلَّذِينَ أُوتُوا۟ ٱلْكِتَٰبَ حِلٌّ لَّكُمْ وَطَعَامُكُمْ حِلٌّ لَّهُمْ ۖ وَٱلْمُحْصَنَٰتُ مِنَ ٱلْمُؤْمِنَٰتِ وَٱلْمُحْصَنَٰتُ مِنَ ٱلَّذِينَ أُوتُوا۟ ٱلْكِتَٰبَ مِن قَبْلِكُمْ﴾ [المائدة، ٥/ ٥].

By the explicit words of the Qurʾān, it is permissible to marry a woman from the People of the Book. Allah Most High says: ﴾*And those chaste women from the believers and from those who were given the Scripture before you [are permitted for you to wed in marriage].*﴿ [Q.5:5.] The word ﴾*chaste*﴿ here (*al-muḥṣanāt*) refers to those women who are unblemished. As for the *muḥṣanāt* mentioned in *sūra al-Nisāʾ* to whom marriage is forbidden, it refers to those who are already married.

It is also said that the *muḥṣanāt* are those free women to whom marriage is permitted, and that for this reason it is not allowed to marry the handmaidens among the People of the Book—but the soundest position is the former for a number of reasons.

Firstly, freedom is not a prerequisite to marry a Muslim woman.

Secondly, Allah mentions chastity (*iḥṣān*) with respect to both women and men, as He says: ﴾*So when you give to them their reward [their dowry] in a chaste manner. ...*﴿ [Q.5:5.] This is without doubt the chastity of temperance, and is coupled with the chastity that describes the woman.

Thirdly, Allah—Glorified and Exalted is He!—mentions

the fine and wholesome things of foods and the fine and wholesome of those who are taken in marriage, as He says: ﴾*Today the fine and wholesome things are permitted to you, and the food of those who received the Scripture is permitted to you, and those chaste women from the believers and from those who were given the Scripture before you [are permitted for you to wed in marriage].*﴿ [Q.5:5.][1]

وَالْـمَقْصُودُ أَنَّ اللهَ سُبْحَانَهُ أَبَاحَ لَنَا الْـمُحْصَنَاتِ مِنْ أَهْلِ الْكِتَابِ، وَفَعَلَهُ أَصْحَابُ نَبِيِّنَا ﷺ فَتَزَوَّجَ عُثْمَانُ نَصْرَانِيَّةً، وَتَزَوَّجَ طَلْحَةُ بْنُ عُبَيْدِ اللهِ نَصْرَانِيَّةً، وَتَزَوَّجَ حُذَيْفَةُ يَهُودِيَّةً.

قَالَ عَبْدُ اللهِ بْنُ أَحْمَدَ: سَأَلْتُ أَبِي عَنِ الْـمُسْلِمِ يَتَزَوَّجُ النَّصْرَانِيَّةَ، أَوِ الْيَهُودِيَّةَ؟ فَقَالَ: مَا أُحِبُّ أَنْ يَفْعَلَ ذَلِكَ، فَإِنْ فَعَلَ فَقَدْ فَعَلَ ذَلِكَ بَعْضُ أَصْحَابِ النَّبِيِّ ﷺ.

What this means is that Allah—Glorified and Exalted is He!—has permitted for us to marry the chaste women from the People of the Book. This, furthermore, was the practice of the Prophet's Companions ﷺ: ʿUthmān married a Christian woman; Ṭalḥa married a Christian woman; and Ḥudhayfa married a Jewish woman. ʿAbd Allah the son of Imam Aḥmad said: "I asked my father about a Muslim who marries a Christian or Jewish woman. He replied: 'I dislike that he does that; however, if he does it then [it suffices that] some of the Prophet's Companions ﷺ did it, too.'"[2]

وَقَدْ تَأَوَّلَتِ الشِّيْعَةُ الْآيَةَ عَلَى غَيْرِ تَأْوِيلِهَا، فَقَالُوا: الْـمُحْصَنَاتُ مِنَ الْـمُؤْمِنَاتِ مَنْ كَانَتْ مُسْلِمَةً فِي الْأَصْلِ، ﴿وَٱلْمُحْصَنَٰتُ مِنَ ٱلَّذِينَ أُوتُوا۟

---

[1] •Ibn al-Qayyim, *Aḥkām ahl al-dhimma*, 2:794.

[2] Narrated by •al-Khallāl in *Aḥkām ahl al-milal*, p. 159 §448. •Ibn al-Qayyim in *Aḥkām ahl al-dhimma*, 1:795.

ٱلْكِتَـٰبَ مِن قَبْلِكُمْ﴾ [المائدة، ٥/ ٥] مَنْ كَانَتْ كِتَابِيَّةً، ثُمَّ أَسْلَمَتْ.

قَالُوا: وَحَمَلَنَا عَلَى هَذَا التَّأْوِيْلِ قَوْلُهُ تَعَالَى: ﴿وَلَا تَنكِحُوا۟ ٱلْمُشْرِكَـٰتِ حَتَّىٰ يُؤْمِنَّ﴾ [البقرة، ٢/ ٢٢١]، وَأَيُّ شِرْكٍ أَعْظَمُ مِنْ قَوْلِهَا: «اللهُ ثَالِثُ ثَـلَاثَةٍ»؟ وَقَوْلُهُ تَعَالَى: ﴿وَلَا تُمْسِكُوا۟ بِعِصَمِ ٱلْكَوَافِرِ﴾ [الممتحنة، ٦٠/ ١٠]، وَأَجَابَ الْجُمْهُورُ بِجَوَابَيْنِ:

أَحَدُهُمَا: أَنَّ الْـمُرَادَ بِالْـمُشْرِكَاتِ الْوَثَنِيَّاتُ.

قَالُوْا: وَأَهْلُ الْكِتَابِ لَا يَدْخُلُوْنَ فِي لَفْظِ «الْـمُشْرِكِيْنَ» فِي كِتَابِ اللهِ تَعَالَى. قَالَ تَعَالَى: ﴿لَمْ يَكُنِ ٱلَّذِينَ كَفَرُوا۟ مِنْ أَهْلِ ٱلْكِتَـٰبِ وَٱلْمُشْرِكِينَ مُنفَكِّينَ﴾ [البينة، ٩٨/ ١]، وَقَالَ تَعَالَى: ﴿إِنَّ ٱلَّذِينَ ءَامَنُوا۟ وَٱلَّذِينَ هَادُوا۟ وَٱلصَّـٰبِـِٔينَ وَٱلنَّصَـٰرَىٰ وَٱلْمَجُوسَ وَٱلَّذِينَ أَشْرَكُوٓا۟﴾ [الحج، ٢٢/ ١٧].

وَكَذَلِكَ الْكَوَافِرُ الْـمَنْهِيُّ عَنِ التَّمَسُّكِ بِعِصْمَتِهِنَّ إِنَّمَا هُنَّ الْـمُشْرِكَاتُ، فَإِنَّ الْآيَةَ نَزَلَتْ فِي قِصَّةِ الْـحُدَيْبِيَةِ، وَلَـمْ يَكُنْ لِلْمُسْلِمِيْنَ زَوْجَاتٌ مِنْ أَهْلِ الْكِتَابِ إِذْ ذَاكَ، وَغَايَةُ مَا فِي ذَاكَ التَّخْصِيْصُ، وَلَا مَحْذُوْرَ فِيْهِ إِذَا دَلَّ عَلَيْهِ دَلِيْلٌ.

اَلْـجَوَابُ الثَّانِي: جَوَابُ الإِمَامِ أَحْمَدَ، قَالَ فِي رِوَايَةِ ابْنِهِ صَالِحٍ: قَالَ اللهُ تَعَالَى: ﴿وَلَا تَنكِحُوا۟ ٱلْمُشْرِكَـٰتِ حَتَّىٰ يُؤْمِنَّ﴾ [البقرة، ٢/ ٢٢١]، وَقَالَ فِي سُورَةِ الْـمَائِدَةِ، وَهِيَ آخِرُ مَا أُنْزِلَ مِنَ الْقُرْآنِ: ﴿وَٱلْمُحْصَنَـٰتُ مِنَ ٱلَّذِينَ أُوتُوا۟ ٱلْكِتَـٰبَ مِن قَبْلِكُمْ﴾ [المائدة، ٥/ ٥].

The Shiites misinterpreted this Qurʾānic verse and said that the chaste women among the believers are those who were born into Islam, and that the chaste women ﴾*from those who were given the Scripture before you*﴾[1] are those who were Christians or Jews that subsequently embraced Islam. They claim: "Our basis for this interpretation is the statement of Allah Most High '*And do not marry idolatresses until they believe.*'[2] What idolatry is more heinous than their claim that Allah is 'the Third of Three' [the Trinitarian doctrine]? Allah also says: '*And do not maintain marriage bonds with disbelieving women.*'"[3]

The scholarly majority (*al-jamhūr*) have provided two answers to this argument:

1. The intended meaning of "idolatresses" in the verse are literally those who worship idols. Thus, they assert that the People of the Book are not included in the term "idolaters" in the Book of Allah Most High. Allah Most High says: "*Those who disbelieved among the People of the Book and the idolaters were not to part ways [from disbelief] until there came to them clear evidence.*"[4] Allah Most High also said: "*Indeed, those who believe and those who are Jews, Sabians, Christians, and Magians, and those who associated partners [with Allah]. . .*"[5]

Likewise with regard to the "disbelieving women" with whom it is forbidden to have ties of marriage: they are polytheists only, because the verse was revealed during the events surrounding the armistice of Ḥudaybiya, and at that time the Muslims did not have wives from the People of the Book. At any rate, the most that can be said is that this verse is qualified, and thus there is no harm in [marrying a woman from the People of the Book] since there are revealed proofs in support of it.[6]

2. Imam Aḥmad said, in the narration of his son Ṣāliḥ:

---

[1] Qur'ān 5:5.

[2] Ibid 2:221.

[3] Ibid., 60:10.

[4] Ibid., 98:1.

[5] Ibid., 22:17.

[6] •Ibn al-Qayyim, *Aḥkām ahl al-dhimma*, 1:797

> "Allah Most High says: *'And do not marry idolatresses until they believe.'*[1] He also says in *sūra al-Māʾida*, which contains the final verses revealed in the Qurʾān: *'And those chaste women from the believers and from those who were given the Scripture before you [are permitted for you to wed in marriage].'*"[2]

This elaborate account of Ibn al-Qayyim's stance on non-Muslims' entrance in the Sacred Mosque, attending their funerals and the issues of the meat of their slaughtered animals has aimed to promote awareness of those contemporary people who relish extremist views about non-Muslims despite their more or less identical views though. Their beliefs and ideas are not far from what Ibn Taymiyya or Ibn al-Qayyim hold. Their extremist stance not only fatally damage the teachings of interfaith harmony but also foment social and legal woes for the expatriate Muslims of European countries. It is imperative, therefore, to make our ever-changing thoughts and beliefs of the modern world compatible to the teachings of the Qurʾān and Sunna and the pious predecessors.

---

[1] Qurʾān 2:221.

[2] Narrated by •al-Khallāl in *Aḥkām ahl al-milal*, pp. 164–165 §467. •Ibn al-Qayyim in *Aḥkām ahl al-Dhimma*, 1:797.

Part II

اَلْبَابُ الثَّانِي عَشَرَ

أَقْسَامُ الدِّيَارِ فِي الإِسْلَامِ

CHAPTER TWELVE

CATEGORIES OF THE ABODES

ISLAM INTENDS TO BRING ABOUT A DYNAMIC, COHESIVE AND PEACEFUL society. Jihad is a comprehensive word loaded with multiple connotations. It encompasses individual life as well as persistent struggle to reform national and international affairs. A voluminous book by the present author on jihad is in process and will soon see daylight, with a peculiar feature of unveiling several aspects to this subject first time. Meanwhile, *al-Jihād al-Akbar*—Arabic, Urdu and *The Supreme Jihad*—English have already been published.

The extremist elements, militants and terrorist forces and groups have done very serious damage to the Islamic concept of jihad. Naming terrorism, massacres and bloodshed as jihad, they have brought defame to Islam and distorted its teachings and identity. The subject of this treatise being relations of Muslims and non-Muslims, the dissertation on categories of abodes has been included in this work.

According to the Islamic rules, the inhabitants of the countries of the world are divided into different abodes premised on their religions and state of affairs such as the Abode of Islam (*Dār al-Islām*), the Abode of Reconciliation (*Dār al-Ṣulḥ*), the Abode of Treaty (*Dār al-ʿAhd*), The Abode of Peace (*Dār al-Amn*) and the Abode of War (*Dār al-Ḥarb*). While in modern times, we find full display of extremism and violence due to wrong interpretation of religion, the division of countries into various abodes too is accomplished the way they like. Different gangs and groups kick off terrorism in the name of jihad wherever they feel like due to their peculiar misanthropist idiosyncrasies and heretic beliefs. That leads to civil strife, mayhem, massacres and carnage. If asked about legal basis of the homicide and genocide they perpetrate they say: "this is 'the abode of war' so we are justified to slay the hostile people whether Muslims or non-Muslims." It is against this perspective that the legal truths have been penned on the following pages to analyse and explain the division of abodes these people maliciously make to cause deviation and bring defame to the

Islamic beliefs.

12.1 THE ABODE OF ISLAM (*DĀR AL-ISLĀM*)

Imams and jurists have defined 'the Abode of Islam' in several ways. Here is a brief survey of these definitions.

1. Abū Yaʿlā al-Ḥanbalī (210–307 AH), in his treatise *al-Muʿtamad fī uṣūl al-Dīn* (p. 276), has premised the definition of the Abode of Islam on the issuance and supremacy of Islamic Law vis-à-vis non-Islamic rules instead of predicating it on the enforcement of Islamic Law in isolation. He has pronounced:

وَكُلُّ دَارٍ كَانَتِ الْغَلَبَةُ فِيْهَا لِأَحْكَامِ الْإِسْلَامِ دُوْنَ أَحْكَامِ الْكُفْرِ فَهِيَ دَارُ إِسْلَامٍ.

> "Every country, where, in comparison to non-Islamic Law, Islamic Law is held supreme, falls into the category of Abode of Islam."

2. Ibn al-Mufliḥ al-Ḥanbalī (717–762 AH), declaring the prevalence and supremacy of Islamic Law as the basis of the definition of 'Abode of Islam', has opined:

فَكُلُّ دَارٍ غَلَبَ عَلَيْهَا أَحْكَامُ الْـمُسْلِمِيْنَ فَدَارُ الإِسْلَامِ.

> "Every territory where the rules of the Muslims predominate is considered the Abode of Islam."[1]

3. lbn al-Qayyim al-Ḥanbalī (691–751 AH), in his *Aḥkām ahl al-dhimma* (2:728), has proclaimed that if the Muslims dwell in a particular territory where Islamic laws are entered into force, it will be considered as the Abode of Islam. In support of his position, he has referred to the opinion held by the majority of the jurists:

قَالَ الْـجَمْهُوْرُ: دَارُ الْإِسْلَامِ هِيَ الَّتِي نَزَلَـهَا الْـمُسْلِمُونَ وَجَرَتْ عَلَيْهَا أَحْكَامُ الْإِسْلَامِ.

[1] •Ibn al-Mufliḥ, *al-Ādāb al-sharʿiyya*, 1:211.

"The majority opinion holds that the Abode of Islam is the land where Muslims dwell and Islamic pillars are enforced (and practised)."

4. Al-Shawkānī (d. 1255 AH) has defined it in the following way:

وَدَارُ الْإِسْلَامِ مَا ظَهَرَتْ فِيْهِ الشَّهَادَتَانِ وَالصَّلَاةُ، وَلَمْ تَظْهَرْ فِيْهَا خَصْلَةٌ كُفْرِيَّةٌ.

"The Abode of Islam is the land wherein a system is instituted on the formula of affirming the Oneness of Allah, witnessing the Messengership of the Prophet and establishing the ritual prayers, and that does not manifest any feature of disbelief."[1]

5. Shaykh Muhammad Abū Zahra (1898–1974 CE) has defined the Abode of lslam in these words:

دَارُ الْإِسْلَامِ هِيَ الدَّوْلَةُ الَّتِي تُحْكَمُ بِسُلْطَانِ الْمُسْلِمِينَ وَتَكُوْنُ الْمَنَعَةُ وَالْقُوَّةُ فِيْهَا لِلْمُسْلِمِينَ.

"The Abode of Islam is the state where the authority and governance of the Muslim rulers prevail, and the Muslims own its defence and military might."[2]

12.1.1 How Does an Abode of Islam Morph into an Abode of Disbelief and Abode of War?

1. Imam Muhammad b. Aḥmad al-Sarakhsī (d. 483 AH) has given a detailed description of the stance of the great Imam Abū Ḥanīfa (d. 150 AH) shared also by his two disciples—Imam Muhammad and Imam Abū Yūsuf—popularly known as *Ṣāḥibayn*. Their position on how an Abode of Islam becomes an Abode of Disbelief and Abode of War has appeared as follows:

عِنْدَ أَبِي حَنِيفَةَ إِنَّمَا تَصِيرُ دَارُهُمْ دَارَ الْحَرْبِ بِثَلَاثِ شَرَائِطَ:

---

[1] •Al-Shawkānī, *al-Sayl al-jarār*, 4:575.

[2] •Abū Zuhra, *al-ʿAlāqāt al-duwaliyya fī al-Islām*, p. 56.

أَحَدُهَا: أَنْ تَكُونَ مُتَاخِمَةً أَرْضَ التُّرْكِ لَيْسَ بَيْنَهَا وَبَيْنَ أَرْضِ الْحَرْبِ دَارٌ لِلْمُسْلِمِينَ.

وَالثَّانِي: أَنْ لَا يَبْقَى فِيهَا مُسْلِمٌ آمِنٌ بِإِيْمَانِهِ، وَلَا ذِمِّيٌّ آمِنٌ بِأَمَانِهِ.

وَالثَّالِثُ: أَنْ يُظْهِرُوا أَحْكَامَ الشِّرْكِ فِيهَا.

وَعَنْ أَبِي يُوسُفَ وَمُحَمَّدٍ: إِذَا أَظْهَرُوا أَحْكَامَ الشِّرْكِ فِيهَا فَقَدْ صَارَتْ دَارُهُمْ دَارَ حَرْبٍ.

According to Imam Abū Ḥanīfa, a land of the Muslims becomes an Abode of War—*dār al-ḥārb*—when three conditions are met:

1. The neighbouring country of an Abode of Islam is an Abode of War and no other Muslim country forms a corridor between the two.
2. Muslim citizens become unsafe and insecure along with their faith and non-Muslim citizens find themselves deprived of safety that their peace treaty had already guaranteed them.
3. The non-Muslim combatants and aggressors capture it and make the non-Islamic and polytheistic law prevail.

In the view of Imam Abū Yūsuf and Imam Muhammad, such a land morphs into the Abode of War when the invading non-Muslim forces seize it and enter into force the non-Muslim and polytheistic rules.[1]

2. In *Badāʾiʿ al-ṣanāʾiʿ*, Imam ʿAlāʾ al-Dīn al-Kāsānī (d. 587 AH) elaborated on this edict issued by Imam Abū Ḥanīfa. He writes:

قَالَ أَبُو حَنِيْفَةَ: إِنَّهَا لَا تَصِيرُ دَارَ الْكُفْرِ إِلَّا بِثَلَاثِ شَرَائِطَ:

أَحَدُهَا: ظُهُورُ أَحْكَامِ الْكُفْرِ فِيهَا.

[1] •Al-Sarakhasī, *al-Mabsūṭ*, 10:114.

وَالثَّانِي: أَنْ تَكُوْنَ مُتَاخِمَةً لِدَارِ الْكُفْرِ.

وَالثَّالِثُ: أَنْ لَا يَبْقَى فِيْهَا مُسْلِمٌ وَلَا ذِمِّيٌّ آمِنًا بِالْأَمَانِ الْأَوَّلِ وَهُوَ أَمَانُ الْـمُسْلِمِينَ.

Imam Abū Ḥanīfa holds that unless three conditions are met, an Abode of Islam cannot turn into an Abode of War (*dār al-ḥarb*):

Firstly, non-Islamic rules are enforced.

Secondly, it abuts an Abode of War.

Thirdly, neither a Muslim nor a non-Muslim citizen remains secure under the umbrella of the peace treaty concluded with the non-Muslims by the Muslims.[1]

3. In *Durr al-mukhtār*, ʿAlaʾ al-Dīn al-Ḥaskafī (d. 1088 AH) has also quoted the same edict of Imam Abū Ḥanīfa with regard to the Abode of Islam developing into an Abode of War. He said:

لَا تَصِيرُ دَارُ الْإِسْلَامِ دَارَ حَرْبٍ إِلَّا بِأُمُورٍ ثَـلَاثَةٍ:

بِإِجْرَاءِ أَحْكَامِ أَهْلِ الشِّرْكِ.

وَبِاتِّصَالِـهَا بِدَارِ الْـحَرْبِ.

وَبِأَنْ لَا يَبْقَى فِيْهَا مُسْلِمٌ أَوْ ذِمِّيٌّ آمِنًا بِالأَمَانِ الْأَوَّلِ.

An Abode of Islam cannot take the shape of an Abode of War (*dār al-ḥārb*) without the following three conditions:

1. The laws of polytheists are entered into force.
2. It borders an Abode of War.
3. No Muslim or non-Muslim citizen remains protected under the peace treaty of the Muslims with the non-Muslims.[2]

4. Ibn Qudāma al-Ḥanbalī (d. 620 AH) has also taken an account of

[1] •Al-Kāsānī, *Badāʾiʿ al-ṣanāʾiʿ*, 8:130.

[2] •Al-Ḥaṣkafī, *al-Durr al-mukhtār*, 4:174–175.

the stipulations mentioned by Imam Abū Ḥanīfa. He said:

قَالَ أَبُو حَنِيْفَةَ: لَا تَصِيْرُ دَارَ حَرْبٍ حَتَّى تَجْمَعَ فِيْهَا ثَلَاثَةَ أَشْيَاءَ:

أَنْ تَكُونَ مُتَاخِمَةً لِدَارِ الْحَرْبِ لَا شَيْءَ بَيْنَهُمَا مِنْ دَارِ الإِسْلَامِ.

الثَّانِي: أَنْ لَا يَبْقَى فِيهَا مُسْلِمٌ وَلَا ذِمِّيٌّ آمِنٌ.

الثَّالِثُ: أَنْ تُجْرَى فِيهَا أَحْكَامُهُمْ.

According to Imam Abū Ḥanīfa, the Abode of Islam does not turn into an Abode of War until three conditions are met:

1. It borders an Abode of War with no commonality of any feature of the Abode of Islam.
2. Neither a Muslim nor a non-Muslim is in a state of peace.
3. The rules of non-Muslims are in effect.[1]

5. Shaykh Muhammad b. Aḥmad b. ʿArafa al-Dasūqī al-Mālikī (d. 1230 AH) has opined:

بِلَادُ الْإِسْلَامِ لَا تَصِيْرُ دَارَ حَرْبٍ بِأَخْذِ الْكُفَّارِ لَهَا بِالْقَهْرِ مَا دَامَتْ شَعَائِرُ الْإِسْلَامِ قَائِمَةً فِيْهَا. ...

بِلَادُ الْإِسْلَامِ لَا تَصِيْرُ دَارَ حَرْبٍ بِمُجَرَّدِ اسْتِيْلَائِهِمْ عَلَيْهَا بَلْ حَتَّى تَنْقَطِعَ إِقَامَةُ شَعَائِرِ الْإِسْلَامِ عَنْهَا، وَأَمَّا مَا دَامَتْ شَعَائِرُ الْإِسْلَامِ أَوْ غَالِبُهَا قَائِمَةً فِيْهَا فَلَا تَصِيْرُ دَارَ حَرْبٍ.

As long as the Signs of Islam (*shaʿāʾir al-Islām*) persist, the lands of *dār al-Islām* do not turn into *dār al-ḥārb* just because the disbelievers seize them by force....

Until the Signs of Islam give way and remain no more in practice, the mere upper hand of disbelievers cannot alter the status of Muslim countries and transform them into *dār al-ḥārb*. So long as Islamic rituals are in practice and

[1] •Ibn Qudāma, *al-Mughnī fī fiqh al-Imām Aḥmad b. Ḥanbal*, 9:25–26.

predominant, Muslim lands do not become *dār al-ḥārb.*[1]

6. Shaykh Aḥmad b. Muhammad al-Ṣawī al-Khalwatī al-Mālikī (d. 1241 AH) has also taken the same position in his work *Bulgha al-sālik lī-aqrab al-masālik ʿalā Sharḥ al-ṣaghīr li Aḥmad al-Dardīr* (2:187).

7. Elucidating the Salafi standpoint on the issue, al-Shawkānī writes:

> إِنْ كَانَتِ الْأَوَامِرُ وَالنَّوَاهِي فِي الدَّارِ لِأَهْلِ الْإِسْلَامِ بِحَيْثُ لَا يَسْتَطِيعُ مَنْ فِيْهَا مِنَ الْكُفَّارِ أَنْ يَتَظَاهَرَ بِكُفْرِهِ إِلَّا لِكَوْنِهِ مَأْذُوْنًا لَهُ بِذَلِكَ مِنْ أَهْلِ الْإِسْلَامِ فَهَذِهِ دَارُ إِسْلَامٍ، وَلَا يَضُرُّ ظُهُورُ الْخِصَالِ الْكُفْرِيَّةِ فِيهَا لِأَنَّهَا لَمْ تَظْهَرْ بِقُوَّةِ الْكُفَّارِ وَلَا بِصَوْلَتِهِمْ كَمَا هُوَ مُشَاهَدٌ فِي أَهْلِ الذِّمَّةِ مِنَ الْيَهُوْدِ وَالنَّصَارَى وَالْمُعَاهِدِينَ السَّاكِنِينَ فِي الْمَدَائِنِ الْإِسْلَامِيَّةِ، وإِذَا كَانَ الْأَمْرُ الْعَكْسَ فَالدَّارُ بِالْعَكْسِ.
>
> If the Islamic commands and prohibitions are enforced and practised in a country and the disbelievers are not in a position to proclaim their disbelief except that they have a permission from the believers to reside there, it is regarded as an Abode of Islam. It may be noted that the manifestation of the features of disbelief will not do it any harm as they cannot gain currency due to the disbelievers' meagre power and influence. The living conditions of the Jews and the Christians and the non-Muslims with whom there is a peace treaty in Muslim countries provide ample evidence to prove this. However, if matters are reversed, then the status of the abode will be reversed, too (i.e., it will morph into an Abode of Disbelief).[2]

12.1.2 THE STRINGENT CONDITIONS FOR THE ABODE OF WAR

The preceding comparative study of the ideas and concepts propounded

---

[1] •Al-Dasūqī, *Ḥāshiya ʿalā al-Sharḥ al-kabīr*, 2:188.

[2] •Al-Shawkānī, *al-Sayl al-jarār*, 4:575.

by Imam Abū Ḥanīfa (d. 150 AH) and a host of other imams has revealed that the Islamic state will only transform into an Abode of Disbelief or an Abode of War when the following stringent conditions are met:

1. The non-Islamic and polytheistic laws dominate the Abode of Islam: idolatry instead of the belief in the Oneness of Allah prevails; the rules of non-Muslims instead of the Divine and Prophetic laws enter into force; and the Muslim faith and practices are banned.
2. The Muslim and non-Muslim inhabitants are deprived of the protection and security that was conferred on them by the earlier Islamic state—the non-Muslim government completely takes over.
3. The Signs and Rituals of Islam—the call to prayer, the ritual prayers, fasting, pilgrimage and the Alms-due—all of the pillars are abolished.
4. The Muslim community does not enjoy a majority any longer.

It should be noted that the status of an Abode of Islam for a Muslim state is impaired only when it completely meets these conditions. Thus, no one has the right to declare an Islamic state an Abode of War and unleash a spree of violence, tribulations and killings. If a Muslim country meets all but one of the preceding conditions, its status as an Abode of Islam remains intact. Quoting the same edict of Imam Abū Ḥanīfa, Imam Abū Jaʿfar al-Ṭāḥāwī (d. 321 AH) added the following sentence:

إِنْ فُقِدَ شَيْءٌ مِنْ ذَلِكَ لَمْ تَكُنْ دَارَ حَرْبٍ.

> "If any of these conditions are unmet, it will not become *dār al-ḥārb* (and will continue as *dār al-Islām*)."[1]

12.1.3 The Rationale for The Stringent Conditions Regarding the Abode of War

Imam al-Sarakhasī said in *al-Mabsūṭ* (10:114):

أَبُو حَنِيفَةَ يَعْتَبِرُ تَمَامَ الْقَهْرِ وَالْقُوَّةِ، لِأَنَّ هَذِهِ الْبَلْدَةَ كَانَتْ مِنْ دَارِ الْإِسْلَامِ،

---

[1] •Al-Ṭāḥāwī, *Mukhtaṣar ikhtilāf al-ʿulamāʾ*, 3:469.

مُحْرَزَةً لِلْمُسْلِمِينَ فَلَا يَبْطُلُ ذَلِكَ الْإِحْرَازُ إِلَّا بِتَمَامِ الْقَهْرِ مِنَ الْـمُشْرِكِينَ، وَذَلِكَ بِاسْتِجْمَاعِ الشَّرَائِطِ الثَّلَاثِ، لِأَنَّهَا إِذَا لَـمْ تَكُنْ مُتَّصِلَةً بِالشِّرْكِ فَأَهْلُهَا مَقْهُورُونَ بِإِحَاطَةِ الْـمُسْلِمِينَ بِهِمْ مِنْ كُلِّ جَانِبٍ، فَكَذَلِكَ إِنْ بَقِيَ فِيهَا مُسْلِمٌ أَوْ ذِمِّيٌّ آمِنٌ فَذَلِكَ دَلِيلُ عَدَمِ تَمَامِ الْقَهْرِ مِنْهُمْ.

Imam Abū Ḥanīfa considers full spectrum dominance [as a condition], because the said land was the Abode of Islam and a safe haven for the Muslims, and that cannot be cancelled out unless the polytheists gain full control [over it]—and that is only when the three conditions are met. If (in such a case) the polytheist rules are not promoted, it implies that the idolaters are hemmed in from all sides by the besieging Muslims. In a like manner, if the Muslim and non-Muslim citizens are in peace, it implies that the non-Muslims have not attained complete control.

Citing the fatwa issued by the great Imam Abū Ḥanīfa, Imam ʿAlāʾ al-Dīn al-Kāsānī al-Ḥanafī (d. 587 AH) writes in *Badāʾiʿ al-ṣanāʾiʿ* (7:131):

وَجْهُ قَوْلِ أَبِي حَنِيفَةَ أَنَّ الْـمَقْصُودَ مِنْ إِضَافَةِ الدَّارِ إِلَى الْإِسْلَامِ وَالْكُفْرِ لَيْسَ هُوَ عَيْنَ الْإِسْلَامِ وَالْكُفْرِ، وَإِنَّمَا الْـمَقْصُودُ هُوَ الْأَمْنُ وَالْـخَوْفُ. وَمَعْنَاهُ أَنَّ الْأَمَانَ إِنْ كَانَ لِلْمُسْلِمِينَ فِيهَا عَلَى الْإِطْلَاقِ، وَالْـخَوْفُ لِلْكَفَرَةِ عَلَى الْإِطْلَاقِ، فَهِيَ دَارُ الْإِسْلَامِ، وَإِنْ كَانَ الْأَمَانُ فِيهَا لِلْكَفَرَةِ عَلَى الْإِطْلَاقِ، وَالْـخَوْفُ لِلْمُسْلِمِينَ عَلَى الْإِطْلَاقِ، فَهِيَ دَارُ الْكُفْرِ. وَالْأَحْكَامُ مَبْنِيَّةٌ عَلَى الْأَمَانِ وَالْـخَوْفِ لَا عَلَى الْإِسْلَامِ وَالْكُفْرِ، فَكَانَ اعْتِبَارُ الْأَمَانِ وَالْـخَوْفِ أَوْلَى، فَمَا لَـمْ تَقَعِ الْـحَاجَةُ لِلْمُسْلِمِينَ إِلَى الِاسْتِئْمَانِ بَقِيَ الْأَمْنُ الثَّابِتُ فِيهَا عَلَى الْإِطْلَاقِ، فَلَا تَصِيرُ دَارَ الْكُفْرِ.

The rationale behind the statement of Imam Abū Ḥanīfa is

that the annexation of a '*dār*' (abode) with *Islām* and *kufr* is not because of Islam or *kufr per se*. Its implied intent is peace and terror (the Abode of Islam denotes an Abode of Peace and the Abode of Disbelief signifies an Abode of Terror). This means if the Muslims of a country enjoy absolute peace and protection while the disbelievers live under absolute fear (until the Islamic government guarantees their protection), the country is an Abode of Islam. However, if the disbelievers breathe in absolute peace while the Muslims live in absolute fear, the country is (unequivocally) an Abode of Disbelief.

So the application of rules is premised on peace and fear instead of Islamic faith or its rejection (i.e., *kufr*). What matters then is whether the state of peace or fear is supreme. So long as the Muslims are not in need of seeking security and the existing security arrangements persist, the land will not morph into an Abode of Disbelief—*dār al-kufr*.

12.1.4 The Inaptness of Declaring an Abode of Islam an Abode of Disbelief due to Predominant Corruption

The Salafi scholar al-Shawkānī (d. 1255 AH) has also stated:

إِلْـحَاقُ دَارِ الْإِسْلَامِ بِدَارِ الْكُفْرِ بِمُجَرَّدِ وُقُوعِ الْـمَعَاصِي فِيْهَا عَلَى وَجْهِ الظُّهُورِ لَيْسَ بِمُنَاسِبٍ لِعِلْمِ الرِّوَايَةِ وَلَا لِعِلْمِ الدِّرَايَةِ.

According to the reported and the acquired knowledge (the teachings of the Qur'ān and Sunna and the application of reason and intellect), declaring an Abode of Islam as the Abode of Disbelief on the ground of predominant corruption and acts of disobedience is inapt and inappropriate.[1]

12.1.5 Absolute Power and Dominance are a Must for a Place to Be Judged as an Abode of War

According to Imam Abū Ḥanīfa, an Abode of Islam cannot change

[1] •Al-Shawkānī, *Nayl al-awṭār*, 8:179.

into an Abode of War unless a hostile power assumes absolute and total control. An abode does not undergo change through only partial control. Abū Ḥanīfa maintains that the basis for change is not Islam or *kufr per se*, but rather the basis is security and fear.

As already mentioned, Imam ʿAlāʾ al-Dīn al-Kāsānī al-Ḥanafī, after citing the edict of Imam Abū Ḥanīfa, said:

وَجْهُ قَوْلِ أَبِي حَنِيفَةَ أَنَّ الْـمَقْصُوْدَ مِنْ إِضَافَةِ الدَّارِ إِلَى الْإِسْلَامِ وَالْكُفْرِ لَيْسَ هُوَ عَيْنُ الْإِسْلَامِ وَالْكُفْرِ، وَإِنَّمَا الْـمَقْصُودُ هُوَ الْأَمْنُ وَالْـخَوْفُ.

> The underlying logic of Imam Abū Ḥanīfa's statement is that annexing '*Dār*' (abode) with *Islām* and *kufr* purposely implies peace and terror (the Abode of Islam denotes an Abode of Peace and the Abode of Disbelief signifies an Abode of Terror).[1]

Furthermore, Imam Abū Ḥanīfa holds that the relevance of applying the rules is predicated on peace and terror instead of Islamic faith or *kufr*. The significance, therefore, of peace and fear is supreme. So long as Muslims are not in need of seeking security and the existing security arrangements endure, the land will not transform into an Abode of Disbelief—*dār al-kufr*.[2]

12.1.6 The Viewpoint of al-Thānwī on the Abode of War

Al-Thānwī has cited a quote from Imam Jamāl al-Dīn b. ʿImād al-Dīn al-Ḥanafī's *Fūṣūl al-ahkām fī usūl al-aḥkām* in his famous book *Kashshāf isṭilāḥāt al-funūn* (1:466):

وَلَا خِلَافَ فِي أَنَّهُ يَصِيْرُ دَارُ الْـحَرْبِ دَارَ الْإِسْلَامِ بِإِجْرَاءِ بَعْضِ أَحْكَامِ الْإِسْلَامِ فِيْهَا.

> There is no disagreement that *dār al-ḥārb* becomes *dār al-Islām* due to the enforcement of some of the Shariah laws

[1] •Al-Kasānī, *Badāʾiʿ al-ṣanāʾiʿ*, 7:131.

[2] Ibid.

therein (and continues to be so long as the rules operate).[1]

Describing the third condition on the change of the Abode of Islam into the Abode of War, he writes:

وَثَالِثُهَا زَوَالُ الْأَمَانِ الْأَوَّلِ، أَيْ لَـمْ يَبْقَ مُسْلِمٌ وَلَا ذِمِّيٌّ آمِنًا إِلَّا بِأَمَانِ الْكُفَّارِ، وَلَـمْ يَبْقَ الْأَمَانُ الَّذِي كَانَ لِلْمُسْلِمِ بِإِسْلَامِهِ.

[A]nd the third condition is that the treaty of peace concluded earlier will not be operative and in force any longer. Neither a Muslim nor a non-Muslim citizen enjoys protection save by one granted by the disbelievers, and there no longer remains the security that a Muslim enjoyed through his Islam.[2]

Al-Thānwī further writes with reference to Imam ʿAlī b. Muhammad b. Ismāʿīl al-Isbījābī al-Samarqandī (d. 535 AH):

إِنَّ الدَّارَ مَحْكُوْمَةٌ بِدَارِ الْإِسْلَامِ بِبَقَاءِ حُكْمٍ وَاحِدٍ فِيْهَا كَمَا فِي الْعِمَادِيِّ، وَفَتَاوَى عَالَـمْغِيْر، وَفَتَاوَى قَاضِي خَانْ وَغَيْرِهَا.

An abode is determined as *dār al-Islām* by there remaining even a single (Islamic) ruling—as mentioned in *ʿImādī*, *Fatāwā ʿĀlamgīrī*, and *Fatāwā Qāḍī Khān*, etc.[3]

12.1.7 A Country Practicing Islamic Teachings and Signs cannot be Declared an Abode of War

Ibn Qudāma al-Ḥanbalī has written with reference to Imam Abū Ḥanīfa that, according to the latter, an Abode of Islam does not become an Abode of War until it meets three conditions. The second among them reads: "Not a single Muslim and non-Muslim citizen is in peace."

Ibn Qudāma added: "[In that case] it will be an Abode of Disbelief. (However, legally, it will not be an Abode of Disbelief or Abode of

[1] Ibid.

[2] •Al-Thānwī, *Kashshāf iṣṭilāḥāt al-funūn*, 1:466.

[3] Ibid.

War)."[1]

Shaykh Muhammad b. Aḥmad b. ʿArafa al-Dasūqī al-Mālikī (d. 1230 AH) maintains:

بِلَادُ الْإِسْلَامِ لَا تَصِيْرُ دَارَ حَرْبٍ بِأَخْذِ الْكُفَّارِ لَـهَا بِالْقَهْرِ مَا دَامَتْ شَعَائِرُ الإِسْلَامِ قَائِمَةً فِيهَا.

As long as the Signs (and pillars) of Islam remain in practice and enforced, the Islamic lands—*dār al-Islām*—do not become *dār al-ḥārb* merely because of the upper hand of disbelievers.[2]

12.1.8 No Land can be Declared an Abode of War Only Due to Disbelievers' Rule and Authority

The jurists of the Mālikī school uphold:

بِلَادُ الْإِسْلَامِ لَا تَصِيْرُ دَارَ حَرْبٍ بِمُجَرَّدِ اسْتِيْلَائِهِمْ عَلَيْهَا.

Until the Signs and pillars of Islam are in practice, mere hegemony (or rule and authority) and coercive measures (like financial restrictions) of disbelievers cannot alter the status of Muslim countries into *Dār al-Ḥarb*].[3]

Ibn Taymiyya said:

وَأَمَّا مَنْ لَـمْ يَكُنْ مِنْ أَهْلِ الْـمُمَانَعَةِ وَالْـمُقَاتَلَةِ كَالنِّسَاءِ وَالصِّبْيَانِ وَالرَّاهِبِ وَالشَّيْخِ الْكَبِيْرِ وَالْأَعْمَى وَالزَّمِنِ وَنَحْوِهِمْ فَلَا يُقْتَلُ عِنْدَ جُمْهُوْرِ الْعُلَمَاءِ.

A majority of jurists maintain that all non-combatants whether (they are) from women, children, priests, the elderly,

---

[1] •Ibn Qudāma, *al-Mughnī fī fiqh al-Imām Aḥmad b. Ḥanbal*, 9:26.

[2] •al-Dusūqī, *Ḥāshiya ʿalā al-Sharḥ al-kabīr ʿalā Mukhtaṣar Khalīl li al-Dardīr*, 2:188.

[3] Ibid.

the blind, the infirm and the like are not allowed to be killed.[1]

Ibn al-Qayyim stated in his book *Aḥkām ahl al-dhimma*: "If Muslims are residing in a particular territory and Islamic laws are implemented in it, such a state would be an Abode of Islam." He cited the majority opinion of the jurists:

دَارُ الإِسْلَامِ هِيَ الَّتِي نَزَلَهَا الْمُسْلِمُونَ وَجَرَتْ عَلَيْهَا أَحْكَامُ الإِسْلَامِ.

The Abode of Islam is the land in which the Muslims have settled and Islamic pillars are practiced.[2]

12.2 The Abode of Reconciliation (*Dār al-Ṣulḥ*)

An Abode of Reconciliation is the non-Islamic state which enters into a treaty of reconciliation with an Islamic state on some predetermined conditions.

12.2.1 The Difference between the Abode of Treaty and the Abode of Reconciliation

Most of the jurists and imams do not find any difference between the Abode of Treaty and the Abode of Reconciliation. However, Imam al-Shāfiʿī described a slight difference between these two. According to him:

> An Abode of Treaty is a territory or a non-Muslim country, which enters into a treaty of peace with an Islamic state. Moreover, an Abode of Reconciliation refers to a non-Islamic country or a territory, which was at war with an Islamic state, and then agreed to reconciliation with the Islamic state to withdraw from war on certain conditions. So long as the reconciliation is sustained and armed conflict abates, the territory is regarded as an Abode of Reconciliation.

Imam al-Shāfiʿī has described in *Kitāb al-umm* (4:182) the situation in which an Abode of War becomes an Abode of Reconciliation:

---

1 •Ibn Taimiyya, *Majmūʿ al-Fatāwā*, 28:354.

2 •Ibn al-Qayyim, *Aḥkām ahl al-dhimma*, 2:728.

إِذَا غَزَا الْإِمَامُ قَوْمًا فَلَمْ يَظْهَرْ عَلَيْهِمْ حَتَّى عَرَضُوْا عَلَيْهِ الصُّلْحَ عَلَى شَيْءٍ. ... فَعَلَيْهِ أَنْ يَقْبَلَهُ مِنْهُمْ.

When an Islamic state is at war with a non-Islamic state and they present the proposal of reconciliation to the Islamic state during the war, before their victory, then it is incumbent upon the Islamic state to agree to reconciliation.[1]

In accordance with Imam al-Shāfiʿī's view, if an Islamic state reconciles with a warring state, then that state will be changed from an Abode of War to an Abode of Reconciliation.

Defining the concept of Abode of Reconciliation, Sh. Muhammad Tāj al-ʿArūsī writes in *Fiqh al-jihād wa al ʿalaqāt al-duwaliyya fī al-Islām*:

هِيَ الَّتِي لَمْ يَظْهَرْ عَلَيْهَا الْمُسْلِمُوْنَ وَعَقَدَ أَهْلُهَا الصُّلْحَ بَيْنَهُمْ وَبَيْنَ الْمُسْلِمِينَ عَلَى شَيْءٍ.

It is a territory where Muslims have not overcome [militarily] and in which its inhabitants conclude a treaty of reconciliation with the Muslims according to certain terms.[2]

12.2.2 Instructions to Fulfil Agreements with the Abode of Reconciliation

In *sūra al-Nisāʾ*, Allah has ordered Muslims to fulfil their agreements with non-Muslims with utmost sincerity and honesty:

﴿إِلَّا ٱلَّذِينَ يَصِلُونَ إِلَىٰ قَوْمِۭ بَيْنَكُمْ وَبَيْنَهُم مِّيثَٰقٌ أَوْ جَآءُوكُمْ حَصِرَتْ صُدُورُهُمْ أَن يُقَٰتِلُوكُمْ أَوْ يُقَٰتِلُوا۟ قَوْمَهُمْ ۚ وَلَوْ شَآءَ ٱللَّهُ لَسَلَّطَهُمْ عَلَيْكُمْ فَلَقَٰتَلُوكُمْ ۚ فَإِنِ ٱعْتَزَلُوكُمْ فَلَمْ يُقَٰتِلُوكُمْ وَأَلْقَوْا۟ إِلَيْكُمُ ٱلسَّلَمَ فَمَا جَعَلَ ٱللَّهُ لَكُمْ عَلَيْهِمْ سَبِيلًا﴾

1 •Al-Shāfiʿī, *al-Umm*, 4:184.

2 •Al-Urūsī, *Fiqh al-jihād wa al-ʿalaqāt al-duwaliyya fī al-Islām*, p. 333.

﴾But (do not fight) those who have allied with a people that between you and them there is a (peace) treaty, or who (losing heart) come to you in such a state that their breasts are afflicted (with this obsession) whether they should fight you or their own people. If Allah had so willed, He (strengthening their hearts) would have given them supremacy over you. Then they would certainly have fought you. So if they keep away from you and do not fight you and send you (a message) for peace, then (in the interest of peace) Allah has left no way open for you (to launch any aggression) against them.﴿[1]

The next verse mentions that if some miscreants and troublemakers commit wrongdoing and terrorism, then it is essential that they are eliminated so that society can be protected from their evils:

﴿فَإِن لَّمْ يَعْتَزِلُوكُمْ وَيُلْقُوٓاْ إِلَيْكُمُ ٱلسَّلَمَ وَيَكُفُّوٓاْ أَيْدِيَهُمْ فَخُذُوهُمْ وَٱقْتُلُوهُمْ حَيْثُ ثَقِفْتُمُوهُمْ ۚ وَأُوْلَـٰٓئِكُمْ جَعَلْنَا لَكُمْ عَلَيْهِمْ سُلْطَـٰنًا مُّبِينًا﴾

﴾So if they do not give up (fighting against you, nor) send you any (message for) peace, (nor) hold their hands off (their disruptive activities), then seize (and capture) them and kill them wherever you find them. And it is they against whom We have granted you unrestricted authority.﴿[2]

Imam Fakhr al-Dīn al-Rāzī (d. 606 AH) wrote in his commentary on the above verse:

وَالْمَعْنَى ﴿فَإِن لَّمْ يَعْتَزِلُوكُمْ﴾ وَلَمْ يَطْلُبُوا الصُّلْحَ مِنْكُمْ وَلَمْ ﴿وَيَكُفُّوٓاْ أَيْدِيَهُمْ فَخُذُوهُمْ وَٱقْتُلُوهُمْ حَيْثُ ثَقِفْتُمُوهُمْ﴾. قَالَ الأَكْثَرُوْنَ: وَهَذَا يَدُلُّ عَلَى أَنَّهُمْ إِذَا اعْتَزَلُوا قِتَالَنَا وَطَلَبُوا الصُّلْحَ مِنَّا وَكَفُّوْا أَيْدِيَهِمْ عَنْ إِيْذَائِنَا

---

[1] Qurʾān 4:90.

[2] Ibid., 4:91.

لَـمْ يَجُزْ لَنَا قِتَالُهُمْ وَلَا قَتْلُهُمْ.

Many exegetes have stated that this verse signifies that when they (the disbelievers) eschew mischief and refrain from killing us, and want to reconcile with us, then it does not remain permissible for us to kill them.[1]

Similarly, verse 12 of *sūra al-Tawba* warns of chastisement for those transgressors who breach promises and covenants. It was revealed:

﴿وَإِن نَّكَثُوٓاْ أَيۡمَٰنَهُم مِّنۢ بَعۡدِ عَهۡدِهِمۡ وَطَعَنُواْ فِي دِينِكُمۡ فَقَٰتِلُوٓاْ أَئِمَّةَ ٱلۡكُفۡرِ إِنَّهُمۡ لَآ أَيۡمَٰنَ لَهُمۡ لَعَلَّهُمۡ يَنتَهُونَ﴾

﴿And if after making a promise (for peaceful bilateral relations), they break their oaths, (and restore the state of war,) and taunt you with sarcasm in your Dīn (Religion), then wage (defensive) war against (those) chieftains of disbelief (to eliminate any chance of mischief, violence and revolt)—surely, their oaths are not worth any regard—so that they may desist (from their mischief-mongering).﴾[2]

The very next verse of *sūra al-Tawba* enjoins fighting against those who breached the promise, ostracized Allah's Messenger ﷺ and his Companions ﷺ from Mecca and initiated aggression, invasion and ordeals:

﴿أَلَا تُقَٰتِلُونَ قَوۡمٗا نَّكَثُوٓاْ أَيۡمَٰنَهُمۡ وَهَمُّواْ بِإِخۡرَاجِ ٱلرَّسُولِ وَهُم بَدَءُوكُمۡ أَوَّلَ مَرَّةٍۚ أَتَخۡشَوۡنَهُمۡۚ فَٱللَّهُ أَحَقُّ أَن تَخۡشَوۡهُ إِن كُنتُم مُّؤۡمِنِينَ﴾

﴿Will you not fight a people who broke their oaths (violating the peace treaty and restoring the state of war), and decided to banish the Messenger (ﷺ) whilst the first time it is they who initiated war against you? Do you fear them? But Allah has more right that you should fear Him,

---

[1] •Al-Rāzī, *al-Tafṣīr al-kabīr*, 1:179.

[2] Qur'ān 9:12.

provided you are believers.﴾[1]

Commenting on this verse, Imam al-Wāḥidī (d. 468 AH) said:

وَأَرَادَ بِنكْثِ الْيَمِيْنِ هَهُنَا أَنَّهُمْ نَقَضُوْا عَهْدَ الصُّلْحِ بِالْحُدَيْبِيَةِ، وَأَعَانُوْا بَنِي بَكْرٍ عَلَى خُزَاعَةَ، وَهُمْ كَانُوْا حُلَفَاءَ رَسُوْلِ اللهِ ﷺ ... وَقَالَ جَمَاعَةٌ مِنَ الْمُفَسِّرِيْنَ: وَأَرَادَ أَنَّهُمْ قَاتَلُوْا حُلَفَاءَكَ خُزَاعَةَ، فَبَدَأُوْا بِنَقْضِ الْعَهْدِ ... قَالَ ابْنُ عَبَّاسٍ وَالسُّدِّيُّ وَمُجَاهِدٌ يَعْنِي بَنِي خُزَاعَةَ وَذَلِكَ أَنَّ قُرَيْشاً أَعَانَتْ بَنِي بَكْرٍ عَلَيْهِمْ.

Here breaking oaths connotes that they broke the treaty of Ḥudaybiya and supported Banū Bakr against Banū Khuzāʿa, while the latter were the allies of the Messenger of Allah ﷺ. Some of the exegetes[2] hold that it means they fought against the allies of the Messenger of Allah ﷺ—Banū Khuzāʿa. In this way, they violated the treaty. According to Ibn ʿAbbās, al-Suddī and Mujāhid, it refers to Banū Khuzāʿa, because the people of Quraysh pitted and supported Banū Bakr against them.[3]

Ibn Kathīr has interpreted this verse in the following manner:

اَلَّذِيْنَ هَمُّوْا بِإِخْرَاجِ الرَّسُوْلِ مِنْ مَكَّةَ. ... وَقَوْلُهُ: ﴿وَهُم بَدَءُوكُمْ أَوَّلَ مَرَّةٍ﴾. قِيْلَ: الْمُرَادُ بِذَلِكَ يَوْمُ بَدْرٍ ... وَقِيْلَ الْمُرَادُ نَقْضُهُمُ الْعَهْدَ وَقِتَالُهُمْ مَعَ حُلَفَائِهِمْ بَنِي بَكْرٍ لِخُزَاعَةَ أَحْلَافِ رَسُوْلِ اللهِ ﷺ حَتَّى سَارَ إِلَيْهِمْ رَسُوْلُ اللهِ ﷺ عَامَ الْفَتْحِ.

[Regarding the clause] "*Those who planned to exile the*

[1] Ibid., 9:13.

[2] •Al-Baghawī, *Maʿālim al-tanzīl*, 2:273. •al-Qurṭubī, *al-Jāmiʿ li aḥkām al-Qurʾān*, 8:55. •Ibn Ḥayyān, *al-Baḥr al-muḥīṭ*, 5:17. •Ibn Kathīr, *Tafsīr al-Qurʾān al-ʿAẓīm*; 4:60. •al-Shawkānī, *Fatḥ al-qadīr*, 2:343.

[3] •Al-Wāḥidī, *al-Wasīṭ fī tafsīr al-Qurʾān al-Majīd*, 2:481.

> *Messenger of Allah ﷺ from Mecca...,*" in view of some of the exegetes, it refers to the battle of Badr, though others have interpreted it as the breach of the treaty of peace by the polytheists of Mecca with Muslims and the aiding their allies, Banū Bakr, and fighting against the allies of the Messenger of Allah ﷺ, Banū Khuzāʿa, until the Messenger of Allah ﷺ marched on Mecca in the year of conquest.[1]

With respect to the Abode of Reconciliation, Imam al-Jaṣṣāṣ has quoted a statement of Muhammad b. al-Ḥasan in *Aḥkām al-Qurʾān* (5:83). In it he says that demolishing the places of worship belonging to non-Muslims located in the Muslim majority areas is strictly prohibited, and their security is a constitutional obligation of the Islamic state. Imam Muhammad b. al-Ḥasan has said:

فِيْ أَرْضِ الصُّلْحِ إِذَا صَارَتْ مِصْرًا لِلْمُسْلِمِيْنَ، لَمْ يُهْدَمْ مَا كَانَ فِيْهَا مِنْ بِيْعَةٍ أَوْ كَنِيْسَةٍ أَوْ بَيْتِ نَارٍ.

> When a land under reconciliation becomes a territory of the Muslims, then no church, sanctuary, or Zoroastrian temple that was there before should be demolished.[2]

12.2.3 Preference of Reconciliation and Compromise for the Establishment of Peace

In *sūra al-Anfāl*, the Muslims have been inspired to adopt reconciliation to restore and stabilize peace and security. Allah has ordained:

﴿وَإِن جَنَحُواْ لِلسَّلْمِ فَٱجْنَحْ لَهَا وَتَوَكَّلْ عَلَى ٱللَّهِۚ إِنَّهُۥ هُوَ ٱلسَّمِيعُ ٱلْعَلِيمُ ٦١ وَإِن يُرِيدُوٓاْ أَن يَخْدَعُوكَ فَإِنَّ حَسْبَكَ ٱللَّهُ﴾

> ﴾*And if they (the combatant or hostile disbelievers) incline to peace and reconciliation, you also incline to it and put your trust in Allah. Surely, He alone is All-Hearing, All-Knowing. And if they seek to deceive you, then surely Allah*

[1] •Ibn Kathīr, *Tafsīr al-Qurʾān al-Aẓīm*, 2:340.

[2] •Al-Jaṣṣāṣ, *Aḥkām al-Qurʾān*, 5:83.

is Sufficient for you.﴾[1]

Despite all the peace making and reconciliatory actions, if an opponent breaks the treaty and comes out with open enmity, then the treaty can be terminated on the grounds of equality. The Muslims are instructed to be patient, if the opponent does not act against the treaty. In this regard, Allah Most High has said:

﴿وَإِمَّا تَخَافَنَّ مِن قَوْمٍ خِيَانَةً فَٱنۢبِذْ إِلَيْهِمْ عَلَىٰ سَوَآءٍۚ إِنَّ ٱللَّهَ لَا يُحِبُّ ٱلْخَآئِنِينَ﴾

﴿*And if you apprehend treachery from a people, then throw their promise back to them on the basis of equality. Indeed, Allah does not like the treacherous.*﴾[2]

What could be a better testimony to believe that Islam is a religion of peace, security and reconciliation than the truth to which Allah guided His exalted Messenger ﷺ: to provide asylum to a polytheist if he seeks it? Allah says:

﴿وَإِنْ أَحَدٌ مِّنَ ٱلْمُشْرِكِينَ ٱسْتَجَارَكَ فَأَجِرْهُ حَتَّىٰ يَسْمَعَ كَلَٰمَ ٱللَّهِ ثُمَّ أَبْلِغْهُ مَأْمَنَهُۥۚ ذَٰلِكَ بِأَنَّهُمْ قَوْمٌ لَّا يَعْلَمُونَ﴾

﴿*And if any of the idolaters seeks asylum with you, provide him with protection until he listens to the Words of Allah. Then escort him to his haven. This is because these people do not possess the knowledge (of the truth).*﴾[3]

12.3 THE ABODE OF TREATY (*DĀR AL-ʿAHD*)

Defining the Abode of Treaty, Shaykh Abū Zahra (1897–1974 CE) writes:

وهَذِهِ الْبِلَادُ هِيَ الَّتِي كَانَ بَيْنَهَا وَبَيْنَ الْـمُسْلِمِينَ عَهْدٌ.

---

[1] Qurʾān 8:61–62.

[2] Ibid., 8:58.

[3] Ibid., 9:6.

> (An Abode of Treaty) refers to those states where Muslims and non-Muslims are bound by a treaty.[1]

Shaykh Abū Zahra speaks about the differences between the two states (the Abode of Islam and the Abode of Reconciliation) with mutual harmony and consent about the conditions of agreement. He opines that the conditions of both states may be different, relative to their respective power and might, or weaknesses and limitations.

فَأَهْلُهَا يَعْقِدُوْنَ صُلْحًا مَعَ الْـحَاكِمِ الْإِسْلَامِيِّ عَلَى شُرُوْطٍ تُشْتَرَطُ مِنَ الْفَرِيْقَيْنِ، وَهَذِهِ الشُّرُوْطُ تَخْتَلِفُ قُوَّةً وَضَعْفًا عَلَى حَسْبِ مَا يَتَرَاضَى عَلَيْهِ الطَّرْفَانِ، وَعَلَى حَسْبِ هَذِهِ الْقَبَائِلِ وَتِلْكَ الدَّوْلَةِ قُوَّةً وَضَعْفًا، وعَلَى مِقْدَارِ حَاجَتِهَا إِلَى مُنَاصَرَةِ الدَّوْلَةِ الْإِسْلامِيَّةِ.

> The rulers of this territory (combatants) reconcile with the current Islamic state on the conditions determined by the parties (to the conflict). These conditions may differ according to the mutual agreement based on the control and weakness of the tribes and governments, and it may also differ according to the need of support and assistance of the Islamic state.[2]

An Abode of Treaty can also be defined as:

> All the non-Islamic states that are in a long-term or permanent peace treaty with the Islamic states, whether or not they enter into the condition of immigration or citizenship, are included in an Abode of Treaty.
> It is the firm responsibility of the Islamic state to fulfil all the terms and conditions of the treaty.

12.3.1 Qur'ānic Injunction to Fulfil Agreements with an Abode of Treaty

Allah Most High commanded Muslims to complete the terms of the

---

[1] •Abū Zuhra, *al-ʿAlāqāt al-duwaliyya fī al-Islām*, p. 58.

[2] Ibid., p. 59.

treaties with the tribes of the disbelievers who did not break the treaty and did not rebel against the state of Medina. In *sūra al-Tawba*, Allah Most High said:

﴿إِلَّا ٱلَّذِينَ عَٰهَدتُّم مِّنَ ٱلْمُشْرِكِينَ ثُمَّ لَمْ يَنقُصُوكُمْ شَيْـًٔا وَلَمْ يُظَٰهِرُوا۟ عَلَيْكُمْ أَحَدًا فَأَتِمُّوٓا۟ إِلَيْهِمْ عَهْدَهُمْ إِلَىٰ مُدَّتِهِمْ ۚ إِنَّ ٱللَّهَ يُحِبُّ ٱلْمُتَّقِينَ﴾

﴿Except those idolaters with whom you made an agreement, who then did not show any latitude (in executing the treaty) and who did not support (or reinforce) anyone against you. So fulfil the treaty with them till the end of the term. Surely, Allah loves those who fear Him.﴾[1]

In the commentary on the above verse, Imam al-Wāḥidī has said:

قَوْلُهُ ﴿إِلَّا ٱلَّذِينَ عَٰهَدتُّم مِّنَ ٱلْمُشْرِكِينَ﴾ قَالَ الْمُفَسِّرُوْنَ: اسْتَثْنَى اللهُ طَائِفَةً وَهُمْ بَنُوْ ضَمْرَةَ هِيَ مِنْ كِنَانَةَ أَمَرَ النَّبِيُّ ﷺ بِإِتْمَامِ عُهُوْدِهِمْ، وَكَانَ قَدْ بَقِيَ لَهُمْ مِنْ مُدَّةِ عَهْدِهِمْ تِسْعَةُ أَشْهُرٍ وَقَوْلُهُ: ﴿لَمْ يَنقُصُوكُمْ شَيْـًٔا﴾ أَيْ مِنْ شُرُوْطِ الْعَهْدِ ﴿وَلَمْ يُظَٰهِرُوا۟ عَلَيْكُمْ أَحَدًا﴾ لَمْ يُعَاوِنُوْا عَلَيْكُمْ عَدُوًّا ﴿فَأَتِمُّوٓا۟ إِلَيْهِمْ عَهْدَهُمْ إِلَىٰ مُدَّتِهِمْ﴾ أَيْ إِلَى انْقِضَاءِ مُدَّتِهِمْ.

About the words of Allah Most High: *﴿Except those idolaters with whom you made an agreement﴾*, the interpreters said: "Allah has given an exception to a group named Banū Ḍamra, a tribe of Banū Kināna. The Messenger of Allah ﷺ gave instructions to complete the term of the agreement with them, as there were nine months left till the end the term. Then Allah Most High said: *﴿Who then did not show any latitude﴾* in executing the treaty, which refers to the conditions of the treaty *﴿and who did not support (or reinforce) anyone against you﴾* and they did not help your enemies, *﴿So fulfil the treaty with them till the end of the*

---

[1] Qur'ān 9:4.

term﴾, that is, until the period of agreement ends."[1]

Later, in another verse of *sūra al-Tawba*, Allah Most High ordered the Muslim state to complete the term of the treaty signed with the non-Muslim states. The Qur'ān reveals:

﴿كَيْفَ يَكُونُ لِلْمُشْرِكِينَ عَهْدٌ عِندَ ٱللَّهِ وَعِندَ رَسُولِهِۦٓ إِلَّا ٱلَّذِينَ عَٰهَدتُّمْ عِندَ ٱلْمَسْجِدِ ٱلْحَرَامِ ۖ فَمَا ٱسْتَقَٰمُوا۟ لَكُمْ فَٱسْتَقِيمُوا۟ لَهُمْ ۚ إِنَّ ٱللَّهَ يُحِبُّ ٱلْمُتَّقِينَ﴾

﴿*(How) can there be a promise for the polytheists with Allah and His Messenger (ﷺ) except for those with whom you have made a treaty near the Sacred Mosque (at al-Ḥudaybiya)? So as long as they remain true to (the treaty with) you, remain true to them. Surely, Allah loves those who fear Him.*﴾[2]

This is an ample proof of the veracity of the Dīn [religion] of Islam as a religion of peace and security. The people of Medina were not allowed to use force and take up arms against the people of Mecca until the Meccans themselves breached their promise on the treaty of Ḥudaybiya and attacked and killed the allies of the state of Medina.

A study of the biography of Allah's Messenger ﷺ will unfold that he concluded two kinds of treaties with non-Muslim communities.

1. A Temporary or Long-Term Treaty.
2. A General Treaty.

12.3.1.1 A Temporary or Long-Term Treaty

The best example of a temporary treaty or a long-term treaty was the pact of Ḥudaybiya, which came into effect in the sixth year after migration to Medina, between the state of Medina and the pagans of Mecca. This peace treaty laid aside war for ten years between these two states. In this way, both states were tied to the treaty of peace and the state of war was suspended.

---

[1] •Al-Wāḥidī, *al-Wasīṭ fī tafsīr al-Kitāb al-ʿAzīz*, 2:479.

[2] Qur'ān, 9:7.

1. Imam al-Shāfiʿī (150–204 AH) has described the duration of the temporary or long-term treaty of Ḥudaybiya:

كَانَتِ الْـهُدْنَةُ بَيْنَهُ وَبَيْنَهُمْ عَشْرَ سِنِينَ.

> The treaty of Ḥudaybiya between him (Allah's Messenger ﷺ) and the people of Mecca was for ten years.[1]

Abū Dāwūd has reported in *al-Sunan*

أَنَّهُمُ اصْطَلَحُوا عَلَى وَضْعِ الْـحَرْبِ عَشْرَ سِنِينَ يَأْمَنُ فِيهِنَّ النَّاسُ وَعَلَى أَنَّ بَيْنَنَا عَيْبَةً مَكْفُوفَةً وَأَنَّهُ لَا إِسْلَالَ وَلَا إِغْلَالَ.

> "They (the Quraysh) reconciled that they will observe the truce and honour a ten-year no-war pact. People will reside in peace during that period, and no differences and spite will load the hearts of both the parties, and they will neither backbite each other nor express any malice face to face."[2]

2. Ibn al-Qayyim al-Ḥanbalī, in his book *Zād al-maʿād fī hady Khayr al-ʿIbād* (3:299), has expressed his views about this treaty between the Muslims of Medina and the people of Mecca. He said:

وَجَرَى الصُّلْحُ بَيْنَ الْـمُسْلِمِينَ وأَهْلِ مَكَّةَ علَى وَضْعِ الْـحَرْبِ عَشْرَ سِنِيْنَ.

> The truce between the Muslims and the people of Mecca was to be in effect for ten years.

In the light of this treaty, the state of Medina was considered an Abode of Islam, and the State of Mecca was considered an Abode of Treaty. The state of Medina conformed to the treaty, until the people of Quraysh themselves breached it.

3. Imam ʿAbd al-Malik b. Hishām (d. 218 AH), on the authority of Ibn Isḥāq (d. 150 AH), reported the details of the violation of the treaty of

---

[1] •Al-Shāfiʿī, *al-Umm*, 4:189. •al-Bayhaqī in *al-Sunan al-kubrā*, 9:221.

[2] •Abū Dāwūd, *al-Sunan*, 3:86 §2766

Ḥudaybiya:

فَلَمَّـا تَظَاهَرَتْ بَنُو بَكْرٍ وَقُرَيْشٍ عَلَى خُزَاعَةَ، وَأَصَابُوا مِنْهُمْ مَا أَصَابُوا، وَنَقَضُوا مَا كَانَ بَيْنَهُمْ وبَيْنَ رَسُولِ اللهِ ﷺ مِنَ الْعَهْدِ وَالْـمِيْثَاقِ بِمَا اسْتَحَلُّوا مِنْ خُزَاعَةَ، وَكَانُوْا فِي عَقْدِهِ وَعَهْدِهِ.

> Banū Bakr (allies of the polytheists of Mecca) and Quraysh attacked Khuzāʿa (the allies of the Messenger of Allah ﷺ) and inflicted on them suffering and killings, breaching the treaty which was between them and the Messenger of Allah ﷺ.[1]

4. Imam Abū Jaʿfar b. Jarīr al-Ṭabarī (224–310 AH), in his commentary *Tafsīr Jāmiʿ al-bayān fī tafsīr al-Qurʾān* (10:82), also cited the violation of the treaty of Ḥudaybiya by the polytheists of Mecca. He said: "The people of Mecca did not stick to the treaty and breached it by pitting and supporting Banū Bakr (the allies of Quraysh) against the allies of the Messenger of Allah ﷺ (Banū Khuzāʿa)."
5. Imam Abū Ḥasan ʿAlī b. Aḥmad al-Wāḥidī (d. 468 AH) said about the treachery of the polytheists and their violation of the truce in his commentary on the verse of *sūra al-Tawba*:

﴿وَتَأْبَىٰ قُلُوبُهُمْ﴾ الْوَفَاءَ بِهِ ﴿وَأَكْثَرُهُمْ فَـٰسِقُونَ﴾ غَادِرُوْنَ نَاقِضُوْنَ لِلْعَهْدِ.

> ﴿*Their hearts abstain*﴾ from maintaining the treaty, ﴿*and the majority of them are corrupt*﴾, that is, traitorous and betrayers of the treaty.[2]

12.3.1.2 The General Treaty of Peace and Reconciliation

12.3.1.2.1 The Pact of Medina

Here are some of the articles of the pact of Medina. They highlight

---

[1] •Ibn Hishām, *al-Sīra al-Nabawiyya*, 5:48.

[2] •Al-Wāḥidī, *al-Wasīṭ fī tafsīr al-Kitāb al-ʿAzīz*, 1:454–455.

some distinctive features of the first written constitution of humanity.

1. Weaving unity amongst all the communities of Medina at the state level, Allah's Messenger ﷺ said:

إِنَّهُمْ أُمَّةٌ وَاحِدَةٌ مِنْ دُونِ النَّاسِ.

> "These communities shall be as one unified [constitutional and political] body, distinct from (other) people."[1]

2. Establishing a separate political identity and brotherhood for Muslims, the Prophet ﷺ said:

وَأَنَّ الْـمُؤْمِنِينَ بَعْضُهُمْ مَوَالِي بَعْضٍ دُوْنَ النَّاسِ.

> "As compared to other communities, all believers are brothers to one another."[2]

3. Providing the guarantee of equity, equality, security, justice and support to the Jews who entered into the pact and accepted the writ of the state of Medina, Allah's Messenger ﷺ said:

مَنْ تَبِعَنَا مِنْ يَهُودٍ فَإِنَّ لَهُ النَّصْرَ وَالْأُسْوَةَ غَيْرَ مَظْلُوْمِينَ وَلَا مُتَنَاصِرِيْنَ عَلَيْهِمْ.

> "The Jews who obey our rule shall be given assistance and equality. They shall not be wronged, nor will anyone be supported against them."[3]

4. In the first article of the pact of Medina, Muslims are regarded as the allies of the Jews. In article twenty-eight, the Jews and other non-Muslims are given a separate identity along with religious freedom. The Messenger of Allah ﷺ clarified:

---

1 •Ibn Hishām, *al-Sīra al-Nabawiyya*, 3:32. •Ibn Kathīr , *al-Bidāya wa al-nihāya*, 3:224.

2 •Ibn Hishām, *al-Sīra al-Nabawiyya*, 3:33. •Ibn Kathīr, *al-Bidāya wa al-nihāya*, 3:225.

3 •Ibn Hishām, *al-Sīra al-Nabawiyya*, 3:33. •Ibn Kathīr, *al-Bidāya wa al-nihāya*, 3:225.

إِنَّ يَهُودَ بَنِي عَوْفٍ أُمَّةٌ مَعَ الْمُؤْمِنِينَ، لِلْيَهُودِ دِينُهُمْ وَلِلْمُسْلِمِينَ دِينُهُمْ مَوَالِيهِمْ وَأَنْفُسُهُمْ، إِلَّا مَنْ ظَلَمَ أَوْ أَثِمَ فَإِنَّهُ لَا يُوتِغُ إِلَّا نَفْسَهُ وَأَهْلَ بَيْتِهِ.

"The Jews of Banū ʿAwf (non-Muslim minorities) shall be considered a single political unity with the believers. As for Jews, they have their religion (*dīn*), and as for Muslims, they have their Religion (*Dīn*). And he who commits wrongdoing or sins will not harm anyone else other than himself and his family."[1]

12.3.1.2.2 Developing Political Unity to Stabilize the State and Establish Peace

The Messenger of Allah ﷺ clarified:

لَا فَضْلَ لِعَرَبِيٍّ عَلَى أَعْجَمِيٍّ وَلَا لِعَجَمِيٍّ عَلَى عَرَبِيٍّ وَلَا لِأَحْمَرَ عَلَى أَسْوَدَ وَلَا أَسْوَدَ عَلَى أَحْمَرَ إِلَّا بِالتَّقْوَى

"An Arab has no superiority over a non-Arab, nor does a non-Arab has any superiority over an Arab. A white has no superiority over a black, and a black has no superiority over a white. The standard of superiority is piety (*taqwā*) alone."[2]

Describing the sociopolitical freedom of all groups and the nature of their relations with Muslims, the Messenger of Allah ﷺ said:

وَكُلُّ طَائِفَةٍ تَفْدِي عَانِيَهَا بِالْمَعْرُوفِ وَالْقِسْطِ بَيْنَ الْمُؤْمِنِينَ.

"Every group shall pay the penalty equally and justly and free their prisoners from the custody of Muslims."[3]

---

[1] •Ibn Hishām, *al-Sīra al-Nabawiyya*, 3:34. •Ibn Kathīr, *al-Bidāya wa al-nihāya*, 3:225.

[2] Set forth by •Aḥmad b. Ḥanbal in *al-Musnad*, 5:411 §23536. •al-Ṭabarānī in *al-Muʿjam al-awsaṭ*, 5:86 §4749. •al-Bayhaqī in *Shuʿab al-īmān*, 4:289 §5137.

[3] Cited by •Ibn Hishām in *al-Sīra al-Nabawiyya*, 2:501. •al-Bayhaqī in *al-Sunan al-kubrā*, 8:106 §16147–16148. •Ibn Kathīr in *al-Bidāya wa al-nihāya*, 3:224. •Dr Hamīd Ullāh in *al-Wathāʾiq al-siyasīyya*, p. 41.

12.3.1.2.3 Allah's Messenger ﷺ is the Founder of the Concept of Integration

The Messenger of Allah ﷺ united all the communal groups into a single community despite their religious, linguistic, and racial differences, and became the founder of the concept of integration—the sole means of remedying the socio-civilizational and cultural conflicts and enigmas devouring the modern world.

Today we are engaged in a marathon struggle at global level to win religious, social, cultural and economic freedoms for every class and community of human society. The Messenger of Islam, however, bestowed upon humanity these freedoms, especially the religious freedom—not only for the Jews but all the tribes and ethnic entities more than fourteen centuries ago. He ﷺ proclaimed:

إِنَّ يَهُودَ بَنِي عَوْفٍ أُمَّةٌ مَعَ الْـمُؤْمِنِينَ.

> "The Jews of Banū ʿAwf—non-Muslim citizens—shall be considered a single political unity with the believers."[1]

Thus he knitted them into a single community along with the Muslims.

12.3.1.2.4 The Pact of Najrān

Allah's Messenger ﷺ had guaranteed the security of the lives and properties of the people of Najrān. The instrument of protection was an agreement concluded between the Messenger of Allah ﷺ and the Christians of Abyssinia. This agreement, the pact of Najrān brought about in the Prophet's period, is a concrete and practical evidence of his protection of human rights—especially the right of religious freedom and security. In that regard, the Messenger of Allah ﷺ issued this guarantee:

وَلِنَجْرَانَ وَحَاشِيَتِهَا ذِمَّةُ اللهِ وَذِمَّةُ مُحَمَّدٍ النَّبِيِّ رَسُوْلِ اللهِ، عَلَى دِمَائِهِمْ وَأَنْفُسِهِمْ وَأَرْضِهِمْ وَأَمْوَالِهِمْ وَمِلَّتِهِمْ وَرَهْبَانِيَّتِهِمْ وَأَسَاقِفَتِهِمْ وَغَائِبِهِمْ

[1] •Ibn Hishām, *al-Sīra al-Nabawiyya*, 3:34.

وَشَاهِدِهِمْ وَغَيْرِهِمْ وَبَعْثِهِمْ وَأَمْثِلَتِهِمْ، لَا يُغَيَّرُ مَا كَانُوْا عَلَيْهِ، وَلَا يُغَيَّرُ حَقٌّ مِنْ حُقُوقِهِمْ وَأَمْثِلَتِهِمْ، لَا يُفْتَنُ أُسْقُفٌ مِنْ أُسْقُفِيَّتِهِ، وَلَا رَاهِبٌ مِنْ رَهْبَانِيَّتِهِ، وَلَا وَاقِفٌ مِنْ وَقَافِيَتِهِ، عَلَى مَا تَحْتَ أَيْدِيْهِمْ مِنْ قَلِيْلٍ أَوْ كَثِيْرٍ، وَلَيْسَ عَلَيْهِمْ رَهَقٌ.

"Indeed, Najrān and her allies are under the guarantee of Allah and the guarantee of the Messenger of Allāh ﷺ. They are to be protected in their blood, lives, lands, wealth, religion, monks and priests, those who are present amongst them and those who are absent, their animals and caravans, and their places of worship. They should not be forced to change their religion. There will be no change in their rights and the rights of their places of worship. No priest or monk, and no leader or servant of places of worship shall be removed from their places or possessions, be they plentiful or scarce, and no one should suffer fear or danger."[1]

The Messenger of Allah ﷺ awarded a constitutional and legal status to the security of people in treaty through his covenants, treaties and commandments.[2]

These details clarify that it is not permissible to declare non-Muslim states as Abodes of War when they are under treaties and agreements of peace and reconciliation. On the contrary, they fall into the category of the Abodes of Treaty. Therefore, those who revolt, rebel and murder, and breach the treaty with the Abode of Treaty are declared misguided and evicted from the pale of Islam. The Prophet ﷺ said: "They are not from me." He removed them from his *Umma*. Abū Hurayra ﷺ related that Allah's Messenger ﷺ warned against the masterminds and instigators of turmoil, saying:

---

[1] Cited by •Ibn Saʿd in *al-Ṭabaqāt al-kubrā*, 1:288, 358. •Abū Yūsuf in *al-Kharāj*, 78. •Abū ʿUbayd al-Qāsim b. Sallām in *Kitāb al-amwāl*, p. 244–245 §503. •Ibn Zanjawayh in *Kitāb al-amwāl*, pp. 449–450 §732. •al-Balādhurī in *Futūḥ al-buldān*, p. 90.

[2] Cited by •Ibn Zanjaways in *Kitāb al-amwāl*, pp. 450–451 §732.

مَنْ خَرَجَ مِنَ الطَّاعَةِ وَفَارَقَ الْجَمَاعَةَ فَمَاتَ، مَاتَ مِيتَةً جَاهِلِيَّةً، وَمَنْ قَاتَلَ تَحْتَ رَايَةٍ عِمِّيَّةٍ يَغْضَبُ لِعَصَبَةٍ أَوْ يَدْعُوْ إِلَى عَصَبَةٍ أَوْ يَنْصُرُ عَصَبَةً فَقُتِلَ فَقِتْلَةٌ جَاهِلِيَّةٌ، وَمَنْ خَرَجَ عَلَى أُمَّتِي يَضْرِبُ بَرَّهَا وَفَاجِرَهَا وَلَا يَتَحَاشَى مِنْ مُؤْمِنِهَا وَلَا يَفِي لِذِي عَهْدٍ عَهْدَهُ فَلَيْسَ مِنِّي وَلَسْتُ مِنْهُ.

> "Whoever rebels against the writ of the Muslim state [and challenges its authority] and separates himself from the community [*jamāʿa*] and then dies, he dies the death of one in a state of *jāhilīyya* [pre-Islamic time of ignorance]. And whoever fights under a blind banner, becomes angry for the sake of ignorant bigotry, calls to ignorant bigotry and gives support to blind bigotry and is then killed, his death is one of *jāhilīyya*. And whoever secedes from my nation [and rebels against the state, raising legions and troops], killing its righteous and sinful members and feels no compunction [in killing] its believers and does not fulfil the oath of the one from whom an oath is taken, then he is not from me and I am not from him."[1]

The hadith of the Messenger of Allah ﷺ clearly mentions that the one who violently rebels against an Abode of Treaty does not belong to the *Umma*.

12.4 The Abode of Peace (*Dār al-Amn*)

Against the backdrop of the modern era, we can describe an Abode of Peace in the following way:

> The Abode of Peace includes those non-Islamic states that never behaved aggressively or engage in combat or military actions against the Muslim state. They are neither enemies, nor has any treaty of peace been concluded with them, nor

[1] Set forth by •Muslim in *al-Ṣaḥīḥ*: *Kitāb al-imāra* [The Book of Leadership], chapter: "The Obligation to Stick to the Main Body of the Muslims in the Time of Trials," 3:1476–1477 §1848. •Aḥmad b. Ḥanbal in *al-Musnad*, 2:296, 488. •al-Nasāʾī in *al-Sunan*: *Kitāb taḥrīm al-dam* [The Book on the Prohibition of Bloodshed], 7:123 §4114.

did any such situation arise to work out any agreement—such are the countries that fall into the category of Abode of Peace.

It must be borne in mind that an Abode of War is the state engaged in war with another state. The rest of the states are Abodes of Treaty and Abodes of Peace through the treaty of peace of the United Nations; they are not Abodes of War. In modern times, by virtue of the United Nations, all countries, including the United States of America, Great Britain, and other non-Muslim countries, are the Abodes of Treaty and the Abodes of Peace.

12.4.1 The Hanafī Stance on the Abode of Islam

The Ḥanafī jurists have figuratively regarded all those non-Islamic combating or non-combating states as the Abodes of Islam where the Muslims are allowed to openly practise the signs and rituals of Islam. In their view, any non-Muslim country becomes an Abode of Islam when Islamic rules are openly practised.

In the view of Imam Abū Ḥanīfa, an Abode of Islam does not mean the territory where Muslims dwell; nor does an Abode of Disbelief indicate a country where disbelievers abide. In view of the Hanafīs, the annexation of *dār* (abode) with *Islām* and *kufr* does not connote Islam or *kufr*; it rather refers to peace and fear. The rules will be applied on the basis of peace and fear and will not be premised on Islam and *kufr*. In this connection, see once again the statement of Imam al-Kāsānī that has appeared in *Badāʾiʿ al-ṣanāʾiʿ* already quoted in the preceding pages:

وَجْهُ قَوْلِ أَبِي حَنِيفَةَ أَنَّ الْـمَقْصُودَ مِنْ إِضَافَةِ الدَّارِ إِلَى الْإِسْلَامِ وَالْكُفْرِ
لَيْسَ هُوَ عَيْنَ الْإِسْلَامِ وَالْكُفْرِ، وَإِنَّمَا الْـمَقْصُودُ هُوَ الْأَمْنُ وَالْـخَوْفُ.

The rationale of the statement of Imam Abū Ḥanīfa's is that the annexation of '*dār*' (abode) with *Islām* and *kufr* is not because of Islam or *kufr per se*. Its implied intent is peace and fear. The Abode of Islam denotes an Abode of Peace and the Abode of Disbelief signifies an Abode of Terror.[1]

According to the great Imam Abū Ḥanīfa, the Abode of Islam and

---

[1] •Al-Kāsānī, *Badāʾiʿ al-ṣanāʾiʿ*, 7:131.

the Abode of Disbelief do not imply the religion Islam and its denial i.e., *kufr*. They rather connote that any state where there is security for Muslims is regarded as an Abode of Islam, and any state where there is no guarantee of peace and protection for the Muslims or non-Muslims is deemed an Abode of Disbelief. They are not distinguished on the basis of religion. Instead, they are based on peace, security, protection and freedom that have been provided to or withdrawn from them.

The great Imam said:

وَالْأَحْكَامُ مَبْنِيَّةٌ عَلَى الْأَمَانِ وَالْخَوْفِ لَا عَلَى الْإِسْلَامِ وَالْكُفْرِ.

> The rulings (concerning the classification of the abodes) are based on security and fear—not Islam and *kufr* (disbelief).[1]

Taking into account the situations of security and fear is of greater concern. So long as the Muslims are not in need of seeking security, and peace and security already provided endures, the land does not become *dār al-kufr*.

Here are some expositions propounded by the Ḥanafī jurists on this subject.

1. Imam ʿAlāʾ al-Dīn al-Kāsānī al-Ḥanafī (d. 587 AH) declares a non-Muslim country an Abode of Islam on the basis of the manifestation of Islamic rules through implementation (freedom to practise the teachings and rituals of Islam). He writes:

فَنَقُولُ لَا خِلَافَ بَيْنَ أَصْحَابِنَا فِي أَنَّ دَارَ الْكُفْرِ تَصِيرُ دَارَ إِسْلَامٍ بِظُهُورِ أَحْكَامِ الإِسْلَامِ فِيْهَا.

> We (unanimously) proclaim—and there is no difference on this matter among us—that any non-Muslim state becomes an Abode of Islam when Islamic rules and injunctions appear (as freely practised).[2]

2. ʿAlāʾ al-Dīn al-Ḥaṣkafī (d. 1088 AH) has given his viewpoint in *al-Durr al-mukhtār fī sharḥ tanwīr al-abṣār* (4:175):

---

[1] Ibid.

[2] Ibid.

دَارُ الْـحَرْبِ تَصِيْرُ دَارَ الْإِسْلَامِ بِإِجْرَاءِ أَحْكَامِ أَهْلِ الْإِسْلَامِ فِيهَا كَجُمُعَةٍ وَعِيْدٍ، وإِنْ بَقِيَ فِيهَا كَافِرٌ أَصْلِيٌّ وَإِنْ لَـمْ تَتَّصِلْ بِدَارِ الْإِسْلَامِ.

If Islamic pillars enter into practice, like offering the Friday ritual prayer and the ʿīd ritual prayers in any non-Muslim Abode of War, that state becomes an Abode of Islam, though the majority of residents may be non-Muslims and it may not border an Islamic state.

3. The same definition is given by ʿAbd al-Raḥmān b. Shaykh Muhammad b. Sulaymān, generally known as Shaykh Zādah (d. 1078 AH), in *Majmaʿ al-anhur fī sharḥ Multaqā al-abhur* (2:455).

4. In the backdrop of the current scenario, Shaykh Abū Zahra has also mentioned this point of view in his *al-ʿAlāqāt al-duwaliyya fī al-Islām*. According to him, in modern times the whole world has united under one international system. Practising this particular universal law is, in fact, congruous with the Islamic principle of the fulfillment of a treaty. Therefore, from the beginning, all non-Islamic member countries of the United Nations will not be included among the Abodes of War. They will rather fall into the category of the Abode of Treaty, except for the state that is directly at war with a Muslim country. He writes:

إِنَّهُ يَجِبُ أَنْ يُلَاحَظَ أَنَّ الْعَالِـمَ الْآنَ تَجْمَعُهُ مُنَظَّمَةٌ وَاحِدَةٌ قَدِ الْتَزَمَ كُلُّ أَعْضَائِهَا بِقَانُونِهَا وَنَظْمِهَا، وَحُكْمِ الْإِسْلَامِ فِي هَذِهِ: أَنَّهُ يَجِبُ الْوَفَاءُ بِكُلِّ الْعُهُودِ وَالْاِلْتِزَامَاتِ الَّتِي تَلْتَزِمُهَا الدُّوَلُ الْإِسْلَامِيَّةُ عَمَلًا بِقَانُونِ الْوَفَاءِ بِالْعَهْدِ الَّذِي قَرَّرَهُ الْقُرْآنُ الْكَرِيْمُ، وَعَلَى ذَلِكَ لَا تُعَدُّ دِيَارُ الْـمُخَالِفِينَ الَّتِي تَنْتَمِي لِـهَذِهِ الْـمُؤَسَّسَةِ الْعَالَـمِيَّةِ دَارَ حَرْبٍ ابْتِدَاءً، بَلْ تُعْتَبَرُ دَارَ عَهْدٍ.

It is necessary to be aware of the fact that the whole world has been collected under a global system and all its members are under obligation to uphold its rule of law and observe its discipline in letter and spirit. The dictate

> of Islam under this collective and unified system is that the covenants, agreements and restrictions to which the Islamic countries have committed themselves must be fulfilled. The implementation and execution of this law amounts to the fulfilment of the covenant that the Qur'ān has ordained us to implement, for which they have bound themselves with treaties and restrictions. Under these conditions, all non-Muslim countries that are members of the UN cannot be included among the Abodes of War. They rather fall into the category of the Abode of Treaty.[1]

He has expressed this opinion in the light of the following verse of the Holy Qur'ān:

﴿إِلَّا ٱلَّذِينَ عَـٰهَدتُّم مِّنَ ٱلْمُشْرِكِينَ ثُمَّ لَمْ يَنقُصُوكُمْ شَيْـًٔا وَلَمْ يُظَـٰهِرُوا۟ عَلَيْكُمْ أَحَدًا فَأَتِمُّوٓا۟ إِلَيْهِمْ عَهْدَهُمْ إِلَىٰ مُدَّتِهِمْ ۚ إِنَّ ٱللَّهَ يُحِبُّ ٱلْمُتَّقِينَ﴾

﴿Except those idolaters with whom you made an agreement, who then did not show any latitude (in executing the treaty) and who did not support (or reinforce) anyone against you. So fulfil the treaty with them till the end of the term. Surely, Allah loves those who fear Him.﴾[2]

Today, we have so deeply mired ourselves into ignorance that we have deformed our basic Islamic beliefs and are unable to recognize what the Qur'ān has ordered us to practise. We miserably lack Islamic knowledge. The great jurists do not feel any hesitation in calling a non-Muslim state an Abode of Islam on very insignificant conditions. Opposite to them are a small number of terrorists who, owing to a dearth of wisdom, intellect and insight into Islamic law, issue verdicts allowing bloodshed and terrorism in the same countries. If the Western countries like the US, Great Britain, France and others are declared Abodes of War instead of Abodes of Treaty or Abodes of Peace, it will become impermissible for the Muslims to live there anymore, and,

---

[1] •Abū Zuhra, *al-ʿAlāqāt al-duwaliyya fī al-Islām*, p. 60.

[2] Qur'ān 9:4.

under the Islamic Law (Shariah), they will have to migrate from these countries.

12.5 THE ABODE OF WAR (*DĀR AL-ḤARB*)

It is an exceptional case for a non-Muslim state to be an Abode of War. We have already explained that an Abode of War is the country that is at war with a Muslim state. Apart from that, all other countries are Abodes of Peace and Abodes of Treaty, through their international treaty of peace with the United Nations.

Describing the definition of the Abode of War by the Shāfiʿī school of thought, Saʿdī Abū Ḥabīb writes:

دَارُ الْحَرْبِ عِنْدَ الشَّافِعِيَّةِ: بِلَادُ الْكُفَّارِ الَّذِينَ لَا صُلْحَ لَهُمْ مَعَ الْمُسْلِمِينَ.

> The Abode of War, according to the Shāfiʿī jurists, refers to the non-Muslim countries that are not at peace with the Muslim (countries, but, are at war with them).[1]

12.5.1 THE ISLAMIC RULING FOR THE NON-COMBATANTS

Islam does not allow the killing of the non-combatants even during war. It condemns the unjust killings under all circumstances.

Imam Muslim has reported on the authority of Abū Hurayra ﷺ that, granting general asylum to the non-combatants, Allah's Messenger ﷺ said on the day of the conquest of Mecca:

مَنْ دَخَلَ دَارَ أَبِي سُفْيَانَ فَهُوَ آمِنٌ، وَمَنْ أَلْقَى السِّلَاحَ فَهُوَ آمِنٌ، وَمَنْ أَغْلَقَ بَابَهُ فَهُوَ آمِنٌ.

> "He who enters the house of Abū Sufyān is safe; he who lays down his weapon is safe; and he who closes the doors of his house is also safe."[2]

---

[1] •Saʿdī Abū Ḥabīb, *al-Qāmūs al-fiqhī*, p. 84.

[2] Set forth by •Muslim in *al-Ṣaḥīḥ*, 3:1407 §1780. •Abū Dāwūd in *al-Sunan*, 3:162 §3021. •al-Bazzār in *al-Musnad*, 4:122 §1292.

12.5.2 The Qur'ānic Injunction on Excellent Morality with non-Combatants

Great emphasis has been laid in the Qur'ān and hadith on showing character towards non-combatants and treating them with piety and kindness. Allah has ordained in the Qur'ān:

﴿لَّا يَنْهَىٰكُمُ ٱللَّهُ عَنِ ٱلَّذِينَ لَمْ يُقَٰتِلُوكُمْ فِى ٱلدِّينِ وَلَمْ يُخْرِجُوكُم مِّن دِيَٰرِكُمْ أَن تَبَرُّوهُمْ وَتُقْسِطُوٓاْ إِلَيْهِمْ ۚ إِنَّ ٱللَّهَ يُحِبُّ ٱلْمُقْسِطِينَ ٨ إِنَّمَا يَنْهَىٰكُمُ ٱللَّهُ عَنِ ٱلَّذِينَ قَٰتَلُوكُمْ فِى ٱلدِّينِ وَأَخْرَجُوكُم مِّن دِيَٰرِكُمْ وَظَٰهَرُواْ عَلَىٰٓ إِخْرَاجِكُمْ أَن تَوَلَّوْهُمْ ۚ وَمَن يَتَوَلَّهُمْ فَأُوْلَٰٓئِكَ هُمُ ٱلظَّٰلِمُونَ﴾

﴾Allah does not forbid you to be good to them and treat them with equity and justice who did not fight against you on (the question of) Dīn (Religion), nor did they drive you out of your homes (i.e., homeland). Surely, Allah likes those who conduct themselves with equity and justice. Allah only forbids you to befriend those who fought against you on (account of) the Dīn (Religion) and drove you out of your homes (i.e., homeland) and aided (your enemies) in expelling you. And whoever makes friends with them, it is they who are the wrongdoers.﴿[1]

1. Ibn al-Jawzī (510–579 AH) has written in his commentary on the said verse:

قَالَ الْمُفَسِّرُونَ: هَذِهِ الآيَةُ رُخْصَةٌ فِي صِلَةِ الَّذِينَ لَمْ يَنْصِبُوا الْحَرْبَ لِلْمُسْلِمِينَ وَجَوَازُ بِرِّهِمْ وَإِنْ كَانَتِ الْمُوَالَاةُ مُنْقَطِعَةً مِنْهُمْ.

According to the exegetes, this holy verse of the Qur'ān concedes us leave, excuse and justification to be gentle and nice towards those who are not involved in fighting against

[1] Qur'ān 60:8–9.

the Muslims, even though they have already breached the alliance.[1]

2. In his commentary on this verse, Imam al-Qurṭubī (284–380 AH) writes:

هَذِهِ الآيَةُ رُخْصَةٌ مِنَ اللهِ تَعَالَى فِي صِلَةِ الَّذِينَ لَمْ يُعَادُوا الْمُؤْمِنِيْنَ وَلَمْ يُقَاتِلُوهُمْ.

This verse provides a concession to treat with excellence those who neither feel hostility nor wage combat against the Muslims.[2]

3. Ibn Kathīr writes while interpreting this verse:

أَيْ لَا يَنْهَاكُمْ عَنِ الإِحْسَانِ إِلَى الْكَفَرَةِ الَّذِيْنَ لَا يُقَاتِلُونَكُمْ فِي الدِّينِ وَلَمْ يُظَاهِرُوا أَيْ يُعَاوِنُوا عَلَى إِخْرَاجِكُمْ كَالنِّسَاءِ وَالضَّعَفَةِ مِنْهُمْ.

Allah does not prohibit you from being good to those non-Muslims who do not fight against you because of your *Dīn* (Religion), nor do they help others in expelling your women and elderly persons from their country.[3]

12.5.3 The Affectionate Behaviour of Medina towards non-Combatants

To facilitate a better understanding of this subject, it is worthwhile to narrate an episode from the holy life of the exalted Messenger of Allah ﷺ. In the days when the Messenger of Allah ﷺ was the head of the state in Medina, Mecca was an Abode of Treaty. Through his munificence, largesse, mercy and benevolence, the Messenger of Allah ﷺ turned the callous breasts of the Meccans into loving hearts.

1. The famous historian al-Yaʿqūbī (d. 274 AH) writes:

---

[1] •Ibn al-Jawzī, *Zād al-masīr*, 8:237.

[2] •Al-Qurṭubī, *al-Jāmiʿ li aḥkām al-Qurʾān*, 18:59.

[3] •Ibn Kathīr, *Tafsīr al-Qurʾān al-Aẓīm*, 4:350.

فَبَعَثَ إِلَيْهِمْ بِشَعِيْرِ ذَهَبٍ وَقِيلَ نَوَى ذَهَبٍ مَعَ عَمْرِو بْنِ أُمَيَّةَ الضَّمْرِيِّ وَأَمَرَهُ أَنْ يَدْفَعَهُ إِلَى أَبِي سُفْيَانَ بْنِ حَرْبٍ وَصَفْوَانَ بْنِ أُمَيَّةَ بْنِ خَلْفٍ وَسَهْلِ بْنِ عَمْرٍو وَيُفَرِّقُهُ ثَلَاثًا ثَلَاثًا. فَامْتَنَعَ صَفْوَانُ بْنُ أُمَيَّةَ وَسَهْلُ بْنُ عَمْرٍو مِنْ أَخْذِهِ، وَأَخَذَهُ أَبُو سُفْيَانَ كُلَّهُ وَفَرَّقَهُ عَلَى فُقَرَاءِ قُرَيْشٍ.

> The Prophet ﷺ sent them (the disbelievers of Mecca) lumps (pieces) of gold through ʿAmr b. Umayya al-Ḍamrī and ordered him to hand all of the wealth to Abū Sufyān b. Ḥarb, Ṣafwān b. Umayya b. Khalf and Sahl b. ʿAmr, giving a one-third share to each. When Ṣafwān b. Umayya and Sahl b. ʿAmr refused to accept it, Abū Sufyān distributed the whole wealth amongst the indigent of the Quraysh.[1]

2. The eminent authority, Imam Muhammad b. Aḥmad al-Sarakhsī, has narrated this event in these words:

بَعَثَ رَسُولُ اللهِ ﷺ خَمْسَ مِائَةِ دِينَارٍ إِلَى مَكَّةَ حِينَ قُحِطُوا، وَأَمَرَ بِدَفْعِ ذَلِكَ إِلَى أَبِي سُفْيَانَ بْنِ حَرْبٍ وَصَفْوَانَ بْنِ أُمَيَّةَ؛ لِيُفَرِّقَا عَلَى فُقَرَاءِ أَهْلِ مَكَّةَ. فَقَبِلَ ذَلِكَ أَبُو سُفْيَانَ، وَأَبَى صَفْوَانُ.

> When Mecca was struck by drought, the Messenger of Allah sent 500 dinars to Mecca with the instruction to hand this wealth to Abū Sufyān b. Ḥarb and Ṣafwān b. Umayya so that they both distribute it amongst the destitute of Mecca. Abū Sufyān accepted it while Ṣafwān refused."[2]

Such was the conduct of Allah's Messenger ﷺ, the first head of the first Islamic state, towards his sworn enemies. He helped the peaceful civilian population of non-Muslims financially and supported them at the time of drought.

---

[1] •Al-Yaʿqūbī, *al-Tārīkh*, 2:56.

[2] •Al-Sarakhsī, *Sharḥ Kitāb al-siyar al-kabīr*, 1:70.

12.5.4 The Stand of the Imams and Hadith-Scholars on non-Combatants

1. In his *Aḥkām ahl al-dhimma* (1:165), Ibn al-Qayyim al-Ḥanbalī said about the conduct of the Prophet's Companions ﷺ towards non-combatants:

فَإِنَّ أَصْحَابَ النَّبِيِّ ﷺ لَمْ يَقْتُلُوْهُمْ حِيْنَ فَتَحُوا الْبِلَادَ، وَلِأَنَّهُمْ لَا يُقَاتِلُونَ، فَاشْبَهُوا الشُّيُوخَ وَالرُّهْبَانَ.

> Indeed, when the Prophet's Companions ﷺ conquered the various lands, they did not kill them [farmers and merchants], because they did not fight [against them], and so in that sense they [the civilians] resembled the elderly and the religious leaders.

2. Non-Muslim employees working in the households of non-Muslim employers in the conquered areas are not to be killed, and no kind of tax can be imposed upon them. This is the decree of the Shariah with regard to them. Ibn al-Qayyim stated the same thing, quoting ʿAbd Allāh b. ʿUmar ﷺ:

إِنَّ الْعَبْدَ مَحْقُونُ الدَّمِ فَأَشْبَهَ النِّسَاءَ وَالصِّبْيَانَ.

> The blood of a servant is inviolable, and is thereby similar to that of women and children.[1]

3. Imam al-Awzāʿī (88–157 AH) took a similar view about the non-combatants:

لَا يُقْتَلُ الْحَرَّاثُ إِذَا عُلِمَ أَنَّهُ لَيْسَ مِنَ الْمُقَاتِلَةِ.

> Farmers are not to be killed [during war] if it is known that they are not from the combatants.[2]

4. In in *al-Mughnī fī fiqh al-Imām Aḥmad b. Ḥanbal al-Shaybānī*,

---

[1] •Ibn al-Qayyim, *Aḥkām ahl al-dhimma*, 1:172–173.

[2] •Ibn Qudāma, *al-Mughnī*, 9:251. •Ibn al-Qayyim, *Aḥkām ahl al-dhimma*, 1:165.

Ibn Qudāma al-Maqdisī (d. 620 AH) wrote about the non-combatant farmers:

فَأَمَّا الْفَلَّاحُ الَّذِي لَا يُقَاتِلُ فَيَنْبَغِي أَنْ لَا يُقْتَلَ، لِمَا رُوِيَ عَنْ عُمَرَ بْنِ الْخَطَّابِ ﷺ أَنَّهُ قَالَ: اتَّقُوا اللهَ فِي الْفَلَّاحِينَ، الَّذِينَ لَا يَنْصَبُونَ لَكُمْ فِي الْحَرْبِ.

> As for the farmer who is a non-combatant, he should not be killed, because it was narrated from ʿUmar b. al-Khaṭṭāb ﷺ that he said, "Fear Allah regarding the farmers who do not wage war against you."[1]

When two countries are in a state of war, it is forbidden in Islam to slay peaceful and non-combatant civilians, let alone commit mass killings in peacetime while the victims are non-combatant peaceful citizens.

The teachings of the Qur'ān, hadith, and the practices and statements of the Companions ﷺ and the expositions and exegeses of the jurists and hadith scholars all vividly reveal that Islamic countries are permitted to fight only those people and forces in the Abode of War that are directly taking part in hostilities. According to Islamic teachings, non-combatants and civilians must remain safe and secure during war. At the present time, under the United Nations, all countries, including the United States of America and Great Britain, and even their citizens are regarded as Abodes of Treaty, Abodes of Peace and Abodes of Islam. However, if someone is directly at war with them, that is a separate case.

12.5.5 Why Medina was Chosen for Migration

Equipped with unsheathed swords, the disbelievers of Mecca sieged the Prophet's inviolable abode. Under these conditions, the place selected for emigration was Yathrib, which was also an ancient abode of the People of the Book. At the first and the second allegiance at ʿUqba, dozens of people received the opportunity to be in the blessed

---

[1] •Ibn Qudāma al-Maqdisī, *al-Mughnī*, 9:251. •al-Bayhaqī in *al-Sunan al-kubrā*, 9:91 §1738.

company of the Messenger of Allah. They were also the People of the Book belonging to the members of the ʿAws and Khazraj tribes of Medina.

The question is, what was the reason of their stimulation for such a quick acceptance of Islam and inclination towards faith in such a brief span of time? In fact, they had already read in the Bible and the Torah about the raising of the Final Messenger of Allah in their scripture. They were aware of the signs of his appearance. The seed of faith had already been planted in their hearts when they beheld him at Minā, and were bestowed the cognizance of the esteemed status and the great dignity of the Holy Prophet. They then worked for the mission of Islam in Medina as the representatives and supporters of Islam even though they had not witnessed the splitting of the moon like the disbelievers of Mecca did, nor did they witness the journey of Ascension and other great miracles. The people of the Book were blessed with a mindset compatible with Islam—the blessing that had not touched the Meccan disbelievers and polytheists. So the People of the Book started paving the way for the Messenger's arrival in Medina well before his migration. Moreover, those who became the "supporters" (*anṣār*) of the Meccan Companions too were formerly the People of the Book. It was as though they had the instinct and predilection of accepting Islam much more than others. For the same reason, the prospects of the acceptance of the prophethood of the Holy Prophet ﷺ too were brighter in Medina as compared to Mecca under the rule of oppressive and tyrant disbelievers. That was the underlying reason why Medina was selected as an abode of emigration.

12.5.6 The Difference of Pace and Number Between the Meccan and Medinan People in Accepting Islam

In Mecca, the Prophet spent forty years before and thirteen years after the commissioning of his prophethood. In a long span of fifty-three years, an over three hundred people embraced faith, besides the advent of several mighty miracles of the Prophet during this period. Contrarily, about 10,000 Muslims of Medina accompanied the Holy Prophet in the 8th year of migration to conquer Mecca. This manifests how quickly and in what great numbers the people in Medina professed faith as compared to the idolaters and disbelievers of Mecca. The basic reason for this wide difference was that the Meccans were totally opposed to the concept of faith in the Oneness of God. Originally, they also denied prophethood, messengership, revelation, and the divine teachings.

The People of the Book, however, were at an advantage because they were well acquainted with all these concepts and teachings and were inclined to faith. The only stumbling block in the way of faith for them was that the Prophet was raised in Banī Ismāʿīl instead of Banī Israel, even though they had settled in the city of date-palms, Medina, centuries before, only for the reason that, according to their Scripture, the Final Messenger of Allah ﷺ was to appear there. Many of their generations had passed, waiting for the arrival of the Holy Prophet. They were not originally opposed to faith; rather, they were waiting for it. Nevertheless, most of them felt jealous, became malicious, and deviated to disbelief when they saw that the Final Messenger whom they were waiting for a long time hailed from Banī Ismāʿīl, yet several of those with a sound temperament became the believers.

12.6 The Prophet ﷺ Integrated the Jews and the Muslims into a Collective Unity Through the Pact of Medina

The pact of Medina, which the Holy Prophet ﷺ concluded with the non-Muslims after migrating to Medina, is another historical step towards peace making. In drawing up this constitution, the People of the Book were mutual partners with the Muslims. The text of the pact of Medina has been narrated by all the imams who wrote on the Prophet's biography and history. Many of them have reported the text fully or partially. The document has reached us through Imam Ibn Shihāb al-Zuhrī, who reported through the following authorities:

Imam Ibn Isḥāq in *al-Sīra*, Imam Abū ʿUbayd al-Qāsim b. Sallām and Imam Ḥumayd b. Zanjawayh in *Kitāb al-Amwāl*, Ibn Hishām in *al-Sīra*, al-Suhaylī in *al-Rawḍ al-Unf*, Ibn Sayyid al-Nās in *ʿAyūn al-Athar*, Ḥāfiẓ Ibn Kathīr in *al-Bidāya wa al-Nihāya*, al-Nawayrī in *al-Nihāya*, Ibn al-Athīr al-Jazarī in *al-Nihāya*, Imam Manṣūr b.

al-Ḥasan in *Nathar al-Durar*, al-Sāghānī in *al-ʿAbāb*, Ibn Taymiya in *al-Ṣārim al-Maslūl*, Ibn al-Qayyim in *Aḥkām ahl al-Dhimma*, Imam al-Bayhaqī in *al-Sunan al-Kubrā*, Imam al-Zarqānī in *Sharḥ al-Mawāhib al-Laduniyya*, and others.

Here are the opening words of the pact of Medina:

هَذَا كِتَابُ رَسُوْلِ اللهِ ﷺ بَيْنَ الْـمُؤْمِنِيْنَ وَأَهْلِ يَثْرِبَ وَمُوَادَعَتِهِ يَهُوْدَهَا، مَقْدَمَهُ الْـمَدِيْنَةَ ... أَنَّ رَسُوْلَ اللهِ ﷺ كَتَبَ بِهَذَا الْكِتَابِ: هَذَا كِتَابٌ مِنْ مُحَمَّدٍ النَّبِيِّ رَسُوْلِ اللهِ ﷺ، بَيْنَ الْـمُؤْمِنِيْنَ وَالْـمُسْلِمِيْنَ مِنْ قُرَيْشٍ وَأَهْلِ يَثْرِبَ، وَمَنْ تَبِعَهُمْ فَلَحِقَ بِهِمْ، فَحَلَّ مَعَهُمْ، وَجَاهَدَ مَعَهُمْ، إِنَّهُمْ أُمَّةٌ وَاحِدَةٌ مِنْ دُوْنِ النَّاسِ.

> "This is a constitutional agreement after the arrival of the Messenger of Allah to Medina between the believers who migrated from Mecca and the people of Yathrib, and the Jews have been made a party to this reconciliatory agreement. . . This is a written constitution given by the Messenger and the Prophet of Allah. This shall be governing the relations between the Muslims of Quraysh, the people of Yathrib (the citizens of Medina) and those who shall follow them and become attached to them (politically) and fight along with them to defend the state of Medina. The aforementioned communities shall formulate one Constitutional Unity *i.e.*, *Umma* as distinct from (other) people."[1]

Imam Ibn Isḥāq has also reported the opening text in these words:

كَتَبَ رَسُوْلُ اللهِ ﷺ كِتَاباً بَيْنَ الْـمُهَاجِرِيْنَ وَالْأَنْصَارِ، وَادَعَ فِيْهِ يَهُوْدَ وَعَاهَدَهُمْ، وَأَقَرَّهُمْ عَلَى دِيْنِهِمْ وَأَمْوَالِـهِمْ، وَشَرَطَ لَـهُمْ، وَاشْتَرَطَ عَلَيْهِمْ.

---

[1] Cited by •Ḥumayd b. Zanjawayh in *Kitāb al-Amwāl*, 1:393. •Abū ʿUbayd al-Qāsim b. Sallām in *Kitāb al-Amwāl*, 1:393. •Ibn Hishām in *al-Sīra al-Nabawiyya*, 2:497. •Ibn Kathīr in *al-Bidāya wa al-nihāya*, 3:224.

بِسْمِ اللهِ الرَّحْمَنِ الرَّحِيْمِ، هَذَا كِتَابٌ مِنْ مُحَمَّدٍ النَّبِيِّ بَيْنَ الْـمُؤْمِنِيْنَ وِالْـمُسْلِمِيْنَ مِنْ قُرَيْشٍ وَيَثْرِبَ، وَمَنْ تَبِعَهُمْ فَلَحِقَ بِهِمْ وَجَاهَدَ مَعَهُمْ. إِنَّهُمْ أُمَّةٌ وَاحِدَةٌ مِنْ دُوْنِ النَّاسِ.

"The Messenger of Allah inscribed an agreement between the emigrants and the supporters and made the Jews a party to this reconciliatory agreement and maintained their religious and economic freedom, accepting some of their conditions and making them accept certain conditions.

In the name of Allah, Most Compassionate Ever-Merciful. This is a written constitution given by the Prophet Muhammad. It is between the Muslims of Quraysh, the people of Yathrib (the citizens of Medina) and those who shall follow them (politically) and fight along with them (to defend the state of Medina). They all are one Constitutional Community *i.e., Umma* as distinct from (other) people."[1]

From the beginning of this constitution, the Messenger of Allah made the Jews a party to this agreement between the Muslims of Quraysh and the Muslims of Yathrib. They became the allies of the Muslims. They had signed the pact to defend Medina in the event of war along with the Muslims. The Prophet constituted one community or one nation comprising the emigrants, the supporters of Medina and the Jews, declaring:

إِنَّهُمْ أُمَّةٌ وَاحِدَةٌ مِنْ دُوْنِ النَّاسِ.

"They are all one *Umma* distinct from (other) people."

He then enumerated all the tribes who were a party to this agreement and declared their freedom to practise their own religion, customs and traditions. In this connection, the next part of the Holy Prophet's document is noticeable:

---

[1] Cited by •Ibn Hishām in *al-Sīra al-Nabawiyya*, 2:497. •al-Bayhaqī in *al-Sunan al-kubrā*, 8:106. •Ibn Kathīr in *al-Bidāya wa al-nihāya*, 3:224.

١. اَلْـمُهَاجِرُونَ مِنْ قُرَيْشٍ عَلَى رِبَاعَتِهِمْ، يَتَعَاقَلُونَ بَيْنَهُمْ مَعَاقِلَهُمُ الْأُوْلَى، وَهُمْ يَفْدُوْنَ عَانِيَهُمْ بِالْـمَعْرُوْفِ وَالْقِسْطِ بَيْنَ الْـمُؤْمِنِيْنَ.

٢ وَبَنُو عَوْفٍ عَلَى رِبْعَاتِهِمْ، يَتَعَاقَلُوْنَ مَعَاقِلَهُمُ الْأُوْلَى، وَكُلُّ طَائِفَةٍ تَفْدِي عَانِيَهَا بِالْـمَعْرُوفِ وَالْقِسْطِ بَيْنَ الْـمُؤْمِنِينَ.

٣ وَبَنُو الْـخَزْرَجِ عَلَى رِبْعَاتِهِمْ يَتَعَاقَلُوْنَ مَعَاقِلَهُمُ الْأُوْلَى، وَكُلُّ طَائِفَةٍ مِنْهُمْ تَفْدِي عَانِيَهَا بِالْـمَعْرُوْفِ وَالْقِسْطِ بَيْنَ الْـمُؤْمِنِيْنَ.

٤ وَبَنُو سَاعِدَةَ عَلَى رِبَاعَتِهِمْ، يَتَعَاقَلُوْنَ مَعَاقِلَهُمُ الْأُوْلَى، وَكُلُّ طَائِفَةٍ مِنْهُمْ تَفْدِي عَانِيَهَا بِالْـمَعْرُوْفِ وَالْقِسْطِ بَيْنَ الْـمُؤْمِنِينَ.

٥ وَبَنُو جُشَمٍ عَلَى رِبَاعَتِهِمْ، يَتَعَاقَلُوْنَ مَعَاقِلَهُمُ الْأُوْلَى، وَكُلُّ طَائِفَةٍ مِنْهُمْ تَفْدِي عَانِيَهَا بِالْـمَعْرُوْفِ وَالْقِسْطِ بَيْنَ الْـمُؤْمِنِينَ.

٦ وَبَنُو النَّجَّارِ عَلَى رِبَاعَتِهِمْ يَتَعَاقَلُوْنَ مَعَاقِلَهُمُ الْأُوْلَى، وَكُلُّ طَائِفَةٍ مِنْهُمْ تَفْدِي عَانِيَهَا بِالْـمَعْرُوْفِ وَالْقِسْطِ بَيْنَ الْـمُؤْمِنِينَ.

٧ وَبَنُو عَمْرِو بْنِ عَوْفٍ عَلَى رِبْعَاتِهِمْ يَتَعَاقَلُوْنَ مَعَاقِلَهُمُ الْأُوْلَى، وَكُلُّ طَائِفَةٍ تَفْدِي عَانِيَهَا بِالْـمَعْرُوفِ وَالْقِسْطِ بَيْنَ الْـمُؤْمِنِينَ.

٨ وَبَنُو النَّبِيْتِ عَلَى رِبَاعَتِهِمْ يَتَعَاقَلُوْنَ مَعَاقِلَهُمُ الْأُوْلَى، وَكُلُّ طَائِفَةٍ مِنْهُمْ تَفْدِي عَانِيَهَا بِالْـمَعْرُوْفِ وَالْقِسْطِ بَيْنَ الْـمُؤْمِنِينَ.

٩ وَبَنُو أَوْسٍ عَلَى رِبَاعَتِهِمْ يَتَعَاقَلُوْنَ مَعَاقِلَهُمُ الْأُوْلَى، وَكُلُّ طَائِفَةٍ مِنْهُمْ تَفْدِي عَانِيَهَا بِالْـمَعْرُوْفِ وَالْقِسْطِ بَيْنَ الْـمُؤْمِنِينَ.

1. The emigrants from Quraysh shall be responsible for their ward and they shall, according to their approved practice, jointly pay the blood money in mutual collaboration,

and shall secure the release of their prisoners by paying the ransom with righteousness and justice between the believers.

2. And the emigrants from Banū ʿAwf shall be responsible for their ward and they shall, according to their formal approved practice, jointly pay the bloodmoney in mutual collaboration and shall secure the release of their prisoners by paying the ransom with righteousness and justice between the believers.
3. And the emigrants from Banū al-Khazraj shall be responsible for their ward and they shall, according to their formal approved practice, jointly pay the bloodmoney in mutual collaboration and every group shall secure the release of their prisoners by paying the ransom with righteousness and justice between the believers.
4. And the emigrants from Banū Sāʿida shall be responsible for their ward and they shall, according to their formal approved practice, jointly pay the bloodmoney in mutual collaboration and every group shall secure the release of their prisoners by paying the ransom with righteousness and justice between the believers.
5. And the emigrants from Banū Jusham shall be responsible for their ward and they shall, according to their formal approved practice, jointly pay the bloodmoney in mutual collaboration and every group shall secure the release of their prisoners by paying the ransom with righteousness and justice between the believers.
6. And the emigrants from Banū al-Najjār shall be responsible for their ward and they shall, according to their formal approved practice, jointly pay the bloodmoney in mutual collaboration and every group shall secure the release of their prisoners by paying the ransom with righteousness and justice between the believers.
7. And the emigrants from Banū ʿAmr b. ʿAwf shall be responsible for their ward and they shall, according to their formal approved practice, jointly pay the bloodmoney in

mutual collaboration and every group shall secure the release of their prisoners by paying the ransom with righteousness and justice between the believers.

8. And the emigrants from Banū al-Nabīt shall be responsible for their ward and they shall, according to their formal approved practice, jointly pay the bloodmoney in mutual collaboration and every group shall secure the release of their prisoners by paying the ransom with righteousness and justice between the believers.
9. And the emigrants from Banū Aws shall be responsible for their ward and they shall, according to their formal approved practice, jointly pay the bloodmoney in mutual collaboration and every group shall secure the release of their prisoners by paying the ransom with righteousness and justice between the believers.[1]

12.6.1 The Prophetic Pronouncement: "The Jews Together with the Muslims are One Nation"

Creating a single *Umma* by joining the Jews with the Muslims has been clearly mentioned on another occasion in the document. The words in the document dictated by the Holy Prophet ﷺ are noticeable:

إِنَّ يَهُودَ بَنِي عَوْفٍ أُمَّةٌ مَعَ الْـمُؤْمِنِينَ، لِلْيَهُودِ دِينُهُمْ وَلِلْمُسْلِمِيْنَ دِينُهُمْ، مَوَالِيهِمْ وَأَنْفُسُهُمْ.

"Certainly, the Jews of Banū ʿAwf (non-Muslim minorities) shall be considered a community along with the believers. However, the Jews will follow their own religion and the Muslims will practise their own *Dīn*. As for the *Umma*, both will be a part of it and their supporters too."[2]

---

[1] Cited by •Ḥumayd b. Zanjawayh in *Kitāb al-amwāl*, 1:394. •Abū ʿUbayd al-Qāsim b. Sallām in *Kitāb al-amwāl*, 1:394. •Ibn Hishām in *al-Sīra al-Nabawiyya*, 2:497–498. •al-Bayhaqī in *al-Sunan al-kubrā*, 8:106. •Ibn Kathīr in *al-Bidāya wa al-nihāya*, 3:224–225.

[2] Cited by •Ibn Hishām in *al-Sīra al-Nabawiyya*, 2:499. •Ḥumayd b. Zanjawayh in *Kitāb al-amwāl*, 1:394. •Ibn Kathīr in *al-Bidāya wa al-nihāya*,

It has been elucidated here that both groups will follow and practise their respective religions freely. However, there is nothing that keeps them from becoming a single community. Becoming an *Umma* this way does not adversely affect the individual identity of either the Muslims or the Jews. Nor do their distinctive religious identities come in their way to becoming a collective body or a single community.

This Prophetic command does not in any way affect the concept of the Muslim *Umma* because when the Muslims were declared one *Umma*, that had religious, legal and communal implications. However, when the Jews together with the Muslims were declared a single *Umma*, that had political, social, defensive and collective connotations. This generates the concept of a constitutional nationality and citizenship. On the basis of this, the Holy Prophet laid the foundation of a multicultural society, which became a model for present-day interfaith tolerance and peaceful co-existence. The classical books and sources have also quoted the words "community of the believers" instead of "community with the believers". It has been quoted like this:

إِنَّ يَهُوْدَ بَنِي عَوْفٍ وَمَوَالِيْهِمْ وَأَنْفُسِهِمْ أُمَّةٌ مِنَ الْمُؤْمِنِيْنَ، لِلْيَهُوْدِ دِيْنُهُمْ، وَلِلْمُؤْمِنِيْنَ دِيْنُهُمْ.

> "Verily, all the Jews of Banū ʿAwf (non-Muslim minorities) and their supporters shall be considered a part of the community of believers. However, they will practice their own religion and the Muslims will follow their *Dīn*."[1]

12.6.2 The Implications of "The Jews of Banū ʿAwf will be a Part of the Muslim Community"

The imams who have reported the words *Ummatan min al-Muʾminīn* (part of the Muslim community) include Imam Abū ʿUbayd al-Qāsim b. Sallām, Imam Ḥumayd b. Zanjawayh, Imam Manṣūr b. al-Ḥusayn al-Ābī, Imam Ibn al-Athīr al-Jazarī, and Imam Muhammad b. Yūsuf

---

3:225.

[1] Cited by •Abū ʿUbayd al-Qāsim b. Sallām in *Kitāb al-amwāl*, p. 263. •Maḥmūd b. ʿUmar al-Zamakhsharī in *al-Fāʾiq fī gharīb al-ḥadīth wa al-āthār*, 2:25.

al-Ṣāliḥī al-Shāmī and others.

This text connotes that despite having separate religions, Muslims and Jews have become the members of the same *Umma* by this reconciliatory agreement. Thus, they will guard, protect, and support each other like members of the same community. Their alliance, therefore, has united them as the member of a single community.

Let us now delve into how the imams of hadith have interpreted the words reported in the hadith.

12.6.2.1 IMAM IBN AL-ATHĪR AL-JAZARĪ

In this series, we first take the interpretation of Imam Ibn al-Athīr al-Jazarī.

He writes in his famous book *al-Nihāya fī gharīb al-ḥadīth wa al-athar*,

وَفِيْهِ: إِنَّ يَهُوْدَ بَنِي عَوْفٍ أُمَّةٌ مِنَ الْـمُؤْمِنِيْنَ. يُرِيْدُ: أَنَّهُمْ بِالصُّلْحِ الَّذِي وَقَعَ بَيْنَهُمْ، وَبَيْنَ الْـمُؤْمِنِيْنَ كَجَمَـاعَةٍ مِنْهُمْ، كَلِمَتُهُمْ وَأَيْدِيْهِمْ وَاحِدَةٌ.

> "'Certainly, the Jews of Banū ʿAwf are included in the community of believers'—indicate that the status of the Jews determined by the agreement is that they are like the part of the believers' community. The words and the deeds of both of them will be considered as one."[1]

It means that if one group of them promises to some other community or tribe, the other group will also be equally responsible to keep that promise as if he has promised himself. Likewise, if one group provides someone shelter, the other will be equally bound and will honour it as if he has been responsible for providing the shelter. If some action has been taken against any one of them, it will be considered an action against their own community. Similarly, their support and opposition will be considered the one. In short, the Jews and the Muslims will be considered the members of the same community.

Imam Ibn al-Athīr has gone into further details when commenting

---

[1] Cited by •Ibn al-Athīr in *al-Nihāya fī gharīb al-ḥadīth wa al-athar*, chapter of *al-hamza* with *mīm*, 1:77.

on this report in his book, *Manāl al-Ṭālib fī Sharḥ Ṭiwāl al-Gharā'ib*:

قَوْلُهُ: وَإِنَّ يَهُوْدَ بَنِي عَوْفٍ أُمَّةٌ مِنَ الْـمُؤْمِنِيْنَ. يُرِيْدُ: أَنَّهُمْ بِالصُّلْحِ الَّذِي وَقَعَ بَيْنَهُمْ وَبَيْنَ الْـمُؤْمِنِيْنَ، فَصَارَتْ أَيْدِيْهِمْ وَأَيْدِي مَوَالِيْهِمْ مَعَ الْـمُؤْمِنِيْنَ وَاحِدَةٌ عَلَى عَدُوِّ الْـمُؤْمِنِيْنَ، كَأُمَّةٍ مِنَ الْـمُؤْمِنِيْنَ، إِلَّا أَنَّ لِـهَؤُلَاءِ دِيْنُهُمْ، وَلِـهَؤُلَاءِ دِيْنُهُمْ، إِلَّا مَنْ ظَلَمَ وَأَثِمَ بِنَقْضِ الْعَهْدِ وَالنَّكْثِ.

"The Prophetic command—'certainly, the Jews of Banū ʿAwf are included in the community of believers'—means that as a result of the covenant between the Jews and the Muslims, the members and supporters of both the groups and their power and strength have become a united force against the Muslims' enemies (the Meccan infidels), and due to this relation of unity, the Jews will also be taken as part of the Muslim community, except that the Muslims will follow their religion and the Jews will practise theirs, unless any of the parties violates the agreement and perpetrates tyranny and oppression."[1]

12.6.2.2 Interpretation by al-Zamakhsharī

According to al-Zamakhsharī:

يَهُوْدُ بَنِي عَوْفٍ بِسَبَبِ الصُّلْحِ الْوَاقِعِ بَيْنَهُمْ وَبَيْنَ الْـمُؤْمِنِيْنَ كَأُمَّةٍ مِنْهُمْ فِي أَنَّ كَلِمَتَهُمْ وَاحِدَةٌ عَلَى عَدُوِّهِمْ. فَأَمَّا الدِّيْنُ فَكُلُّ فِرْقَةٍ مِنْهُمْ عَلَى حِيَالِـهَا إِلَّا مَنْ ظَلَمَ بِنَقْضِ الْعَهْدِ.

"As a result of the agreement between the Muslims and the Jews, the Jews of Banū ʿAwf have become like part of the same community. The words and agreements of both these groups have now become the same against their enemies. As for religion, both will adhere to their respective faiths, except

---

1 •Ibn al-Athīr, *Manāl al-ṭālib fī Sharḥ Ṭiwāl al-gharā'ib*, ḥadīth, the book of Quraysh and al-Anṣār, 1:183.

the ones who wrong by violating the agreement."[1]

12.6.2.3 Interpretation by Ibn Abī ʿUbayd al-Harawī

Imam Ibn Abī ʿUbayd al-Harawī described these connotations first in his book *al-Gharibayn fī al-Qurʾān wa al-Ḥadīth*, as follows:

وَفِيْهِ: إِنَّ يَهُوْدَ بَنِي عَوْفٍ أُمَّةٌ مِنَ الْـمُؤْمِنِيْنَ. يُرِيْدُ: أَنَّهُمْ بِالصُّلْحِ الَّذِي وَقَعَ بَيْنَهُمْ، وَبَيْنَ الْـمُؤْمِنِيْنَ كَأُمَّةٍ مِنَ الْـمُؤْمِنِيْنَ، كَلِمَتُهُمْ وَأَيْدِيْهِمْ وَاحِدَةٌ.

"'Certainly, the Jews of Banū ʿAwf are included in the community of believers' means that the agreement that has been concluded between the Muslims and the Jews implies that the Jews have been made part of the Muslim community. Their words and deeds will now be regarded as one."[2]

12.7 Five other Jewish Tribes were also Included in One Community along with Muslims

Later, like Banū ʿAwf, the Prophet included five other Jewish tribes in one community along with the Muslims. Each one of these tribes was given the same status that was previously owned by Banū ʿAwf. Then their allies too were made part of it in the same way. Moreover, rules were also formulated to govern mutual help and cooperation of betterment as is expected from the members of the same community.

Here are these extensions:

- وَإِنَّ لِيَهُودِ بَنِي النَّجَّارِ مِثْلَ مَا لِيَهُودِ بَنِي عَوْفٍ.
- وَإِنَّ لِيَهُودِ بَنِي الْـحَارِثِ مِثْلَ مَا لِيَهُودِ بَنِي عَوْفٍ.

---

[1] •Al-Zamakhsharī, *al-Fāʾiq fī gharīb al-ḥadīth wa al-athar*, 2:26.

[2] •Al-Harawī, *al-Gharibayn fī al-Qurʾān wa al-ḥadīth*, chapter of *al-ḥamza* with *al-mīm*, 1:107.

- وَإِنَّ لِيَهُودِ بَنِي جُشَمٍ مِثْلَ مَا لِيَهُودِ بَنِي عَوْفٍ.
- وَإِنَّ لِيَهُودِ بَنِي سَاعِدَةَ مَا لِيَهُودِ بَنِي عَوْفٍ.
- وَإِنَّ لِيَهُودِ الْأَوْسِ مِثْلَ ذَلِكَ، إِلَّا مَنْ ظَلَمَ، فَإِنَّهُ لَا يُوْتِغُ إِلَّا نَفْسَهُ وَأَهْلَ بَيْتِهِ. وَأَنَّهُ لَا يَخْرُجُ أَحَدٌ مِنْهُمْ إِلَّا بِإِذْنِ مُحَمَّدٍ ﷺ.
- عَلَى الْيَهُوْدِ نَفَقَتُهُمْ، وَعَلَى الْـمُسْلِمِيْنَ نَفَقَتُهُمْ.
- وَأَنَّ بَيْنَهُمُ النَّصْرَ عَلَى مَنْ حَارَبَ أَهْلَ هَذِهِ الصَّحِيْفَةِ. وَأَنَّ بَيْنَهُمُ النُّصْحَ وَالنَّصِيْحَةَ وَالنَّصْرَ لِلْمَظْلُوْمِ.
- وَأَنَّ الْـمَدِيْنَةَ جَوْفُهَا حَرَمٌ لِأَهْلِ هَذِهِ الصَّحِيْفَةِ.
- وَأَنَّ بَيْنَهُمُ النَّصْرَ عَلَى مَنْ دَهَمَ يَثْرِبَ.
- وَأَنَّهُمْ إِذَا دَعَوْا الْيَهُوْدَ إِلَى صُلْحِ حَلِيْفٍ لَـهُمْ بِالْأُسْوَةِ، فَإِنَّهُمْ يُصَالِـحُوْنَهُ. وَإِنْ دَعَوْنَا إِلَى مِثْلِ ذَلِكَ، فَإِنَّهُ لَـهُمْ عَلَى الْـمُؤْمِنِيْنَ إِلَّا مَنْ حَارَبَ الدِّيْنَ.
- وَأَنَّ يَهُوْدَ الْأَوْسِ وَمَوَالِيْهِمْ وَأَنْفُسِهِمْ مَعَ الْبَرِّ الْـمُحْسِنِ مِنْهُمْ، مِنْ أَهْلِ هَذِهِ الصَّحِيْفَةِ.
- وَأَنَّهُ الْبِرُّ دُوْنَ الْإِثْمِ، وَلَا يَكْسِبُ كَاسِبٌ إِلَّا عَلَى نَفْسِهِ.
- وَإِنَّ أَوْلَاهُمْ بِهَذِهِ الصَّحِيْفَةِ الْبَرُّ الْـمُحْسِنُ.

- The Jews of Banū al-Najjār shall enjoy the same rights as granted to the Jews of Banū ʿAwf.
- The Jews of Banū al-Ḥārith shall also enjoy the same rights as granted to the Jews of Banū ʿAwf.
- The Jews of Banū Jusham shall also enjoy the same rights

as granted to the Jews of Banū ʿAwf.

- The Jews of Banū Saʿida shall also enjoy the same rights as granted to the Jews of Banū ʿAwf.
- The Jews of Banū Aws shall also enjoy the same rights as granted to the Jews of Banū ʿAwf. But he who wrongs will, no doubt, put himself and his family in trouble. No one shall exit the agreement without permission from the (Prophet) Muhammad (blessings and peace be upon him).
- The Jews will be responsible for their maintenance and the Muslims will be responsible for theirs.
- There shall be mutual help between one another against those who engage in war with the allies of this document. There shall be mutual consultation, well-wishing and sincerity over breaching the treaty, and help for the wronged shall be mandatory.
- And the valley of Medina (the plateau surrounded by hills) will be a sanctuary (an abode of peace) for the signatories of this agreement (i.e. fighting among each other here will be forbidden).
- The Muslims and the Jews shall be jointly responsible to defend (the state of) Medina against any outside attack.
- It shall be incumbent upon the Jews to observe and adhere to any peace treaty they are invited to participate in by any of their allies. Likewise, it shall also be incumbent upon the Muslims to observe and adhere to any peace treaty they are invited to. However, a person who fights against the religion of Islam has no right on believers.
- And the Jews of the Aws tribe whether allies or native citizens will enjoy the same rights that have been awarded to the holders of this constitution, and they will extend faithful conduct to the people of the constitution.
- Faithfulness and sincerity will prevail over breaching the treaty. Everyone will be responsible for his doings.
- The pious and the benevolent will be the beneficiary of this agreement.[1]

---

[1] Cited by •Ḥumayd b. Zanjawayh in *Kitāb al-amwāl,* 1:395. •Ibn Hishām in

By comparing this pact with the pact of Ḥudaybiya that was concluded between the Muslims and the disbelievers of Mecca in the 6th year of migration, we can vividly see that its themes, style, conditions and text are altogether different from the agreement that was concluded with the Jews of Medina. The nature of both the agreements is different from the beginning to the end. The pact of Ḥudaybiya contains conditions to maintain truce and peace for ten years. Apart from that, the agreement is void of any overtures of mutuality and cooperation among the two groups. As for the charter of Medina, it has altogether a different set of objectives and matters of mutual interest with the People of the Book that we have already surveyed.

12.8 ABYSSINIA—THE MODEL ABODE OF PEACE

The disbelievers of Mecca impeded the propagation of Islam and made the lives of the Muslims hard and miserable. They intensified their persecutions against the Prophet and his followers. Even influential men who now followed the Prophet were not spared. They were boycotted and several of them were restrained in their own homes. Many of the Muslims with little or no influence were tortured publicly and repeatedly. When the pagan Meccans' hostility against the Muslims became unbearably brutal, the Prophet commanded a group of them, including Uthmān b. ʿAffān and the Holy Prophet's beloved daughter Ruqayya, to migrate to Abyssinia, even though he knew that Abyssinia was a Christian country and its ruler, the Negus, too was a Christian. Since the repute of the King Negus reached the Prophet as a just and kind ruler, he selected this Christian country for the first and second migration.

The Qurʾān has honoured this decision of the Holy Prophet as the corroboration of Almighty Allah's commandment and declared Abyssinia as the best abode for the Muslims. The Qurʾān's declaration about Abyssinia as the safest country for the Companions of the

al-Sīra al-Nabawiyya, 1:331, 2:499–500. •Abū ʿUbayd al-Qāsim b. Sallām in *Kitāb al-amwāl*, 1:224. •al-Ṭabarī, *Tārīkh al-umam wa al-mulūk*, 1:547. •al-Zamakhsharī in *al-Fāʾiq fī gharīb al-ḥadīth wa al-āthār*, 2:25. •al-Dhahabī, *Tārīkh al-Islām*, 1:184. •Ibn Kathīr, *al-Bidāya wa al-nihāya*, 3:66. •al-ʿAynī, *ʿUmda al-qārī*, 7:268.

Prophet has been elaborately interpreted in the subsequent pages.

The disbelievers and idolaters of Mecca were at war with the Muslims. They inflicted atrocities on them and subjected them to extreme form of terrorism and brutality. The Prophet's command to his Companions to migrate to a Christian kingdom portends the difference between the tyranny the disbelievers meted out to the Muslims and the security and the observance of human rights the People of the Book extended to them under the King Negus of Abyssinia. There the Muslims were received well and allowed to practice their religion and live in peace. The Prophet reciprocated this harmony and hospitality towards them as Abyssinia proved to be a model abode of peace for the Muslims.

12.9 The Difference Between the Christian Rule of Abyssinia and the Meccan Rule

Here are some of its salient features:

a. Many of the People of the Book were pious believers

The Qurʾān provides ample evidence about the piety and true faith of the People of the Book. It has been revealed in *sūra al-Aʿrāf*:

﴿وَمِن قَوْمِ مُوسَىٰٓ أُمَّةٌ يَهْدُونَ بِٱلْحَقِّ وَبِهِۦ يَعْدِلُونَ﴾

﴾And a party amongst the people of Mūsā ([Moses] comprises those) who guide to the path of truth and according to that (make judgments based on) justice.﴿[1]

﴿وَإِنَّ مِنْ أَهْلِ ٱلْكِتَـٰبِ لَمَن يُؤْمِنُ بِٱللَّهِ وَمَآ أُنزِلَ إِلَيْكُمْ وَمَآ أُنزِلَ إِلَيْهِمْ خَـٰشِعِينَ لِلَّهِ لَا يَشْتَرُونَ بِـَٔايَـٰتِ ٱللَّهِ ثَمَنًا قَلِيلًا ۗ أُو۟لَـٰٓئِكَ لَهُمْ أَجْرُهُمْ عِندَ رَبِّهِمْ ۗ إِنَّ ٱللَّهَ سَرِيعُ ٱلْحِسَابِ﴾

﴾And indeed, some People of the Book are such that they believe in Allāh, and also (have faith in) the Book that has been revealed to you, and the one which was sent down to them. Their hearts remain subdued before Allāh. And they

[1] Qurʾān 7:159.

do not receive a paltry price for the Revelations of Allāh. They are the ones whose reward lies with their Lord. Indeed, Allāh is Swift at reckoning.﴾[1]

b. As for love, the Christians are closer to the Muslims

﴿لَتَجِدَنَّ أَشَدَّ ٱلنَّاسِ عَدَٰوَةً لِّلَّذِينَ ءَامَنُوا۟ ٱلْيَهُودَ وَٱلَّذِينَ أَشْرَكُوا۟ ۖ وَلَتَجِدَنَّ أَقْرَبَهُم مَّوَدَّةً لِّلَّذِينَ ءَامَنُوا۟ ٱلَّذِينَ قَالُوٓا۟ إِنَّا نَصَٰرَىٰ ۚ ذَٰلِكَ بِأَنَّ مِنْهُمْ قِسِّيسِينَ وَرُهْبَانًا وَأَنَّهُمْ لَا يَسْتَكْبِرُونَ﴾

﴿*You will indeed find the Jews and the polytheists the bitterest of people in their enmity against the Muslims, and the closest in love and affection for the Muslims you will find those who say: 'Indeed, we are Nazarenes (Christians).' This is because amongst them are savants (i.e., scholars of Shariah) as well as monks (i.e., ascetic worshippers) and (moreover) they are not given to arrogance.*﴾[2]

Such wonderful remarks in the Qur'ān about the Christians have never been made with regard to the disbelievers and polytheists even during the periods of reconciliation, armistice and truce. The reason given for this close affinity has been nothing but the presence of the people of Shariah and the spirituality among them. Also among the Muslims, a similar division exists from the days of the Companions and the pious predecessors to the later eras of scholars, luminaries and jurists. There are many things in common between the two communities, even if the means and methods of both of them differ widely with respect to commands and legal issues. The verses quoted above contain a significant segment that relates to the Christians:

﴿وَلَتَجِدَنَّ أَقْرَبَهُم مَّوَدَّةً لِّلَّذِينَ ءَامَنُوا۟ ٱلَّذِينَ قَالُوٓا۟ إِنَّا نَصَٰرَىٰ﴾

﴿*[A]nd the closest in love and affection for the Muslims you will find those who say: 'Indeed, we are Nazarenes*

[1] Ibid 3:199.

[2] Ibid 5:82.

(Christians).'﴾

c. The Qur'ān declared Abyssinia the safest country for the Companions.

With regard to Abyssinia, the Qur'ān has revealed.

﴿وَٱلَّذِينَ هَاجَرُوا۟ فِى ٱللَّهِ مِنۢ بَعْدِ مَا ظُلِمُوا۟ لَنُبَوِّئَنَّهُمْ فِى ٱلدُّنْيَا حَسَنَةً ۖ وَلَأَجْرُ ٱلْـَٔاخِرَةِ أَكْبَرُ ۚ لَوْ كَانُوا۟ يَعْلَمُونَ﴾

﴾*And those who emigrated after they had been subjected to (different kinds of) torture and brutality, We will certainly provide them with a better abode in this (very) world. And the reward in the Hereafter is certainly greater. Would that they knew (this secret)!*﴿[1]

Imam al-Qurṭubī has interpreted this verse in his exegeses, *al-Jāmiʿ li aḥkām al-Qurʾān*:

وَقَالَ قَتَادَةُ: الْـمُرَادُ أَصْحَابُ مُحَمَّدٍ ﷺ، ظَلَمَهُمُ الْـمُشْرِكُونَ بِمَكَّةَ وَأَخْرَجُوهُمْ حَتَّى لَـحِقَ طَائِفَةٌ مِّنْهُمْ بِالْـحَبَشَةِ. ثُمَّ بَوَّأَهُمُ اللهُ تَعَالَى دَارَ الْـهِجْرَةِ، وَجَعَلَ لَـهُمْ أَنْصَارًا مِنَ الْـمُؤْمِنِينَ.

"According to Qatāda, this verse alludes to those Companions whom the Meccan disbelievers subjected to tyranny and ostracized, until one of their groups left for Abyssinia. Thereafter, Allah blessed them with a safe haven in the abode of migration (i.e., Medina) and produced their helpers from amongst the believers."[2]

Both Imam Ibn Abī Ḥātim al-Rāzī and Imam Ibn Jarīr al-Ṭabarī agree that here "the best abode" implies emigration to Abyssinia and, later, to Medina[3] and both these abodes allude to the words, "We will

---

[1] Ibid 16:41.

[2] •Al-Qurṭubī, *al-Jāmiʿ li aḥkām al-Qurʾān*, 10:107.

[3] •Ibn Abī Ḥātim al-Rāzī, *Tafsīr al-Qurʾān al-ʿAẓīm*, 7:2284 §21518. •al-Ṭabarī, *Jāmiʿ al-Bayān fī Tafsīr al-Qurʾān*, 14:107.

certainly provide them with a better abode in this (very) world", in the Qur'ānic verse.

After mentioning emigration to both these places, Imam Makkī b. Abī Ṭālib al-Muqrī writes in *al-Hidāya ilā Bulūgh al-Nihāya* about this verse:

> "This verse does not refer to emigration to Medina but signifies emigration to Abyssinia, because this verse was revealed in Mecca on the occasion of emigration to Abyssinia."[1]

Imam Ibn ʿAtiyya has further explained it in *al-Muḥarrar*:

وَهُمُ الَّذِيْنَ هَاجَرُوْا إِلَى أَرْضِ الْحَبَشَةِ. هَذَا قَوْلُ الْجُمْهُوْرِ، وَهُوَ الصَّحِيْحُ فِي سَبَبِ هَذِهِ الآيَةِ، لِأَنَّ هِجْرَةَ الْمَدِيْنَةِ لَمْ تَكُنْ وَقْتَ نُزُوْلِ الْآيَةِ.

> "And (the verse under reference signifies) the people who immigrated to Abyssinia. That is the saying of the majority and this is what is congruous to the occasion of its revelation, because, chronologically, its revelation precedes the emigration to Medina."[2]

Imam Abū Ḥayān too has concurred in *al-Baḥr al-muḥīt* that this verse refers to the emigration to Abyssinia because the Muslims of Mecca had not yet moved to Medina when this verse was revealed.[3]

After migration, events occurred to the Muslims in Abyssinia that portray how the Negus, the Christian King of Ethiopia, supported the Companions of the Holy Prophet despite the opposition of Quraysh of Mecca. The Holy Prophet's view about the Ethopian king proved a reality. The Christian king not only protected the Muslims, but a spring of love also sprouted from his heart for the Prophet of Islam and his Companions. Almighty Allah provided a peaceful abode to the Muslims whom the tyrannous Meccans had harried and displaced, fomenting crucibles and shedding their blood. Allah Most Exalted bestowed upon the Muslims a blessing in the form of their host—the ruler of Abyssinia, King Negus. Then the Muslims emigrated twice

[1] •Makkī b. Abī Ṭālib al-Muqrī, *al-Hidāya ilā bulūgh al-nihāya*, 6:3996.

[2] •Ibn ʿAtiyya, *al-Muḥarrar al-wajīz fī tafsīr al-kitāb al-ʿazīz*, 3:394.

[3] •Abū Ḥayān, *al-Baḥr al-muḥīt*, 5:492.

in a large number towards the same land and stayed there in peace until the Prophet, along with the rest of the Muslims, migrated from Mecca to Madina. In this connection, Almighty Allah revealed in *sūra al-ʿAnkabūt*:

﴿يَٰعِبَادِيَ ٱلَّذِينَ ءَامَنُوٓاْ إِنَّ أَرۡضِي وَٰسِعَةٞ فَإِيَّٰيَ فَٱعۡبُدُونِ﴾

﴾O My servants who have believed! Surely, My earth is vast, so worship Me alone.﴿[1]

Ibn Kathīr has interpreted this verse in the following way:

لَـمَّا ضَاقَ عَلَى الْـمُسْتَضْعَفِيْنَ بِمَكَّةَ مُقَامُهُمْ بِهَا، خَرَجُوْا مُهَاجِرِيْنَ إِلَى أَرْضِ الْـحَبَشَةِ، لِيَأْمَنُوْا عَلَى دِيْنِهِمْ هُنَاكَ، فَوَجَدُوْا هُنَاكَ خَيْرَ الْـمَنْزِلَيْنِ. أَصْحَمَةُ النَّجَاشِيُّ مَلِكُ الْـحَبَشَةِ، رَحِمَهُ اللهُ، آوَاهُمْ وَأَيَّدَهُمْ بِنَصْرِهِ.

"When the land of Mecca became narrow upon the feeble and weak (companions of the Holy Prophet) and it was unbearable for them to live there, they immigrated to Abyssinia to save their *Dīn*. There they found Negus Aṣḥama, the King of Abyssinia, the best host who extended his full support to the immigrants, helped them and provided them with all the possible facilities."[2]

12.10 The Holy Prophet ﷺ Declared Abyssinia "The Land of Truth"

As mentioned above, the Qurʾān declared Abyssinia as the best abode. Similarly, the Prophet had also affirmed it the land of peace and truth, knowing that the ruler of that country was a Christian.

According to Imam Ibn Isḥāq, when the brutalities perpetrated by the Meccan disbelievers and polytheists exceeded limits and none of the strategies to protect the Muslims proved fruitful, the Prophet commanded the Companions to migrate to Abyssinia. The Prophetic command inherently confirms the evidence of the Christian land being

---

[1] Qurʾān 29:56.

[2] •Ibn Kathīr, *Tafsīr al-Qurʾān al-ʿAẓīm*, 6:290.

an abode of peace for the insecure Muslims of Mecca.

This is important to remember that this migration took place in the month of Rajab, after the 5th year of the pronouncement of Prophethood [*Nubuwwa*]. In the beginning, our master ʿUthmān b. ʿAffān and his wife Ruqayya, the venerable daughter of the Prophet, along with 15 people, migrated. Later, when the Companions heard the news of peace and security in Abyssinia, many more Companions and their wives emigrated, raising the total number of immigrants to eighty two. This is known as the second migration to Abyssinia. The blessed words of the Holy Prophet addressed to the Companions at the time of migration are inspiring:

لَوْ خَرَجْتُمْ إِلَى أَرْضِ الْـحَبَشَةِ، فَإِنَّ بِهَا مَلِكًا لَا يُظْلَمُ عِنْدَهُ أَحَدٌ، وَهِيَ أَرْضُ صِدْقٍ، حَتَّى يَجْعَلَ اللهُ لَكُمْ فَرَجًا. فَخَرَجَ عِنْدَ ذَلِكَ الْـمُسْلِمُونَ مِنْ أَصْحَابِ رَسُولِ اللهِ ﷺ إِلَى أَرْضِ الْـحَبَشَةِ، مَخَافَةَ الْفِتْنَةِ وَفِرَارًا إِلَى اللهِ بِدِينِهِمْ، فَكَانَتْ أَوَّلَ هِجْرَةٍ كَانَتْ فِي الْإِسْلَامِ.

> "'(It is better) if you leave for Abyssinia until Allah makes a way out for you because the king of Abyssinia does not oppress or tyrannize people. That is a land of truth and righteousness. May Allah make it spacious for you!' Hearing this Prophetic command, many Companions left for Abyssinia to escape the sufferings and save their *Dīn*. This was the first ever emigration of the Muslims in the history of Islam."[1]

Imam al-Ṭabarī wrote exactly the same words about the land of Ethiopia (Abyssinia) and its King Negus in *Tārīkh al-Umam wa al-Mulūk*. According to him, the Holy Prophet ﷺ said:

فَإِنَّ بِهَا مَلِكًا لَا يُظْلَمُ عِنْدَهُ أَحَدٌ، وَهِيَ أَرْضُ صِدْقٍ.

> "This country is under the rule of a king who does not wrong anybody and this is a land of truth. (There you can secure

[1] •Ibn Hishām, *al-Sīra al-Nabawiyya*, 1:331.

your rights better.)"[1]

Imam al-Dhahabī and Ibn Kathīr have narrated the same words in *Tārīkh al-Islām* (1:184) and *al-Bidāya wa al-nihāya* (3:55) respectively. Also, Ibn al-Athīr al-Jazarī and numerous other imams of hadith and history have reported the same narration in their books and treatises. Imam Badr al-Dīn al-ʿAynī too has related it in *Kitāb al-Jumuʿa* of *ʿUmda al-qārī sharḥ Ṣaḥīḥ al-Bukhārī*.

12.10.1 The Negus had yet to Know about the Final Messenger

While Abyssinia was chosen for the Muslims to migrate for the protection of their lives, Dīn and faith from the brutalities and atrocities inflicted upon them by the disbelievers and polytheists, the country was also pertinently labelled as a "safe haven" and the "land of truth". It was a Christian land with the Negus, the Christian ruler, in the saddle; he had yet to receive the news of the raising of the Final Messenger. Despite that, the Prophet declared that country an abode of peace for the Muslims to practise their *Dīn* and honoured it with an exalting title: "The Land of Truth". This was said before the king had accepted Islam. Imam Ibn Isḥāq, Imam al-Ṭabarānī and Imam Ibn ʿAsākir narrate from the mother of believers, Umm Salama:

لَـمَّـا نَزَلْنَا أَرْضَ الْـحَبَشَةِ جَاوَرْنَا بِهَا خَيْرَ جَارٍ النَّجَاشِيَّ، أَمِنَّا عَلَى دِيْنِنَا، وَعَبَدْنَا اللهَ لَا نُؤْذَي، وَلَا نَسْمَعُ شَيْئًا نَكْرَهُهُ.

"When we were with the Negus, we were in peace. As for our *Din*, we were free from all fears. So we worshipped Allah (in the free environment) well which we could not practise before. And we did not hear anything unpleasant there."[2]

In like manner, Imam Ibn Isḥāq, Imam Abū Nuʿaym and Imam Ibn ʿAsākir and Ḥāfiẓ Ibn Kathīr have narrated it from Jaʿfar Ibn Abī Ṭālib in *al-Sīra*, *al-Dalāʾil*, *al-Tārīkh* and *al-Bidāya wa al-nihāya*

---

1 •Al-Ṭabarī, *Tārīkh al-umam wa al-mulūk*, 1:547.

2 •Ibn Hishām, *al-Sīra al-Nabawiyya*, 1:341.

respectively that when the Negus heard of the virtues and teachings of the Final Messenger of Allah, he was in tears. Then he audaciously said in his court:

مَرْحَباً بِكُمْ وَبِمَنْ جِئْتُمْ مِنْ عِنْدِهِ، أَشْهَدُ أَنَّهُ رَسُوْلُ الله، وَأَنَّهُ الَّذِي نَجِدُ فِي الْإِنْجِيْلِ، وَأَنَّهُ الرَّسُوْلُ الَّذِي بَشَّرَ بِهِ عِيْسَى ابْنُ مَرْيَمَ، إِنْزِلُوْا حَيْثُ شِئْتُمْ، وَالله، لَوْلَا مَا أَنَا فِيْهِ مِنَ الْـمُلْكِ لَأَتَيْتُهُ حَتَّى أَكُوْنَ أَنَا الَّذِي أَحْمِلُ نَعْلَيْهِ. وَأَمَرَ لَنَا بِطَعَامٍ وَكُسْوَةٍ. ثُمَّ قَالَ: اذْهَبُوْا فَأَنْتُمْ آمِنُوْنَ. مَنْ سَبَّكُمْ غُرِّمَ، مَنْ سَبَّكُمْ غُرِّمَ، مَنْ سَبَّكُمْ غُرِّمَ.

> "I welcome you and the exalted personage from whom you have come to me. I bear witness that he is doubtlessly the true Messenger of Allah and he is certainly the same Prophet we have been reading about in the Bible about whom Jesus, son of Mary, gave the glad tidings. (O Muslims!) You can live here freely wherever you like. By God! Had I not been the ruler of this country, I would have submitted myself to his presence, until I had been given the opportunity to carry his shoes." The Negus then provided us with food and clothing and said: "Go! You will live in peace; whoever scolds you will be punished; whoever scolds you will be punished; whoever scolds you will be punished."[1]

Against the backdrop of atrocities and brutalities of the tyrannous disbelievers and terrorist polytheists of Mecca, Abyssinia, the land of the People of the Book, is declared a Land of Truth, and its righteous Christian ruler is regarded as the protector of the *Dīn* of the Muslims. He is also proving the Prophet's words true by his compliant and conforming actions. Such an exceptional behaviour could never be expected from any tribe or state being run by extremist disbelievers and bigoted polytheists.

---

[1] •Yūsuf al-Ṣāliḥī, *Subul al-hudā wa al-rishād fī sīra khayr al-ʿibād*, chapter no thirteen, 2:391.

12.10.2 THE COMPANIONS' PRAISE FOR THE NEGUS AND HIS RULE

Imam Ibn Hishām and Ibn Kathīr have further narrated from Umm Salama, the mother of the believers, in *al-Sīra* and *al-Bidāya wa al-nihāya* respectively that she said:

> "Some natives rebelled against the King Negus. By God! We never felt as perturbed as we did on that day, fearing that they might topple his government and take over the throne. In that case, it was likely that he would not recognize the rights of Muslims and not provide us protection the way the Negus was doing. The Negus's army and his troops confronted the opposition and we started praying for the victory of the Negus and his government. Suddenly, Zubayr b. al-ʿAwām brought us the glad news that the Negus had been victorious and his enemy had been defeated. By God! We felt so glad that day as we had never felt before."

Two sentences spoken by Umm Salama are of special significance:

١. فَجَعَلْنَا نَدْعُو اللهَ، وَنَسْتَنْصِرُهُ لِلنَّجَاشِيِّ.

٢. أَلَا، أَبْشِرُوْهُ، فَقَدْ أَظْهَرَ اللهُ النَّجَاشِيَّ، فَوَاللهِ، مَا عَلِمْنَا فَرَحْنَا بِشَيءٍ قَطُّ فَرَحَنَا بِظُهُوْرِ النَّجَاشِيِّ.

1. "So we started praying for the Negus's victory."
2. "'Beware! Rejoice! Allah has blessed the Negus with dominance. By God! We do not know if we have ever been so glad on any occasion as we were glad on the day of the Negus's victory."[1]

12.10.3 ALLAH'S EXCELLENT REWARD FOR NEGUS'S EXCELLENT CONDUCT WITH THE MUSLIMS

The mother of the believers, ʿĀʾisha, reported in *Sunan Abī Dāwūd's*

[1] •Ibn Isḥāq, *al-Sīra al-Nabawiyya*, 1:250. •Ibn Hishām, *al-Sīra al-Nabawiyya*, 1:344–345. •Ibn Kathīr, *al-Bidāya wa al-nihāya*, 3:75.

Kitāb al-Jihād (the Book of Striving):

لَـمَّا مَاتَ النَّجَاشِيُّ كُنَّا نَتَحَدَّثُ أَنَّـهُ لَا يَزَالُ يُرَى عَلَى قَبْرِهِ نُورٌ.

> "When the King Negus died, we used to say that there seemed to be always a shower of divine light on his grave."[1]

12.10.4 The Prophet's Excellent Bestowal for Negus's Benevolence Towards the Companions

According to the chapters *al-Janā'iz* (the funeral rites) and *al-Manāqib* (virtues) of *al-Ṣaḥīḥ* of al-Bukhārī and Muslim:

> "When the Negus died, the Prophet himself broke the news to the Companions and prayed over him."[2]

According to the scholars, the Holy Prophet paid back his benevolence with a higher benevolence because there was no one to pray over him in Abyssinia.[3]

12.10.5 When did the Negus Embrace Islam Formally?

The Negus accepted Islam as a result of the letter written to him from the Holy Prophet during the Medinan period while he also wrote to the Caesar of Rome, the Iranian monarchs and the Egyptian rulers, inviting them to embrace Islam. According to Imam al-Zuhrī, all these letters were written simultaneously. The Negus, however, had been showing his generosity to the Muslims, and, expressing his love and affection to the Holy Prophet for more than a decade before, he

---

[1] Set forth by •Abū Dāwūd in *al-Sunan*: *Kitāb al-jihād* [The Book of Jihad], chapter: 'The Light is Spotted near the Grave of a Martyr,' 3:16 §2523.

[2] Set forth by •al-Bukhārī in *al-Ṣaḥīḥ: Kitāb al-janā'iz* [The Book of Funeral Rites], chapter: 'A Man Announcing Someone's Death to the Dead Person's Relatives,' 1:420 §1188, and in *Kitāb al-manāqib* [The Book of Exemplary Virtues], chapter: 'The Death of the Negus', 3:1407–1408 §§3664–3668. •Muslim in *al-Ṣaḥīḥ*: *Kitāb al-janā'iz* [The Book of Funeral Processions], chapter: "Saying '*Allāh akbar*' (God is the Greatest) over the Dead Body", 2:656.

[3] •Ibn Ḥajar al-ʿAsqalānī, *Fatḥ al-Bārī*, 3:188.

entered the fold of Islam.

12.11 The Loyalty of the Muslim Abyssinian Refugees to Abyssinia and its Relevance to the Modern World

The emigration of the oppressed Muslims of Mecca to Abyssinia vividly depicts the nature of relations of the Muslims and non-Muslims. Ponder the model conduct and the teachings of the Messenger of Allah ﷺ when he ordered some of his Companions to migrate to the Christian state of Abyssinia under a Christian king. He directed his Companions ﷺ in these words:

According to Ibn Isḥāq and al-Ṭabarī:

لَوْ خَرَجْتُمْ إِلَى أَرْضِ الْـحَبَشَةِ، فَإِنَّ بِهَا مَلِكًا لَا يُظْلَمُ عِنْدَهُ أَحَدٌ، وَهِيَ أَرْضُ صِدْقٍ.

> "(It would be better) if you immigrate to the land of Abyssinia, for there is a king in whose presence no one is wronged. It is a land of truth and righteousness. (There you can secure your rights better.)"[1]

This hadith shows how the Messenger of Allah ﷺ appreciated the peaceful and protective conduct of a Christian ruler and his Christian state. Concurrently, the loyalty of the Abyssinian refugees to the state of Abyssinia can be better appreciated by considering the help they offered to the king against the rebels when they rose against him and caused tribulation and mischief. The refugees residing in Abyssinia helped the king against the rebels by taking part in the administration of the state. Loyalty to the country of one's residence is not only the practice of the Companions, it is the noble command of Allah's Messenger ﷺ as well. That has also brought forth the reciprocity of the relations of Muslims and non-Muslims towards maintenance of peace and interfaith harmony in a multicultural society.

Islam orders both men and women to adopt the Sunna of Allah's

---

[1] Cited by •Ibn Hishām in al-*Sīra al-Nabawiyya*, 2:164. •al-Ṭabarī in *Tārīkh al-umam wa al-mulūk*, 1:547.

Messenger ﷺ and be loyal to their country, whether they are British, American, French, Italian, European, Danish, or a refugee or non-resident. Islam exhorts Muslims to always be supportive and helpful to society. Islam orders the Muslims to obey the law and strengthen the rule of law where they dwell, to find gainful employment, to earn a living, to get subsidies, to receive, social and economic benefits, pensions and medical support, where one can have the benefits of life, individuality, business, faith and religion, and the freedom of cultural and traditional values; where mosques can be built freely without restraint; where one can go for pilgrimage; where one can establish prayer and keep fasts; where one can call to prayer and broadcast Islamic channels—in short, where one can do anything he or she wants. Therefore, it is clear and self-evident that all these countries are like the Land of Islam (*Dār al-Islām*) and they are definitely categorized as Abode of Peace.

12.11.1 An Analysis of Human Rights in Western and some Muslim Countries (towards the Categories of Abodes)

If you conduct a realistic analysis of the human rights situation, you will find that the religious, communal, economic and social liberties and freedoms that the Muslims enjoy in Western countries are not accessible to them in their own Muslim, especially Arab countries. The Western World offers them all the benefits and liberties—social, political, religious, economic. Besides the freedom to establish educational institutions, Muslims in Western countries are also allowed to build mosques and Islamic centres. It is also possible to take the advantage of grants and other means. All of the benefits available to Muslims in these countries have been introduced by Islam. This society is the Abode of Islam and an Abode of Peace and Security. Therefore, any Muslim who accepts the teachings of the Messenger of Islam wholeheartedly does not have any right to take up a "private jihad" or fight in any part of the world. The abode of peace model of Abyssinia provides sufficient guidance to take the bearing on our way to global peace and harmony.

12.11.2 The Message of Islam—the Establishment of a Global Human Society

The message of Islam is clear regarding global peace and mutual fairness. Islam is the foremost promoter and propagator of peace, justice and equality. Hence, we are to unite against extremism and religious fanaticism and root out terrorism. This is the time for every Muslim to become an embodiment of peace and harmony, love and affection. A Muslim is peace incarnate. He is to rise with the message of Allah's Messenger, which is a message of global peace.

At this juncture, we are to establish, according to the teachings of the Messenger of Islam, a global human society premised on peaceful co-existence—a society where we may live with peace, love, tolerance, mutual respect, honour and dignity, and where there shall be nobility, reverence and security for religion. The message dictates tolerance, moderation, human dignity, honouring freedoms and liberties for the development and prosperity of human society on the planet. We are to alleviate poverty, ignorance, bigotry and extremism and all forms of hatred and terrorism from the world to make it a safe haven for the future generations. That is the only way to establish equality, justice and rule of law and eliminate oppression, coercion and corruption from the surface of the earth.

12.12 Afterword

Respected readers! Peering into the shadows of words spread over the preceding pages, the truth has been demystified that Islam unequivocally teaches to promote sentiments of love and affection, sympathy and compassion, courtesy and proprieties. Being a Din of peace and security its call overwhelms the whole of humanity—all its socio-economic strata, ethnic layers and political divisions. Whatever religion or community one belongs to, the worldly well-being and otherworldly triumph of all humans form the basic elements of Islamic teachings. Against this backdrop should be appreciated the peculiar rulings pertaining to the People of the Book and the principles of permissibility and justification in several matters with the intention to develop trust and nearness and amity as desired by the divine prudence. Only this way will they revisit the rest of their creeds and beliefs. The Prophet's relations with the Jews of Medina and the treaties and contracts with them for smooth sailing in individual, economic, political, diplomatic affairs were the practical manifestation of the sentiments of well-wishing, mutual cooperation and coexistence.

Islamic history is replete with these sentiments of love and regard, well-wishing and peaceful coexistence. The western historians even today forthrightly confess that the People of the Book were better protected and more peaceful in the Islamic state than in Europe during crusades. That relates to the era of Islamic political and cultural dominance over the world. The modern world is a total contradiction. The Muslims have been undergoing a fall for last over three centuries. A large number of Muslims have settled in non-Muslim communities, societies and civilizations as minorities. The Muslim governments are engaged in diverse interactions with the non-Muslim states while this exercise vastly transpires at individual levels. If the Muslims demonstrate hatred and spite towards the non-Muslims, the idolaters and disbelievers, they will face the worse reaction from the opposite side.

Bibliography

Ibn ʿĀdil, Abū Ḥafṣ Sirāj al-Dīn ʿUmar b. ʿAlī. *Al-Lubāb fī ʿulūm al-Kitāb*. Beruit: Dar al-Kutub al-ʿIlmiyya, 1998.

Aḥmad .b. Ḥanbal, Abū ʿAbd Allāh b. Muhammad (164–241/780–855), *al-Musnad,* Beirut, Lebanon: al-Maktab al-Islāmī, 1398/1978.

—. *al-Musnad*. Beruit: Dār al-Kutub al-ʿIlmiyya, 1986.

al-ʿAjlūnī, Abū al-Fidāʾ Ismāʿīl b. Muhammad b. ʿAbd al-Hādī b. ʿAbd al-Ghanī al-Jarrāḥī (1087–1162/1676–1749), *Kashf al-Khifāʾ wa Muzīl al-Ilbās,* Beirut, Lebanon: Muʾassisa al-Risāla, 1405/1985.

Anwar Shāh Kāshmīrī (d. 1353 AH), *Fayḍ al-Bārī ʿalā Ṣaḥīḥ al-Bukhārī*, Beirut, Lebanon: Dār al-Kutub al-ʿIlmiyya, 1426/2005.

Ibn ʿAsākir, Abū al-Qāsim ʿAlī b. al-Ḥasan b. Hibat Allāh b. ʿAbd Allāh b. al-Ḥusayn al-Dimashqī (499–571/1105–1176), *Tārīkh Dimashq al-Kabīr (Tārīkh Madīna Dimashq),* generally known as *Tārīkh Ibn ʿAsākīr,* Beirut, Lebanon: Dār al-Iḥyāʾ al-Turāth al-ʿArabī, 1421/2001.

—. *Tārīkh Dimashq al-kabīr*. Beirut: Dar al-Fikr, 1995.

Ibn Abī ʿĀṣim, Abū Bakr b. ʿAmr al-Ḍaḥḥāk b. Makhlad al-Shaybānī (206–287/822–900), *Al-Diyāt*. Karachi: Idāra al-Qurʾān wa al-ʿUlūm al-Islāmiyya, 1308 AH.

—. *al-Āḥād wa al-Mathānī*, Riyadh, Saudi Arabia: Dār al-Rāya, 1411/1991.

Ibn al-Athīr, Abū al-Ḥasan ʿAlī b. Muhammad b. ʿAbd al-Karīm b. ʿAbd al-Wāḥid al-Shaybānī al-Jazarī (555–630/1160–1233), *al-Kāmil fī al-Tārīkh,* Beirut, Lebanon: Dār al-Ṣādir, 1979.

—. *Manāl al-Ṭālib fī Sharḥ Ṭawāl al-Gharāʾib*. Beirut, Lebanon: Dār al-Maʾmūn li al-Turāth.

—. *al-Nihāya fī gharīb al-ḥadīth wa al-athar*, Beirut, Lebanon: al-Maktaba al-ʿIlmiyya, 1399/1979.

Ibn ʿAṭiyya, Abū Muhammad ʿAbd al-Ḥaqq b. Ghālib b. ʿAbd al-Raḥmān b. Tammām al-Andulusī (d. 542 AH), *al-Muḥarrar al-*

wajīz fī tafsīr al-kitāb al-ʿazīz, Beirut, Lebanon: Dār al-Kutub al-ʿIlmiyya, 1422 AH.

Abū ʿAwāna, Yaʿqūb b. Isḥāq b. Ibrāhīm b. Zayd al-Naysabūrī (230–316/845–928), *al-Musnad,* Beirut, Lebanon: Dār al-Maʿrifa, 1998.

al-ʿAynī, Badr al-Dīn Abū Muhammad Maḥmūd b. Aḥmad b. Mūsā b. Aḥmad b. Ḥusayn b. Yūsuf b. Maḥmūd (762–855/1361–1451), *ʿUmdat al-Qārī Sharḥ ʿalā Ṣaḥīḥ al-Bukhārī,* Beirut, Lebanon: Dār al-Fikr, 1399/1979.

—. *ʿUmdat al-qārī sharḥ Ṣaḥīḥ al-Bukhārī*. Beruit: Dār Iḥyāʾ al-Turāth al-ʿArabī, n.d.

al-Baghawī, Abū Muhammad al-Ḥusayn b. Masʿūd b. Muhammad (436–516/1044–1122), *Maʿālim al-Tanzīl,* Beirut, Lebanon: Dār al-Maʿrifa, 1407/1987.

al-Balādhurī, Aḥmad b. Yaḥyā al-. (d. 279), *Futūḥ al-buldān*, Beirut: Dār al-Kutub al-ʿIlmiyya, 1403/1985.

Ibn ʿAbd al-Barr, Abū ʿUmar Yūsuf b. ʿAbd Allāh b. Muhammad (368–463/979–1071), *Al-Tamhīd li mā fī al-muwaṭṭa min al-maʿānī wa al-asānīd,* Morocco: Wazāt ʿUmūm al-Awqāt waʾs-Suʾūn al-Islāmiyya, 1387 AH.

—. *al-Istidhkār,* Beirut, Lebanon: Dār al-Kutub al-ʿIlmiyya, 2000.

al-Bayhaqī, Abū Bakr Aḥmad b. al-Ḥusayn b. ʿAlī b. ʿAbd Allāh b. Mūsā (384–458/994–1066), *Shuʿab al-Īmān*, Beirut, Lebanon: Dār al-Kutub al-ʿIlmiyya, 1410/1990.

—. *al-Sunan al-Kubrā*, Mecca, Saudi Arabia: Maktaba Dār al-Bāz, 1414/1994.

—. *al-Sunan al-Kubrā*, Mecca, Saudi Arabia: Maktaba Dār al-Bāz, 1410/1990.

—. *Dalāʾil al-Nubuwwa*, Beirut, Lebanon: Dār al-Kutub al-ʿIlmiyya, 1405/1985.

—. *Maʿrifa al-sunan wa al-āthār*, Beirut, Lebanon: Dār al-Kutub al-ʿIlmiyya.

al-Bazzār, Abū Bakr Aḥmad b. ʿAmr b. ʿAbd al-Khāliq al-Baṣrī (210–292/825–905), *al-Musnad* (*al-Baḥr al-zakhār*), Beirut, Lebanon: Muʾassasa ʿUlūm al-Qurʾān, 1409 AH.

al-Bukhārī, Abū ᶜAbd Allāh Muhammad b. Ismāᶜīl b. Ibrahīm b. Mughīra (194–256/810–870), *al-Ṣaḥīḥ*, Beirut, Lebanon, Damascus, Syria: Dār al-Qalam, 1401/1981.

—. *Al-Jāmiᶜ al-ṣaḥīḥ*. Beruit: Dār Ibn Kathīr, 1987.

—. *al-Adab al-Mufrad*, Beirut, Lebanon: Dār al-Bashā'ir al-Islāmiyya, 1409/1989.

—. *Al-Tārīkh al-kabīr*. Beirut, Lebanon: Dar al-Kutub al-ᶜIlmiyaa, 2001.

al-Dāraquṭnī, Abū al-Ḥasan ᶜAlī b. ᶜUmar b. Aḥmad b. al-Mahdī b. Masᶜūd b. al-Nuᶜmān (306–385/918–995), *al-Sunan*, Beirut, Lebanon: Dār al-Maᶜrifa, 1386/1966.

al-Dārimī, Abū Muhammad ᶜAbd Allāh b. ᶜAbd al-Raḥmān (181–255/797–869), *al-Sunan*, Beirut, Lebanon: Dār al-Kitāb al-ᶜArabī, 1407 AH.

al-Dasūqī, Muhammad b. Aḥmad b. ᶜArafa. (d. 1230/1815), *Ḥāshiyat al-Dasūqī ᶜalā al-sharḥ al-kabīr*. Beirut: Dar al-Fikr, n.d.

Abū Dāwūd, Sulaymān b. Ashᶜath b. Isḥāq b. Bashīr al-Sijistānī (202–275/817–889), *al-Sunan*, Beirut, Lebanon: Dār al-Fikr, 1414/1994.

al-Daylamī, Abū Shujāᶜ Shīrawayh b. Shardār b. Shīrawayh al-Daylamī al-Hamdānī (445–509/1053–1115), *Musnad al-Firdaws*, Beirut, Lebanon: Dār al-Kutub al-ᶜIlmiyya, 1986.

Ibn Ḍayyān, Ibrāhīm b. Muhammad b. Sālim (1275–1353), *Manār al-Sabīl*, Riyad, Saudi Arabia: Maktaba al-Maᶜārif, 1405 AH.

al-Dhahabī, Shams al-Dīn Muhammad b. Aḥmad (673–748/1274–1348), *Tārīkh al-Islām*, Beirut, Lebanon: Dār al-Kitāb al-ᶜArabī, 1410/1990.

Ibn Abī al-Dunyā, Abū Bakr ᶜAbd Allāh b. Muhammad b. al-Qurashī (208–281 AH), *Al-Ahwāl*.

Ibn Ḥajar al-ᶜAsqalānī, Aḥmad b. ᶜAlī b. Muhammad b. Muhammad b. ᶜAlī b. Aḥmad al-Kinānī (773–852/1372–1449), *Fatḥ al-Bārī Sharḥ Ṣaḥīḥ al-Bukarī*, Lahore, Pakistan: Dār Nashr al-Kutub al-Islāmiyya, 1401/1981.

al-Ḥākim, Abū ᶜAbd Allāh Muhammad b. ᶜAbd Allāh b. Muhammad (321–405/933–1014), *al-Mustadrak ᶜalā al-Ṣaḥīḥayn*, Beirut, Lebanon: Dār al-Kutub al-ᶜIlmiyya, 1411/1990.

—. *al-Mustadrak ᶜalā al-Ṣaḥīḥayn*, Mecca, Saudi Arabia: Dār al-Bāz.

al-Ḥalabī, ʿAlī b. Burhān al-Dīn (975–1044 AH), *al-Sīra al-Ḥalabiyya (Insān al-ʿUyūn fī Sīrat al-Amīn al-Maʾmūn)*, Beirut, Lebanon: Dār al-Maʿrifa, 1400 AH.

al-Ḥalabī, ʿAlī b. Burhān al-Dīn (d. 1404 AH), *al-Sīra al-Ḥalabiyya*, Beirut, Lebanon: Dār al-Maʿrifa, 1400 AH.

al-Harawī, Abū ʿUbayd Aḥmad b. Muhammad (d. 401 AH), *al-Gharibayn fī al-Qurʾān wa al-Ḥadīth*, Mecca, Saudi Arabia, Maktaba Nazār al-Muṣṭafā al-Bāz, 1419/1999.

al-Ḥaṣkafī, Muhammad ʿAlāʾ al-Dīn b. ʿAlī. *al-Durr al-mukhtār fī sharḥ tanwīr al-abṣār*. Beirut: Dar al-Fikr, 1386 AH.

Ibn Abī Ḥātim al-Rāzī, ʿAbd al-Raḥmān b. Muhammad Idrīs (240–327/854–938), *Tafsīr al-Qurʾān al-ʿAẓīm*. Sayda: al-Maktaba al-ʿAṣriyya, n.d.

al-Haythamī, Nūr al-Dīn Abū al-Ḥasan ʿAlī b. Abī Bakr b. Sulaymān (735–807/1335–1405), *Majmaʿ al-zawāʾid wa manbaʿ al-fawāʾid*, Cairo, Egypt: Dār al-Riyān li al-Turāth & Beirut Lebanon: Dār al-Kitab al-ʿArabī, 1407/1987.

Ibn Ḥayyān, Muhammad b. Yūsuf al-Shahīr al-Andulsī (d. 654/745), *Tafsīr al-Baḥr al-muḥīṭ*, Beirut, Lebanon: Dār Kutub al-ʿIlmiyya, 1422/2001.

Ibn Ḥazm, ʿAlī b. Aḥmad b. Saʿīd b. Ḥazm al-Andalusī (384–456/994–1064), *al-Muḥallā*, Beirut, Lebanon: Dār al-Āfāq al-Jadīd.

Ibn Ḥibbān, Abū Ḥātim Muhammad b. Ḥibbān b. Aḥmad b. Ḥibbān (270–354/884–965), *al-Ṣaḥīḥ*, Beirut, Lebanon: Muʾassisa al-Risāla, 1414/1993.

—. *al-Thiqāt*, Beirut, Lebanon: Dār al-Fikr, 1395 AH.

al-Hindī, Ḥussam al-Dīn, ʿAlāʾ al-Dīn ʿAlī al-Muttaqī (d. 975 AH), *Kanz al-ʿUmmāl fī Sunan al-Afʿāl wa al-Aqwāl*, Beirut, Lebanon: Muʾassisa al-Risāla, 1399/1979.

Ibn Hishām, Abū Muhammad ʿAbd al-Malik (d. 213/828), *al-Sīra al-Nabawiyya*, Beirut, Lebanon: Dār al-Jīl,1411 AH.

—. *Al-Sīra*, Beruit: Muʾassasa al-Risāla, 1993.

ʿAbd b. Ḥumayd, Abū Muhammad b. Naṣr al-Kasī (d. 249/863), *al-Musnad*, Beirut, Lebanon: Dār al-Kutub al-ʿIlmiyya, 1408/1988.

—. *al-Musnad*, Cairo, Egypt: Maktaba al-Sunna, 1408/1988.

al-Ḥusaynī, Ibrahīm b. Muhammad (1054–1120 AH), *al-Bayān wa al-Taʿrīf*, Beirut, Lebanon: Dār al-Kitāb al-ʿArabī 1401 AH.

Ibn Ibrāhīm, Abū Yūsuf Yaʿqūb. *Kitāb al-kharāj*. Beirut: Dār al-Maʿrifa, n.d.

Ibn Isḥāq, Muhammad b. Isḥāq b. Yasār (85–151), *al-Sīrat al-Nabawiyya*, Maʿhad al-Dirāsāt wa al-Abḥāth li-Taʿrīb.

Ibn al-Jaʿd, Abū al-Ḥasan ʿAlī b. Jaʿd b. ʿUbayd Hāshimī (133–230/750–845), *al-Musnad*, Beirut, Lebanon: Muʾassisa Nādir, 1410/1990.

Ibn al-Jārūd, Abū Muhammad ʿAbd Allāh b. ʿAlī (d. 307/919), *al-Muntaqā min al-Sunan al-Musnadā*, Beirut, Lebanon: Muʾassisa al-Kitāb al-Thaqāfiyya, 1418/1988.

al-Jaṣṣāṣ, Aḥmad b.ʿAlī al-Rāzī Abū Bakr (305/370 AH), *Aḥkām al-Qurʾān*, Beirut, Lebanon: Dār al-Iḥyāʾ al-Turāth, 1405 AH.

Ibn al-Jawzī, Abū al-Faraj ʿAbd al-Raḥmān b. ʿAlī b. Muhammad b. ʿAlī b. ʿUbayd Allāh (510–579/1116–1201), *Zād al-Masīr fī ʿIlm al-Tafsīr*, Beirut, Lebanon: al-Maktab al-Islāmī, 1404 AH.

al-Kāsānī, ʿAlāʾ al-Dīn (d. 587 AH), *Badāʾiʿ al-ṣanāʾiʿ fī tartīb al-sharāʾiʿ*, Beirut, Lebanon: Dār al-Kutub al-ʿArabī, 1982 AD.

Ibn Kathīr, Abū al-Fidāʾ Ismāʿīl b. ʿUmar (701–774/1301–1373), *al-Bidāya wa al-Nihāya*, Beirut, Lebanon: Dār al-Fikr, 1419/1998.

—. *Al-Bidāya wa al-nihāya*. Beirut: Maktaba al-Maʿārif, n.d.

—. *Tafsīr al-Qurʾān al-ʿAẓīm*, Beirut, Lebanon: Dār al-Maʿrifa, 1400/1980.

—. *Tafsīr al-Qurʾān al-ʿAẓīm*. Beruit: Dar al-Fikr, 1401 AH.

—. *al-Sīra al-nabawiyya*.

al-Khallāl, Abū Bakr Aḥmad b. Muhammad b. Harūn b. Yazīd al-Baghdādī al-Ḥanbalī (d. 311 AH), *Aḥkām ahl al-milal*, Beirut, Lebanon: Dār al-Kutub al-ʿIlmiyya, 1414/1994.

Ibn Khuzayma, Abū Bakr Muhammad b. Isḥāq (223–311/838–924), *al-Ṣaḥīḥ*, Beirut, Lebanon: al-Maktab al-Islāmī, 1390/1970.

Ibn Mājah, Abū ʿAbd Allāh Muhammad b. Yazīd al-Qazwīnī (209–273/824–887), *al-Sunan*, Beirut, Lebanon: Dār al-Kutub al-ʿIlmiyya, 1419/1998.

—. *al-Sunan*, Beirut, Lebanon: Dār al-Iḥyāʾ al-Turāth al-ʿArabī, 1395/1975.

Mālik, Ibn Anas b. Mālik b. Abī ʿĀmir b. ʿAmr b. Ḥārith al-Aṣbaḥī (93–179/712–795), *al-Muwaṭṭāʾ*, Beirut, Lebanon: Dār Iḥyāʾ al-Turāth al-ʿArabī, 1985.
Makkī b. Abī Ṭālib al-Muqrī, Abū Muhammad Ḥammūsh b. Muhammad b. Mukhtār (d. 437 AH), *al-Hidāya ilā Bulūgh al-Nihāya*, Jāmiʿa al-Shāriqah, 1429/2008.
al-Maqdisī, Muhammad b. ʿAbd al-Wāḥid al-Ḥanbalī, (567–643 AH), *al-Aḥādīth al-Mukhtāra,* Mecca, Saudi Arabia: Maktaba al-Nahda al-Ḥadīthiyya, 1410/1990.
—. *al-Aḥādīth al-Mukhtāra,* Syria: Dār al-Fikr, 1405 AH.
al-Maqdisī, Muhammad b. Mufliḥ, Shams al-Dīn (717–762), *Al-Furūʿ*, Beirut, Lebanon: Dār al-Kutub al-ʿIlmiyya, 1418 AH.
—. *al-Ādāb al-sharʿiyya*, Beirut, Lebanon: Muʾassasa al-Risāla, 1417/1996.
Māturīdī, Abū Manṣūr Muhammad b. Muhammad b. Maḥmūd al-. *Taʾwīlāt Ahl al-Sunna*. Beirut: Muʾassasa al-Risāla, 2004.
Al-Thānwī (d. 1158/1745), *Kashshāf isṭilāḥāt al-funūn*, Lebanon: Maktaba Lubnān.
Muhammad Ḥamīd Ullāh al-Ḥaydar Ābādī al-Hindī, Dr. (d. 1424 AH), *al-Wathāʾiq al-siyasīyya*, Beirut, Lebanon: Dār al-Nafāʾis, 1407 AH.
Muhammad b. Yūsuf al-Ṣāliḥī al-Shāmī (d. 942 AH), *Subul al-Hudā wa al-Rishād fī Sīra Khayr al-ʿIbād*, Beirut, Lebanon: Dār al-Kutub al-ʿIlmiyya, 14214/1993.
al-Mundhirī, Abū Muhammad ʿAbd al-Aẓīm b. ʿAbd al-Qawī b. ʿAbd Allāh b. Salama b. Saʿd (581–656/1185–1258), *al-Targhīb wa al-Tarhīb,* Beirut, Lebanon: Dār al-Kutub al-ʿIlmiyya, 1417 AH.
Muslim, Ibn al-Ḥajjāj Abū al-Ḥasan al-Qushayrī al-Naysābūrī (206–261/821–875), *al-Ṣaḥīḥ,* Beirut, Lebanon: Dār al-Iḥyāʾ al-Turāth al-ʿArabī.
al-Nasāʾī, Aḥmad b. Shuʿayb Abū ʿAbd al-Raḥmān (215–303/830–915), *al-Sunan,* Beirut, Lebanon: Dār al-Kutub al-ʿIlmiyya, 1416/1995.
—. *al-Sunan al-Kubrā,* Beirut, Lebanon: Dār al-Kutub al-ʿIlmiyya, 1411/1991.
al-Nawawī, Abū Zakariyyā Yaḥyā b. Sharaf b. Murrī b. al-Ḥasan b. al-Ḥusayn b. Muhammad b. Jumuʿa b. Ḥizām (631–677/1233–

1278), *Sharḥ Ṣaḥīḥ Muslim,* Karachi, Pakistan: Qādīmī Kutub Khāna, 1375/1956.

Abū Nuʿaym, Aḥmad b. ʿAbd Allāh b. Aḥmad b. Isḥāq b. Mūsā b. Mihrān al-Aṣbahānī (336–430/948–1038), *Musnad al-Imām Abī Ḥanīfa,* Riyad, Saudi Arabia: Maktaba al-Kawthar, 1415 AH.

—. *Dalāʾil al-Nubuwwa,* Hyderabad, India: Majlis Dāʾira Maʿārif ʿUthmāniyya.

Ibn al-Qayyim, Abū ʿAbd Allāh Muhammad b. Abī Bakr Ayyūb al-Zarʿī (691–751/1292–1350), *Zād al-maʿād.* Beirut: Muʾassisa al-Risāla, 1407/1986.

—. *Aḥkām ahl al-dhimma.* Beirut: Dār Ibn Ḥazm, 1997.

Ibn Qudāma, Abū Muhammad ʿAbd Allāh b. Aḥmad al-Maqdasī (d. 620 AH), *al-Mughnī fī Fiqh al-Imām Aḥmad b. Ḥanbal al-Shaybānī,* Beirut, Lebanon: Dār al-Fikr, 1405 AH.

al-Qurāfī, Shihāb al-Dīn al-. *Al-Furūq (Anwār al-burūq fī anwāʿ al-furūq).* Beirut: Dār al-Kutub al-ʿIlmiyya, 1998.

al-Qurashī, Yaḥyā b. Ādam al-. *Kitāb al-Kharāj.* Lahore: al-Maktaba al-Islāmiyya, 1974.

al-Qurṭubī, Abū ʿAbd Allāh Muhammad b. Aḥmad b. Muhammad b. Yaḥyā b. Mufarraj al-Umawī (d. 671 AH), *al-Jāmiʿ li-Ahkām al-Qurʾān,* Beirut, Lebanon: Dār al-Iḥyāʾ al-Turāth al-ʿArabī.

—. *Al-Jāmiʿ li aḥkām al-Qurʾān.* Cairo: Dār al-Shaʿb, 1372 AH.

al-Rabīʿ, b. Ḥabīb b. ʿAmr al-Azdī al-Baṣrī (95–153/713–770), *al-Jāmiʿ al-Ṣaḥīḥ—Musnad al-Imām al-Rabīʿ b. al-Ḥabīb,* Beirut, Lebanon: Dār al-Ḥikma, 1415 AH.

al-Rāzī, ʾhammad b. ʿUmar b. al-Ḥasan b. al-Ḥusayn b. ʿAlī al-Tamīmī (543–606/1149–1210), *al-Tafsīr al-Kabīr,* Tehran, Iran: Dār al-Kutub al-ʿIlmiyya.

ʿAbd al-Razzāq, Abū Bakr b. Hammām b. Nāfiʿ al-Ṣanʿānī (126–211/744–826), *al-Muṣannaf,* Beirut, Lebanon: al-Maktab al-Islāmī, 1403 AH.

Ibn Rushd, Abū Walīd Muhammad b. Aḥmad b. Muhammad b. Rushd al-Qurṭubī (d. 595 AH), *Bidāyat al-Mujtahid,* Beirut, Lebanon: Dār al-Fikr, n.d.

Ibn Saᶜd, Abū ᶜAbd Allāh Muhammad (168–230/784–845), *al-Ṭabaqāt al-Kubrā,* Beirut, Lebanon: Dār Beirut li al-Ṭabat wa al-Nashr, 1398/1978.

al-Sarakhsī, Muhammad b. Aḥmad b. Abī Sahal Shams al-Āʾimma (d. 483), *al-Mabsūṭ*, Beirut, Lebanon: Dār al-Maᶜrifa, 1978 AD.

—. *Sharḥ Kitāb al-siyar al-kabīr*, Beirut, Lebanon: Dār Kutub al-ᶜIlmiyya 1417/1997.

al-Ṣaydāwī, Muhammad b. Aḥmad b. Jumaīᶜ Abū al-Ḥusayn (305–402 AH), *Muᶜjam al-Shuyūkh,* Beirut, Lebanon: Muʾassisa al-Risāla, 1405 AH.

al-Shāfiᶜī, Abū ᶜAbd Allāh Muhammad b. Idrīs b. ᶜAbbās b. ᶜUthmān b. al-Shāfiᶜ al-Qurashī (150–204/767–819), *al-Musnad,* Beirut, Lebanon: Dār al-Kutub al-ᶜIlmiyya.

—. *Al-Umm*. Beirut: Dār al-Maᶜrifa, 1393.

al-Shāmī, Ibn ᶜĀbidīn, Muhammad. *Radd al-muḥtār ᶜalā al-durr al-mukhtār ᶜalā tanwīr al-abṣār*. Beirut: Dar al-Fikr, 1386 AH.

al-Shāṭibī, Abū Isḥāq Ibrāhīm b. Mūsā (d. 790 AH), *al-Muwāfaqāt*, Beirut, Lebanon: Dār al-Maᶜrifa.

al-Shawkānī, Muhammad b. ᶜAlī b. Muhammad (1173–1250/1760–1834), *al-Sayl al-Jarār,* Beirut, Lebanon, Dār al-Kutub al-ᶜIlmiyya, 1405.

—. *Nayl al-Awtār Sharḥ Muntaqā al-Akhbār,* Beirut, Lebanon: Dār al-Fikr, 1402/1982.

—. *Nayl al-awṭār sharḥ Muntaqā al-akhbār*. Beirut: Dār al-Jīl, 1973.

Ibn Abī Shayba, Abū Bakr ᶜAbd Allāh b. Muhammad b. Ibrahīm b. ᶜUthmān al-Kūfī (159–235/776–850), *al-Muṣannaf*, Riyadh, Saudi Arabia: Maktaba al-Rushd, 1409 AH.

—. *al-Muṣannaf*, Karachi, Pakistan: Idāra al-Qurʾān wa al-ᶜUlūm al-Islāmiyya.

al-Shaybānī, Abū Bakr Aḥmad b. ᶜAmr b. al-Ḍaḥḥāk b. Makhlad (206–287/822–900), *al-Āḥād wa al-Mathānī,* Riyadh, Saudi Arabia: Dār al-Rāya, 1411/1991.

al-Shaybanī, Muhammad b. al-Ḥasan b. Farqad Abū ᶜAbd Allāh (132–189 AH), *al-Aṣl al-Maᶜrūf bi-l-Mabsūṭ,* Karachi, Pakistan: Idārat al-Qurʾān wa al-ᶜUlūm al-Islāmiyya.

—. *Kitāb al-ḥujja ʿalā ahl al-Madīna*, Beirut, Lebanon: ʿĀlim al-Kutub, 1403 AH.
al-Ṭabarānī, Abū al-Qāsim Sulaymān b. Aḥmad b. Ayyūb b. Maṭīr al-Lakhmī (260–360/873–971), *al-Muʿjam al-Awsaṭ,* Riyadh, Saudi Arabia: Maktaba al-Maʿārif, 1405/1985.
—. *Al-Muʿjam al-awsaṭ*. Cairo, Egypt: Dār al-Ḥaramayn, 1415 AH.
—. *Al-Muʿjam al-kabīr*. Mosul, Iraq: Maktaba al-ʿUlūm wa al-Ḥikam, 1983.
—. *al-Muʿjam al-Kabīr,* Mosul, Iraq: Matbaʿa al-Zahrāʾ al-Ḥadītha.
—. *al-Muʿjam al-Kabīr,* Cairo, Egypt: Maktaba Ibn Taymiyya.
—. *Musnad al-Shāmiyyīn,* Beirut, Lebanon: Muʾassisa al-Risāla, 1405/1985.
al-Ṭabarī, Abū Jaʿfar Aḥmad Muhammad b. Jarīr b. Yazīd (224–310/839–923), *Tārīkh al-Umam wa al-Mulūk,* Beirut, Lebanon: Dār al-Kutub al-ʿIlmiyya, 1407 AH.
—. *Jāmiʿ al-Bayān fī Tafsīr al-Qurʾān*, Beirut, Lebanon: Dār al-Fikr, 1405 AH.
al-Ṭaḥāwī, Abū Jaʿfar Aḥmad b. Muhammad b. Salama b. Salma b. ʿAbd al-Malik b. Salma (229–321/853–933), *Sharḥ Maʿānī al-Āthār,* Beirut, Lebanon: Dār al-Kutub al-ʿIlmiyya, 1399 AH.
—. *Sharḥ Mushkal al-Āthār,* Beirut, Lebanon: Dār Ṣādir.
—. *Mukhtaṣar ikhtilāf al-ʿulamāʾ*, Beirut, Lebanon: Dār al-Bashāʾir al-Islāmiyya, 1417.
al-Ṭayālisī, Abū Dāwūd Sulaymān b. Dāwūd al-Jārūd (133–204/751–819), *al-Musnad,* Beirut, Lebanon: Dār al-Maʿrifa.
Ibn Taymiyya, Aḥmad b. ʿAbd al-Ḥalīm b. ʿAbd al-Salām al-Ḥarānī (661–728/1263–1328), *Majmūʿ Fatāwā*, Maktaba Ibn Taymiyya.
Ibn Taymiyya, ʿAbd al-Salām b. ʿAbd Allāh b. al-Khaḍar b. Muhammad al-Ḥarānī, Abū al-Barkāt, Mujid al-Dīn (d. 652), *al-Muḥarrar fī al-fiqh ʿalā madhab al-Imām Aḥmad bin Ḥanbal*, Riyadh, Saudi Arabia: Maktaba al-Maʿārif, 1404/1984.
al-Tirmidhī, Abū ʿĪsā Muhammad b. ʿĪsā b. Sūra b. Mūsā b. Ḍaḥḥāk Salmā (210–279/825–892), *al-Sunan,* Beirut, Lebanon: Dār al-Gharb al-Islāmī, 1998.
—. *al-Sunan*. Beirut, Lebanon: Dār Iḥyāʾ al-Turāth al-ʿArabī, n.d.

Abū ʿUbayd, al-Qāsim b. al-Sallām, (d. 244 AH), *al-Amwāl*, Beirut, Lebanon: Dār al-Fikr, 1408 AH.

al-ʿUrūsī, *Fiqh al-jihād wa al-ʿalaqāt al-duwaliyya fī al-Islām.*

al-Wāḥidī, Abū al-Ḥasan ʿAlī b. Aḥmad (d. 468 AH), *al-Wajīz fī tafsīr al-Kitāb al-ʿAzīz*, Damascus, Syria: Dār al-Qalam, 1415/1995.

Abū Yaʿlā, Aḥmad b. ʿAlī b. Mathnā b. Yaḥyā b. ʿĪsā b. al-Hilāl al-Mūṣilī al-Tamīmī (210–307/825–919), *al-Musnad,* Damascus, Syria: Dār al-Maʾmūn li al-Turāth, 1404/1984.

al-Yāʿqūbī, Aḥmad b. Abī Yaʿqūb b. Jaʿfar b. Wahb, *al-Tārīkh*, Beirut, Lebanon: Dār Ṣādir.

Abū Zahra, *al-ʿAlāqāt al-duwaliyya fī al-Islām.*

al-Zamakhsharī, Jār Allāh Abū al-Qāsim Maḥmūd b. ʿUmar b. Aḥmad al-. (467–538/1075–1144), *al-Fāʾiq fī Gharīb al-Ḥadīth wa al-Āthār*, Lebanon: Dār al-Maʿrifa.

Ibn Zanjawayh, Ḥamīd. *Kitāb al-Amwāl.* Riyadh: Markaz al-Malik Fayṣal li al-Buḥūth wa al-Dirāsāt al-Islāmiyya, 1986.

al-Zaylaʿī, Abū Muhammad ʿAbd Allāh b. Yūsuf al-Ḥanafī (d. 762/1360), *Naṣb al-Rāya li-Aḥadīth al-Hidāya,* Egypt: Dār al-Ḥadīth, 1357/1938.